The Changing Face of Management in South East Asia

Edited by Chris Rowley and Saaidah Abdul-Rahman

T0300345

Routledge
Taylor & Francis Group

LONDON AND NEW YORK

First published 2008 by Routledge
2 Park Square, Milton Park, Abingdon, Oxon, OX14 4RN

Simultaneously published in the USA and Canada
by Routledge
711 Third Avenue, New York, NY 10017

Routledge is an imprint of the Taylor & Francis Group

Typeset in Times New Roman by Prepress Projects, Perth, UK

British Library Cataloguing in Publication Data
A catalogue record for this book is available from the British Library

Library of Congress Cataloging in Publication Data
Changing face of management in South East Asia/edited by Chris Rowley and Saaidah Abdul-Rahman.

    p. cm.

    Includes bibliographical references and index.
    ISBN 978-0-415-40544-7 (hardcover: alk. paper)–ISBN
    978-0-415-40543-0 (softcover: alk. paper)–ISBN
    978-0-203-93774-7 (e-book: alk. paper) 1. Personnel management–
    Southeast Asia Case studies. 2. Management–Southeast Asia–Case
    studies. I. Rowley, Chris, 1959– II. Abdul-Rahman, Saaidah. III.
    Changing face of management in Southeast Asia.
HF5549.2.S785C46 2007
658.300959–dc22
                2007024401

ISBN10: 0-415-40543-2 (pbk)
ISBN10: 0-415-40544-0 (hbk)
ISBN10: 0-203-93774-0 (ebk)
ISBN13: 978-0-415-40543-0 (pbk)
ISBN13: 978-0-415-40544-7 (hbk)
ISBN13: 978-0-203-93774-7 (ebk)

The Changing Face of Management in South East Asia

South East Asia has undergone important economic, social and political developments in the last decade. The emergence of China as Asia's largest pool of cheap labour has resulted in remarkable changes in the volume of foreign direct investment it commands, and the 1997 Asian Financial Crisis has undoubtedly influenced managerial practices in the majority of the countries in the region. In response, South East Asian governments and businesses have sought ways of attracting new investors while at the same time intensifying their efforts to retain existing industries.

This important new volume overviews the development of South East Asian management practices, focusing on human resource management (HRM) as an indicator and measure of change. Written by prominent scholars of the region, the book focuses on reform in the human resource (HR) managerial domain, documenting recent changes and assessing current practices from both macro and micro perspectives. The book includes a wealth of detail, covering a wide range of South East Asian countries and examining a mix of organisations and industries. A consistent structure and content is used throughout, with each chapter incorporating 'real life' local organisational and manager case studies, plus vignettes to give 'voice' to practitioners and developments.

The Changing Face of Management in South East Asia is essential reading for anybody with an interest in management, HR or the political, social, cultural and economic profiles of the countries of South East Asia.

Chris Rowley is Professor of Human Resource Management, editor of the leading journal *Asia Pacific Business Review* and Series Editor for Studies in Asia Pacific Business and Asian Studies: Contemporary Issues and Trends. Professor Rowley has published very widely, with over 80 articles, over 60 book chapters and other contributions and 12 edited and sole authored books. He has recently co-edited *Globalization and Labour in the Asia Pacific Region* (2001), *Managing Korean Business* (2002), *The Management of Human Resources in the Asia Pacific Region* (2003) and *Globalization and Competition: Big Business in Asia* (2005). He has also written *The Management of People: HRM in Context* (2003) and regularly contributed to 'Mastering Management Online' from the *Financial Times*.

Saaidah Abdul-Rahman is an independent researcher. She specialises in the areas of Social Policy and Human Resource Management. She has extensive experience as an academic and a consultant to several government agencies and private companies.

Working in Asia

General Editors:
Tim G Andrews
Bristol Business School, University of the West of England,
Keith Jackson
School of Oriental and African Studies, University of London,
and **Chris Rowley**
Cass Business School, City University, London.

This series focuses on contemporary management issues in the Asia-Pacific region. It draws on the latest research to highlight critical factors impacting on the conduct of business in this diverse and dynamic business environment.

Our primary intention is to provide management students and practitioners with fresh dimensions to their reading of standard texts. With each book in the *Working in Asia* series, we offer a combined insider's and outsider's perspective on how managers and their organisations in the Asia-Pacific region are adapting to contemporary currents of both macro- and micro-level change.

The core of data for the texts in this series has been generated by recent interviews and discussions with established senior executives as well as newly-fledged entrepreneurs; with practising as well as aspiring middle managers; and with women as well as men. Our mission has been to give voice to how change is being perceived and experienced by a broad and relevant range of people who live and work in the region. We report on how they and their organisations are managing change as the globalisation of their markets, together with their business technologies and traditions, unfolds.

Drawing together the combined insights of Asian and Western scholars, and practitioners of management, we present a uniquely revealing portrait of the future of working and doing business in Asia.

Titles in the series include:

The Changing Face of Multinationals in Southeast Asia
Tim G Andrews, Nartnalin Chompusri and Bryan J. Baldwin

The Changing Face of Chinese Management
Jie Tang and Anthony Ward

The Changing Face of Japanese Management
Keith Jackson and Miyuki Tomioka

The Changing Face of Management in South East Asia
Edited by Chris Rowley and Saaidah Abdul-Rahman

For our parents – exemplars in many areas

Contents

Boxes

 # Contributors

Saaidah Abdul-Rahman is an independent researcher, specialising in the fields of social policy and human resource management. She graduated from the London School of Economics and Bristol University, UK.

Ahmad D. Habir is a founding faculty member at the IPMI Business School in Jakarta. He received an MBA degree from George Washington University and his PhD from the Australian National University. He also heads a management consulting and training company. He is now Dean of Business Administration, Swiss German University, Jakarta.

Tak Kee Hui is an associate professor at the Department of Decision Sciences, School of Business, National University of Singapore. He has published widely in numerous journals. His research interests are in the areas of applied statistics, applied finance, hospitality and tourism management, as well as strategic human resource management.

Rene E. Ofreneo is Professor and former Dean of the School of Labor and Industrial Relations, University of the Philippines. He has studied economic, labour market and employment relations issues in the Asia-Pacific region.

Krishnan Rajendran is a faculty member at the IPMI Business School in Jakarta. He has extensive experience in human resource management as a manager and consultant in India and Indonesia since 1981. He received his MBA degree from the Weatherhead School of Management, Case Western Reserve University, Cleveland.

Chris Rowley is the inaugural Professor of Human Resource Management at Cass Business School, City University, London, and Director of its Centre for Research in Asian Management and Editor of the leading journal *Asia Pacific Business Review*. He has published widely in the area of Asian business and management with over 20 books, over 80 chapters and entries and over 100 articles.

Sununta Siengthai is Associate Professor of Human Resource Management/ Industrial Relations of the School of Management, Asian Institute of Technology, Thailand.

Uthai Tanlamai is Professor of Business Administration, Faculty of Commerce and Accountancy, Chulalongkorn University, Thailand.

Le Chien Thang is a consultant, Human Resources Advisory Services, Navigos Group, Vietnam. He also teaches human resource management courses for the EMBA Programme at the Asian Institute of Technology, Thailand.

Truong Quang is an Associate Professor in Human Resource Management and Organisational Behaviour at Maastricht School of Management, the Netherlands. He regularly serves as a consultant for several companies and organisations in Vietnam on human resource management matters.

David Wan is Head of the Human Resource Management Unit, and Deputy Head of the Department of Management and Organisation, School of Business, National University of Singapore. He is also a council member of the Singapore HR Institute and co-chairs its Academic Board, School of Human Capital Management. He is an Associate Editor of the *Asian Case Research Journal* and sits on the editorial advisory boards of *Journal of Comparative International Management* and *Research & Practice in HRM*. His research interests include strategic human resource management, industrial relations climate, unionisation process and organisational participation as well as tourism and hospitality management.

Common abbreviations used in the text

ASEAN	Association of South East Asian Nations
BPO	business process outsourcing
CEO	chief executive officer
FDI	foreign direct investment
FIE	foreign-invested enterprise
FOC	foreign-owned company
GDP	gross domestic product
GNP	gross national product
HR	human resource
HRD	human resource development
HRM	human resource management
ILO	International Labour Organization
IT	information technology
JV	joint venture
LOC	locally owned company
MNC	multinational company
PA	performance appraisal
PM	personnel management
PMS	performance management system
SOE	state-owned enterprise
SME	small and medium-sized enterprise
WTO	World Trade Organization

Acknowledgements

Indonesia

The authors would like to extend their appreciation to those managers who were interviewed for the case studies. From PT Austindo, Nusantara Jaya: George S. Tahija, President Director; A. Wahyuhadi, Commissioner; and Tommy Sudjarwadi, Director. From PT Medco Energi Oil and Gas: P. M. Susbandono, Head of HR, Aviv Murtadho, Head of Information Services. From PT Medco Energi Chemicals: Budiarto Idries, Head of HSE and Management Audit.

Malaysia

The authors record their appreciations to the following individuals who were interviewed independently and who imparted data and information that were incorporated in the chapter: Dato Zuraidah Atan; Mr. Madzlan Mansor, General Manager (Human Resouce) UMW Corporation; Mr. Shariff Abdullah Shariff Along, Ajinomoto Malaysia; Professor Mitsuhide Shiraki, Waseda University, Japan. Professor Rowley thanks the British Academy and the Committee for South East Asian Studies for a grant. Dr Saaidah Abdul-Rahman thanks the Japan Institute for Labour Policy and Training for a grant and research facilities.

Thailand

We are grateful to the Royal Thai Government and the Asian Institute of Technology for having provided financial support. Our appreciation is extended in particular to the managers of the case studies who shared with us their HRM practices. Also, 2006 was an auspicious year for Thailand as it marked the 60th year of King Bhumibol Adulyadej's accession to the throne. Over 60 years of His Majesty's benevolent governance and role model, which went back before the time Thailand first started its national five-year social and economic plan, the Thais have benefited significantly from his devoted effort for the development of the country, particularly with respect to rural development and the royal poverty alleviation-related projects. Needless to say, one of the most remarkable dimensions of all the royal projects is human resource development. We therefore dedicate this chapter to His Majesty King Bhumipol Adulyadej. Professor Rowley thanks the British Academy and the Committee for South East Asian Studies for a grant.

The publishers have made every effort to contact authors/copyright holders of works reprinted in *The Changing Face of Management in South East Asia*. This has not been possible in every case, however, and we would welcome correspondence from those individuals/ companies whom we have been unable to trace.

Currencies

Indonesian rupiah (Rp)

1 US$	=	9,220 Rp
1 euro	=	11,563 Rp
1 GBP	=	17,102 Rp

Malaysian ringgit (RM)

1 US$	=	RM3.6
1 euro	=	RM4.6
1 GBP	=	RM6.9

Thai baht (Bt)

1 US$	=	37.4774 Bt
1 euro	=	48.1713 Bt
1 GBP	=	71.1408 Bt

Philippine peso (Php)

1 US$	=	50.50 Php
1 euro	=	64.00 Php
1 GBP	=	94.91 Php

Singaporean dollar (S$)

1 US$	=	1.5619 S$
1 euro	=	1.994 S$
1 GBP	=	2.9756 S$

Vietnam dong (VND)

1 US$	=	16,055 VND
1 euro	=	20,520 VND
1 GBP	=	30,495 VND

Map of South-East Asia

1 Introduction

Rationale, overview and issues

Chris Rowley and Saaidah Abdul-Rahman

- **Overview**
- **South East Asia – how coherent a group?**
- **Country overviews**
- **People management in South East Asia – personnel management versus human resource management?**
- **Human resource management overviews**
- **Globalisation, convergence and an Asian way?**
- **Conclusion**

Introduction

This latest book in the Routledge 'Working in Asia' series continues, but also develops in some fresh ways, the original purpose and conceptualisation of this somewhat unusual book series. The intention was to provide accessible, easy to read and use books written by experts, many local, and which importantly give 'voice' to local managers within organisations, often in a set of case studies or vignettes, to examine the changing 'face' and practice of indigenous management. This in turn would involve some commensurate downplaying of the more research monograph-type content in the books. With the increased interest in Asia the time was ripe for books using such a focus and format.

This particular book is concerned with the changing face of management in South East Asia, focusing on human resource management (HRM) as an indicative example. Other areas of management operate within the same contexts and face some similar changes as HRM outlined in the following chapters, of course. We undertake this journey via an examination of personnel management (PM) and HRM as both a function/profession and set of key practices across a broad range of countries in the South East Asian region set within national contexts. However, we did not want the book to fall into a set of disparate, isolated country-based chapters, but rather be a more integrated and thematic whole. To achieve this objective all the substantive chapters in the book have a standard and common format, structure and content.

The South East Asian region is important, containing several large economies, populations and labour forces. For example, in 2005 Indonesia alone had approaching 160 million people in the prime working age group (16- to 64-year-olds). Some of the economies have rapidly developed and become a destination for foreign direct investment (FDI) and multinational companies (MNC) from a range of different nationalities and in a variety of sectors. For example, in 2005 Singapore's gross domestic product (GDP) per capita was US$29,000 with exports of US$245 billion, while even Vietnam received nearly US$6 billion inward investment. Despite this importance, some of the countries covered in this book tend to be less popular subjects and under-researched, especially in comparison with other Asian countries like Japan and China, albeit with some exceptions (see, for example, Rowley and Warner, 2006).

This introduction is structured in a further set of main parts. These cover an overview and explanation of the book (sequence, structure, cases studies and 'voice'), how coherent a region this is, country sketches, perspectives on PM and HRM, people management and HRM country overviews, the area of globalisation and convergence, especially in relation to Asia, and a conclusion.

Overview

Sequence

Chapter 1 is the introductory chapter. This outlines the aims and objectives of the book and locates it within the wider area. An overview of the structure and content of the rest of the book is also provided. Chapters 2–7 are the substantive chapters. These are country based and written by experts, many of them local, covering six major economies of the region alphabetically: Indonesia, Malaysia, Philippines, Singapore, Thailand and Vietnam. Each chapter focuses on the specific country using the same common format. By doing this, the main contours of management and the evolution of people management, PM and HRM policy and practice at both macro and micro levels is traced in a similar manner. Each chapter incorporates cases and illustrations of two indigenous organisations in the country to provide more specific and empirical information on the country's HRM. In addition, each chapter includes two cases and vignettes of individual managers who have succeeded in plotting exceptional management styles in their companies. Chapter 8 is the concluding chapter, which summarises the main findings and themes of the book, assesses the recent situation in the South East Asian region and discusses the prospects for the future.

Structure

All contributors followed detailed specific guidance to ensure integration, compatibility and consistency across and within every chapter. Thus, all the six country-based chapters have the same sequential structure and format. This not only makes reading easier but also aids explicit comparisons across aspects or dimensions of countries. For example, political, economic and social contexts, labour market features, key HRM practices, and so on, can be quickly identified and even compared as 'stand alone' parts. Furthermore, the bibliographies are important as many students and teachers of international management/HRM and business find it difficult to locate up-to-date sources of information for some of the countries covered in this book, and particularly easily accessible texts written by locals. Thus, all the chapters have the following common structure of nine main parts and sections:

- introduction;
- political, economic and social/cultural background and context;
- key labour market features and developments;
- development of PM and HRM and the HR function and profession;
- HRM practices: employee resourcing, development, rewards and relations;
- case studies of indigenous organisations;
- case studies of individual managers;
- challenges and prospects for HRM;
- conclusion.

Case studies and 'voice'

This is an important and unusual aspect to the book and the series which it forms part of. The 'voice' element in all the chapters comes out clearly in the cases and vignettes. Data for these were collected and compiled in a variety of ways. Sometimes individuals were interviewed directly about their experiences and expectations of the HRM practices described and discussed previously. For instance, the extent to which the experiences and expectations of these individuals conform to local attempts to achieve 'best practice' in the HRM described are sometimes apparent. Some cases highlight enduring constraints and emerging opportunities in local and regional HRM practice and development. Thus, a key purpose and differentiator of this book and its series is to elicit local 'voices' with which readers might identify and feel inspired – or warned – by. This focus is different from more traditional empirical or theoretical, dense and heavy, research monograph-type books.

South East Asia – how coherent a group?

So, to what extent do the constituent countries in the South East Asian region form a meaningfully coherent group? On what basis, other than geographical proximity, might this be? Steeped in antiquity, South East Asia stretches across a large and highly diverse spatial area. Furthermore, there is a widely varied pattern of experiences, such as being colonised and occupied, involving countries ranging from the UK, the Netherlands, France and Spain to the US and Japan.

The region's countries themselves are internally heterogeneous in terms of ethnicity and race (for example, Vietnam has fifty-four and Indonesia hundreds of ethnic groupings) and religions (including Buddhism, Islam and Catholicism), which can be official/state ones or countries can be secular. The region's economies and populations are variegated (Table 1.1), ranging from relatively small city-states like Singapore with a few million inhabitants to the vastness of the Indonesian archipelago and its many millions, the world's fourth most populous country. Other differences include urbanisation, which varies from the almost total urban population of Singapore and approaching the two-thirds level in Malaysia compared with

Table 1.1 South East Asian management – contextual factors (2005)

General statistics	Indonesia	Malaysia	Philippines	Singapore	Thailand	Vietnam
Area (square kilometres)	1,919,440[a]	329,757	300,000	697	513,115	329,314
Population						
Total	241,973,879	26,130,000	84,241,375	4,300,000	65,110,000	83,119,000
Urban (% of total)	47.9[b]	63.0	62.0	99.0	29.9[a]	26.9
Demographics (total and %)						
<15 years	70,414,087 (29.1)	8,719,900 (32.5)	28,428,000 (33.7)	838,000 (19.5)	14,324,288 (22.0)	24,331,852 (29.4)
16–64 years	158,896,958 (65.7)	16,878,000 (63.2)	52,084,000 (61.0)	2,936,000 (68.3)[a]	45,577,280 (70.0)	53,804,699 (65.0)
65+ years	12,662,833 (5.2)	1,150,200 (4.3)	7,747,000 (4.3)	524,600 (12.2)[b]	5,208,832 (8.0)	4,642,958 (5.6)
Employment (total)	94,948,118[c]	10,895,000	32,313,000	2,266,700	36,132,000[b]	42,709,100
By sector (%)						
Agriculture	45	12.9	36.0	n/a	33.72[c]	56.8
Industry	16	36.1[a]	15.5	24.0	22.95	17.9
Services	39	51.0[b]	48.5	76.0	39.22	25.3
Unemployment						
Total	11,899,300[d]	367,000	2,909,000[a]	100,500	663,000	1,836,490
%	11.2[d]	3.5	8.3	3.2	1.9	5.3
Economic						
GDP per capita (US$)	1,277[e]	4,781	1,170	29,000	3,843.7	620
Real GDP growth (%)	5.6[e]	5.3	5.1	6.4	4.5	8.4

Table 1.1 Continued.

General statistics	Indonesia	Malaysia	Philippines	Singapore	Thailand	Vietnam
Sector output (US$ billion)						
Agriculture	37.7[e]	56.8	14.1	n/a	9.12[d]	9.1
Industry	65.26[e]	21.7	31.7	38.3	45.86	17.9
Services	113.645	40.1	52.6	71.5	43.16	16.7
Imports (US$ billion)	63.856[d]	114.2	47.4	213.8	142.45	36.8
Exports (US$ billion)	86.179[d]	141.5	41.3	245.5	139.63l	32.2
Inflation (%)	17.11[d]	3.0	7.6	1.2	4.5[e]	8.5
Inward investment (US$ billion)	6.0[f]	4.7	1.13	19.6	3.35[f]	5.8
Gini coefficient	0.343[c]	0.462[c]	0.46[b]	0.42	0.40–0.44[g]	0.370

Sources: various, from the contributors. See also below for sources for specific country information.

Indonesia
Source: http://education.yahoo.com (2004); www.nscb.gov.ph (2005).
a   Wikipedia (2003).
b   http://globalis.gvu.unu.edu (2005).
c   Biro Pusat Statistik (2005).
d   Bank Indonesia (2005).
e   US Department of State (2005).
f   BKPM (2005).

Malaysia
Source: Economic Planning Unit (2006).
a   Mining, 0.4; manufacturing, 28.7; construction, 7.0.
b   Includes government services.
c   2004.

Philippines

Source: National Statistical Office.

a   April 2005 labour survey using new unemployment definition.
b   2003.

Singapore

a   15–59.
b   60+.

Thailand

a   The number of employed in municipal areas divided by total number of persons in 2005.
b   http://service.nso.go.th/nso/g_data23/stat_23/toc_2/2.1.1-1.xls.
c   For employment by sector, www.bot.or.th/bothomepage/databank/EconData/EconFinance/Download/Tab87.xls, where industry includes manufacturing; electricity, gas and water supply; and construction; services includes wholesale and retail trade; repair of vehicles and personal and household goods; hotels and restaurants; transport, storage and communications; financial intermediation; real estate, renting and business activities; public administration and defence; compulsory social security; education; health and social work; other community, social and personal service activities; private households with employed persons; other (which accounts for the remaining 4.3%).
d   www.bot.or.th/bothomepage/databank/EconData/EconFinance/tab82e.asp (1 US$ = 37.4774 Bt) and as above – searched 2 December 2006.
e   www.bot.or.th.
f   www.bot.or.th/bothomepage/databank/EconData/EconFinance/Download/Tab60.xls (1 US$ = 37.4774 Bt; gross figure = 125,599.69 million Bt).
g   http://en.wikipedia.org/wiki/Gini_coefficient – searched 1 December 2006.

less than one-third in Vietnam. Demographically there is diversity, for example, the under-15s account for one-third of the population in the Philippines but less than one-fifth in Singapore whereas the over-65s account for 12.2 per cent in Singapore but only 4.3 per cent in Malaysia and Thailand. Sectoral employment varies too. Agriculture accounts for no jobs in Singapore and only about one eighth in Malaysia, but well over half in Vietnam. Industry accounts for over one-third of employment in Malaysia, but only one-sixth in the Philippines. Services take over two-thirds of jobs in Singapore and over one-half in Malaysia in contrast to less than one-sixth in Vietnam. Unemployment rates differ too, ranging from less than 2 per cent in Thailand to over 11 per cent in Indonesia. Importantly, these variables, amongst others, help shape the nature of product and factor markets, and in some instances the potential for economic development (Rowley and Warner, 2006).

Economies in the region have developed, although with unevenness temporally and sectorally. Perhaps these can be seen as a part of the so-called 'Asian Miracle' of the late twentieth century? For some commentators Asian achievement was indeed miraculous, although others argue it was more a 'mirage'. For example, the idea of an economic growth 'miracle' was challenged and put down to extraordinary inputs of capital and labour, as opposed to gains in efficiency (Krugman, 1996), with 'perspiration' rather than 'inspiration' being the defining characteristic of the Asian experience, and hard work and persistence the trademarks (Rowley and Warner, 2006). Also, some highlight the role of the interventionist state (Rowley and Warner, 2005). These forces and factors can certainly be seen in the following country overviews and chapters.

Whatever one's views on this Asian phenomenon, the period of high growth rates for Asian economies was interrupted by the 1997 Asian Financial Crisis and its aftermath. The effects for each country in the region varied and were non-standardised (see Rowley and Warner, 2004). Indeed, some economies were resilient and their businesses bounced back in varying degrees, although in some many firms collapsed or languished. We only need to compare the Philippines with Singapore to see the range of impacts and reactions. The crisis also impacted on HRM in different ways. To help understand this variation we present some country overviews and key characteristics.

Country overviews

We now present a set of supplementary, very broad-brush country overviews covering such variables and areas as geographical size, organisation, ethnicity, and political, economic and socio-cultural dimensions. Some recent business-related developments are also added to each country profile.

Indonesia (first paragraph based on Prijadi and Rachmawati, 2002)

Indonesia is the largest country in South East Asia and the world's biggest archipelago with 17,508 islands and islets lying between mainland Asia and Australia. Its large population is unequally distributed with most (62 per cent) on Java alone, an island comprising only a small total (just 7 per cent) of the land area. During the Second World War this former Dutch colony was under Japanese occupation until 1945. It has twenty-seven provinces, sixty-three municipalities and 247 districts. There is racial/ethnic diversity, with four main groups: Melanesian, Proto-Austronesian, Polynesian and Micronesian, subdivided into hundreds of ethnic groupings, with more than 250 local languages. There is no state religion and four major ones are recognised – Christianity, Hinduism, Buddhism and Islam – the last followed by approximately 85 per cent of the population (the largest Muslim population in the world). In terms of its rapid economic development, FDI, especially from Japan and in manufacturing, contribute significantly to growth.

The period since the 1997 Asian Crisis has seen both a shift from corrupt authoritarianism to fledging democracy in Indonesia but also an ending of its former fast economic and social development. For example, unemployment figures shot up from 8 to 13 million and those people living below the poverty line rose to nearly 60 million, almost one half of the population (Chapter 2). The country has continued a struggling recovery with unreformed financial, legal, judicial and state sectors; an exodus of important professional Chinese Indonesians (ethnic Chinese control very large amounts of economic activity although only constituting less than 5 per cent of the population); continuing high costs of doing business; corruption; and political instability with ethnic, religious and labour unrest.

Some recent developments in Indonesia with impacts on business and management include the following example. In 2006 there was a proposal to amend labour laws, weakening minimum wage provisions and reducing entitlements to severance pay while increasing restrictions on the right to strike and possibilities for employers to impose disciplinary measures on workers, described by the Indonesian Trade Union Congress as a 'race to the bottom' in terms of working conditions (ICFTU, 2006).

Malaysia (first paragraph based on Ayudurai *et al.*, 2002)

Malaysia is bordered by Thailand and the Philippines to the north, and Indonesia at all other points. This former British colony gained independence in 1957. It is divided into two regions: Peninsula Malaysia, with eleven states from Johore in the south to the Thai border in the north; and, separated by the South China Sea, Sabah and Sarawak, the two states on the island of Borneo. The multi-racial/ethnic population is classified into two main categories: *Bumiputera* ('sons of the soil'), the Malays and now also including the indigenous peoples of the Peninsular, Sabah and Sarawak; and those who originally came from China, India, Sri Lanka and other parts of Asia. There is a diversity of languages and religions. Islam is the official religion of the Malays. Malaysia is a leading producer and exporter of palm oil, hardwoods, petroleum and pepper, with industrialisation, diversification and encouragement of foreign direct investment (FDI) resulting in steady economic growth and expansion of manufacturing.

Recent developments that impact on business and management in Malaysia include the continuation of positive discrimination in a range of business practices and policies. There is also the question of what to do with companies that have state links and national prestige attached to them. There are approximately forty partially owned state or 'government-linked' companies (GLCs) in the holding company, Khazanah – including Telekom Malaysia, SilTerra, the microchip foundry and Rapid KL, a transportation system operator – with bureaucratic origins as either former monopolists, such as the power firm Tenaga Nasional, or 'pet' government projects, such as Proton (*Economist*, 2005). Under the national car programme the government invested heavily in creating from scratch its own brand vehicle built by Proton. Founded in 1983 with Mitsubishi based models and technology, this protected and heavily subsidised firm has struggled to compete, in contrast to Thailand, which allowed foreign companies majority ownership and gave them tax breaks to build pickup trucks (Leahy, 2006). Therefore, Proton has been in a range of talks with foreign companies such as Volkswagen and China's Chery (Dyer, 2006). However, one issue with these GLCs is that 'political considerations often trump commercial ones' and large-scale redundancies are taboo (*Economist*, 2005: 54). Another example is the crowded and fragmented palm oil sector (it is one of the world's largest producers with growing demand as a biofuel, generating a 23 per cent price rise in just 2006 alone), with the idea (first mooted in 2003 but resisted because of possible job cuts) of merging three state plantations controlled by PNB (the state-run investment equity fund) to form the world's biggest listed producer with market capitalisation of over US$7 billion and sales of US$2 billion (Burton, 2006a).

Philippines (first paragraph based on Ofreneo, 2003)

The Philippines is another archipelago, with more than 7,000 islands. This former colony and occupied (by Spain, America and Japan) area gained independence in 1946. It has fifteen regions and seventy-eight provinces. There are fifty different ethnic groups. While a secular state constitutionally, it is a predominantly Christian country with Catholicism dominant, although with a high concentration of Islamic believers in places, such as parts of Mindanao. Economic development has been uneven, with large agricultural and informal employment, although manufacturing has developed.

The post-1950s import-substituting industry model paved the way for a rapid rise of light industry assembling varied products from imported semi-processed materials (Chapter 4). This was followed in the 1970s by an export-orientated industry model via promoting FDI in processing zones reinforced in the 1980s with economic liberalisation, and further consolidated in the 1990s by integrating the economy regionally and globally. Despite all this the employment share of the industrial sector stagnated at about 16 per cent between 1970 and 2000, with the share of the manufacturing sub-sector actually declining from 11.9 per cent to 10 per cent for the same period (Chapter 4). It was actually the service sector that expanded. Endemic poverty continued with stagnant gross national product (GNP) per capita. Additionally, the importance of remittances back home by overseas Filipino workers became critical as this supported one-quarter of the population and contributed to service sector growth (Ofreneo and Samonte, 2002). Another aspect of services is business process outsourcing (BPO) in which the Philippines led other South East Asian countries as US companies established call centres due to cheaper wages and plentiful college graduates able to offer customer support and interaction with ease owing to their familiarity with American culture and diction (Chapter 4). However, some commentators argue there is still a grave need for more regulatory and economic reform, especially in telecoms, transport and power industries, and for government 'to reduce the cost of doing business and promote competition' (Landingin, 2006: 7).

Singapore (first paragraph based on Low, 2003)

Singapore is composed of one large island, measuring 42 by 23 kilometres, and some smaller islands. It is separated from Peninsular Malaysia by the Straits of Johor and from Indonesia's Riau Islands by the Straits of Singapore. The official languages are Malay, Mandarin, Tamil and English, the last being the language of business and administration. This is a multi-ethnic society with 77 per cent Chinese, 11 per cent Malays, 9 per cent Indians and the rest European. Some 55 per cent are Buddhist and Taoist with the rest Muslim, Hindu and Christian of various denominations. Its 1960s industrialisation was through FDI and MNCs in labour-intensive, low-valued sectors such as textiles and garment manufacturing, developing in the 1980s by upgrading to higher skilled, technology and value-added industries such as electronics, and since the 1990s by the drive to become a more knowledge-based economy. Consequently, the former engines of economic growth have declined.

Of relevance to business and management in Singapore is the internationally admired education and state school system (partly reflecting a Confucian influence) generating top global rankings for science and mathematics and a highly skilled workforce. However, the system has also been criticised for inflexibility. For example, the examination at 12 years of age – which divides students into those going to advanced secondary school and on to university and professional careers from those going to normal high school with less chance of this path – is a crossroads that often determines the rest of a person's life and 'the result is a highly stratified society ruled by an elite of the academically gifted' (Burton, 2006b: 8). There is also criticism of the emphasis on rote learning instead of critical thinking and lack of attention paid to some subjects such as the humanities (80 per cent of primary school class time is devoted to maths, science and languages). Overall, 'the standard national curriculum adheres closely to government goals of creating a skilled, but politically compliant workforce' (ibid.). At the same time there are policies such as the exclusion from employment laws of foreign domestic workers (mainly from the Philippines, Indonesia and Sri Lanka, accounting for 25 per cent of the 600,000 migrant workers), exposing them to abuses (Burton, 2005).

Thailand (first paragraph based on Gullaprawit, 2002)

Thailand borders Laos and Cambodia in the north and east, and Malaysia and the Gulf of Thailand in the south and has two distinct parts: the Chao Phraya River Valley and the Korat Plateau, which form a compact area; and the extension which reaches the Malaysian frontier. The 1932 coup ended 800 years of absolute monarchy. Thailand has seventy-six provinces. Ethnic Thais form 82 per cent of the population and, although many speak different dialects, Bangkok's official Thai language is widespread. The Chinese are the largest ethnic minority. Ethnic Malays are concentrated in the south and constitute a majority of the Muslim population and are the majority or near majority in four of the fourteen southern provinces. Other groups are Indians and Pakistanis, with Cambodians left over from the ancient Khmer Empire and Vietnamese in the north-east. Principal hill tribes include Meos, Karens, Lahus, Lissus and Khas. The vast majority (95 per cent) of Thais are Buddhists. Economic development from the 1960s emphasised agricultural development and import substitution, with manufacturing replacing agriculture as the most important sector from the 1980s.

More recent developments of importance to business and management in Thailand include the 2006 military coup and the later currency and stock market crisis (foreign investors own an estimated US$50 billion in Thai stocks, about 30 per cent of the market) in December 2006 (Kazmin, 2006a). The new government has been trying to clarify the ambiguous foreign ownership laws, which have significant impacts on foreign companies such as Holcim, Norway's Telenor and retailers such as Tesco and Carrefour. This FDI climate has been unsettled by the highly politicised furore over the takeover by Singapore's Temasek Holdings of Shin Corporation, the telecommunications empire founded by the former prime minister. The Foreign Business Act defines a 'foreign company' as a venture with more than 49 per cent foreign equity and bars such firms from engaging in many areas of the economy, particularly service sector businesses. However, for decades the authorities distinguished between nominal equity ownership and actual control of companies – a loophole that let MNCs, operating via complex, multi-layered shareholding structures, have presence and control with 'an aura of Thai ownership' (Kazmin, 2006b: 8). Yet, following the Temasek takeover, the Shin companies could lose their licences for exceeding foreign ownership limits, leaving the FDI framework 'in tatters, shattering confidence in what had long been seemingly acceptable local practices facilitated by legal ambiguity and regulatory forbearance' (ibid.).

Vietnam (first paragraph based on Thao et al., 2003)

Vietnam borders the Gulf of Thailand, the Gulf of Tonkin, the South China Sea, China, Laos and Cambodia. Lowland accounts for about 20 per cent, mountains 40 per cent and hills 40 per cent, with 76 per cent of the country forested. The north consists of highlands and the Red River Delta, the south is divided into coastal lowlands, Giai Truong Son (the central mountains) with its high plateaus and the Mekong River Delta. Following French colonial rule, then Japanese occupation, resistance and division along the seventeenth parallel, US involvement occurred until the 1976 reunification. Vietnam has sixty-one provinces. Most people live in rural areas, with decreasing overall population growth due to the 1986 policy allowing just two children to be born in each family. However, there are still approximately 1 million young people entering the labour force each year (Kazmin, 2006b). There are fifty-four ethnic groupings, with Vietnamese the dominant group, and others including Hoa (Chinese, some 1.8 per cent), Tay, Thai, Khmer, Muong, Nung, Hmong and numerous mountain tribes. The main religions are Buddhism (Mahayana and Theravada), Cao Dai, Hoa Hao, Catholicism, Protestantism, Islam, Hinduism and animism. There are rich natural resources, such as phosphates, coal, manganese, bauxite, chromate, oil and gas and forests. Economic development has shifted from a classic socialist market economy and state-owned enterprises (SOEs) towards a more mixed economy following the *Doi Moi* reforms of the 1980s and organisational diversity, albeit with socialist traits still retained and visible.

More recent events of importance to business and management in Vietnam display both sides of the paradoxical Vietnamese system – trying to operate more like an open economy but keeping socialist characteristics. On the one hand there has been some marketisation, for instance the rush of companies listing (or 'equitising') on the two small stock exchanges (fifty-two companies in Ho Chi Minh and sixteen in the newer Hanoi one) with the two-year tax incentive ending in 2007 (Kazmin, 2006c). For example, in November 2006 Vietnam's largest private commercial bank, Asia Commercial Bank (30 per cent foreign owned, the maximum allowed), listed (Kazmin and Daniel, 2006). FPT (in which Texas Pacific Group and Intel Capital already had a stake), Vietnam's largest IT company with sales of US$517 million and 6,000 employees in 2005 with a series of outsourcing contracts for companies in Japan and Europe, planned to list (Kazmin, 2006d).

On the other hand there has been the continuation of former views and practices in Vietnam. For example, there was a high profile case in 2006 that seriously alarmed foreign banks and business groups who expressed concern that authorities were criminalising what they considered to be normal business practices (Kazmin, 2006e). Basically, an Incombank employee lost money in speculative foreign currency trading causing an economic loss to the state, a crime in Vietnam. So, Incombank demanded that ABN-Amro, the counterparty bank, compensate it for the lost funds (ibid.). The jailing without charge for months of one Incombank and two ABM employees and payment of US$4.5 million in compensation illustrate the continuing risks of dealing with Vietnamese state banks (Kazmin, 2006f).

A similar paradox can be witnessed in FDI and MNC manufacturing and infrastructure development, as seen in the following examples. Nike set up in Vietnam in 1995 and, while many other MNCs left, it stayed and it is now the second largest manufacturer of Nike-branded products (after China), employing 160,000 people making shoes and apparel, 30 per cent of the company's global supply and 9 per cent of Vietnam's manufactured exports (Kazmin, 2006f). However, there are concerns over the already stained infrastructure, sluggish government bureaucracy and intensified competition to find and retain skilled workers, even managers and executives (ibid.). There is the interesting example of the continuation of Vietnam's socialist ethos, for instance, rather than build a handful of large-scale ports in strategic locations the government prefers to distribute benefits of economic growth equally via building smaller ports in every province (ibid.).

People management in South East Asia – PM versus HRM?

So, we now have a broad overview of our six countries in South East Asia. What about their people management? Before we embark on a similar broad-brush overview of this we need to recall the debate this collection reflects – that is, the idea that there are various perspectives and approaches to people management and that PM and HRM are different and there have been moves from the former to the latter (see Rowley, 2003). We do this by using the distinctions and analysis in Rowley (2003). This cogently argues that it is important to outline three tensions in the field of HRM and which run through the four HRM areas used in the later country-based chapters.

Perspectives, approaches and views in HRM

First, universal versus contingent perspectives can be applied to HRM. The universal view in management believes we can find the optimum approach to dealing with each area. For instance, the notions of 'benchmarking' and 'best practices' fit here. This approach claims that it is possible both to identify the most effective way to manage, as in HRM, and that these practices are also readily transferable. While not a new area, ideas such as globalisation have given such universalistic views renewed vigour. However, an alternative view to this is a contingent perspective. This argues that methods and general approaches in management, and especially HRM, vary and are dependent on a range of factors. They are influenced by the specific circumstances and environments of the organisation. This includes not only size and sector, but also location, with its particular frameworks of institutions and culture. This latter perspective makes the production of a transferable 'one size fits all' HRM prescriptive prognosis very difficult, even within one country.

A second tension concerns the area of HRM policies and practices in terms of their integration versus their independent, stand-alone, free-standing nature. For some commentators more than just HRM usage is required. There is a need for HRM congruence and complimentarity. This 'joined up', integrated HRM can be in two dimensions: horizontal (with internal fit across HRM areas) and vertical (with external fit between HRM and management of the organisation and business strategies and environment). This sort of view is in stark contrast to the 'pick and mix' approach to HRM practices.

Third, a further tension is between the opposing camps in HRM practice itself. On the one hand there is a common desire for simple, cheap practices that are usable and complied with. However, on the other hand, the drive and search to overcome possible limitations and biases in some HRM practices leads to ever more complex, costly methods, but which may in turn be less likely to be carried out. One problem is that such HRM practice may come to be increasingly seen as 'chores', imposing extra paperwork, bureaucracy and costs on busy managers and employees.

These tensions can be seen in Figure 1.1. These tensions again indicate that there may often be no 'right' answer to HRM questions.

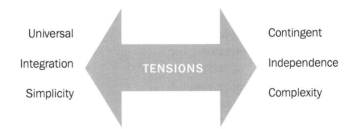

Figure 1.1 Tensions within HRM. Source: Rowley (2003)

A strategic role?

A second part of locating the book's contents in the HRM area is in terms of the 'newness' and 'distinctiveness', or otherwise, of HRM. PM and HRM are often used to refer to the same set of issues and activities and used interchangeably. The rise of the term HRM and its replacement of the motif of PM in lexicons and jobs has emerged, particularly since the 1980s (see Chapters 2 and 3 for examples). However, it is worth recognising some suggested differences between PM and HRM and how the area is seen to have become more central to management. For some, HRM was simply 'old wine in new bottles' while for others it was what 'good' PM should have been all along. Nevertheless, for some commentators distinctions could, however roughly, be made. Some of these can be seen in Table 1.2.

Thus, a key PM/HRM distinction revolves around the concepts of strategy, integration and implementation. This raises a set of related questions, as follows. How strategically do organisations use the HRM function? How integrated are HR policies and decisions with both key business decisions at the strategic level and with each other? Do line managers, rather than HR managers, play a role in developing and implementing HRM?

Furthermore, reports of the take-up of HRM-type practices needs to be tempered by the following. First, practices hailed as 'new' can actually have been in use for some time with newness simply reflecting re-labelling. Second, attempts to introduce change may rarely occur in a strategic and planned way, but rather in an incremental or ad hoc fashion. Third, resistance to change not only from employees but also from managers with preference for previous working practices is to

Table 1.2 PM and HRM compared and contrasted

Dimension	PM	HRM
Implementation	Specialists	Line
Stance	Reactive	Proactive
Practices	Ad hoc	Integrated
Timescale	Short term	Long term
Importance to business	Marginal	Key
Level	Operational	Strategic

Source: Rowley (2003).

be expected. Fourth, many HRM experiments are often less than successful. Fifth, rather than a case of simple and comprehensive HRM absorption there can be more fragmented and nuanced take-up. Indeed, one way to see this is that there are different levels and degrees in HRM application and acceptance.

Levels and degrees of HRM

Rather than seeing HRM as an undifferentiated bloc we can distinguish three levels (system, policy, practice) in HRM (Becker and Gerhart, 1996), with each one having a spectrum of degrees (Kostova, 1999), ranging from imposition and simple enactment through to being fully accepted. This produces a far more nuanced image of HRM (Rowley and Benson, 2002; 2004; Rowley *et al.*, 2004). Such distinctions can be seen in Figure 1.2. We now have a more complex and three-dimensional view of HRM rather than the overly simplified 'yes' or 'no' we are too often given.

In sum, while there is concern to make HRM a key component of senior management decision-making, in practice it may be that few companies have been successful in strategically integrating HRM with the competitive strategy of organisations. The extent to which HRM is applied and accepted can also be distinguished.

HRM overviews

Next we provide a broad-brush overview of HRM in each of the countries, taken mainly from the relevant chapters in the book with extra points added where necessary. The important initial point of the disparate range of HRM between, and within, countries needs to be reinforced. Some of these variations can be explained by some of the commonly used factors in employment research. Of importance here is the nature of the organisation itself, such as whether it is a locally owned company (LOC), an indigenous or foreign MNC subsidiary, a joint venture (JV) or foreign-invested enterprise (FIE) and its nationality and percentage ownership patterns. Others factors include those in Figure 1.2. Of course this limits and makes difficult the idea of being able to say that HRM in a particular country 'x' is 'y'. Nevertheless, we give a broad-brush overview of HRM's main contours.

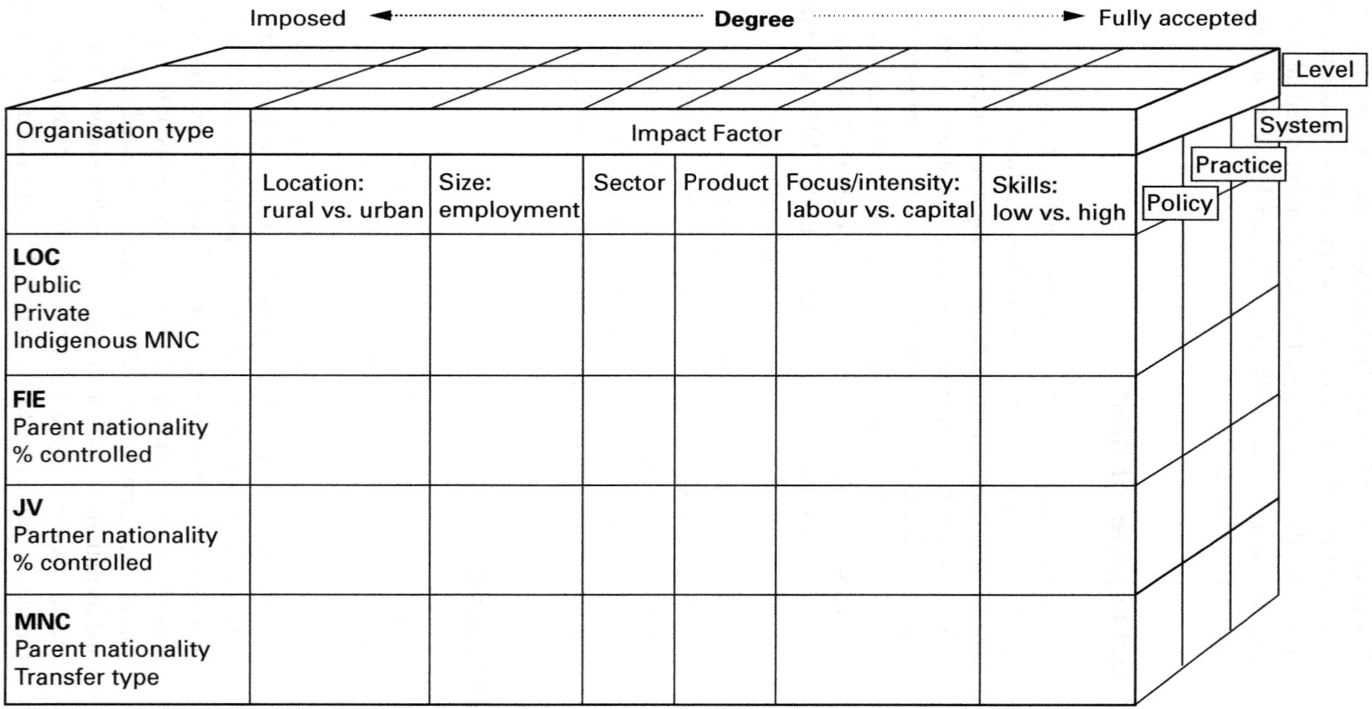

Imposed ⟶ **Degree** ⟵ Fully accepted

Level

System

Practice

Policy

Impact Factor

Organisation type	Location: rural vs. urban	Size: employment	Sector	Product	Focus/intensity: labour vs. capital	Skills: low vs. high
LOC Public Private Indigenous MNC						
FIE Parent nationality % controlled						
JV Partner nationality % controlled						
MNC Parent nationality Transfer type						

Figure 1.2 Impacts on HRM: organisation, level and degree

Indonesia

Traditionally PM did not enjoy high status or have an important role in management and was regarded as a necessary administrative function – especially under the former authoritarian regime with its tight controls and rules and regulations requiring monitoring and compliance – reinforcing an administrative mindset. There has been some cosmetic change, such as the renaming of departments and managers with HR and board-level placements. However, HRM still lacks the status of other management functions, such as marketing or finance. HRM's major responsibility is still seen as keeping records, complying with regulations and processing pay, leave and training and organising company gatherings and outings. Yet, despite this administrative role, widespread discrimination on grounds of gender (despite equality laws) and ethnicity and race (managers picking people from their own ethnic pools) remains. Also, there are limits to how prevalent and 'typical' any practices can be given that 70 per cent of the workforce are in the informal sector with different people management applied.

In terms of the four areas of HRM we can note the following. Regarding employee resourcing some large and well-known organisations maintain their own recruitment centres and there is high labour turnover in the private sector, especially services. With employee development there is little training that needs analysis. Employee rewards include a minimum wage policy while there is the common 'thirteenth month' payment and some development of performance-related pay. With employee relations, the fear of communism led to a government-controlled labour movement to limit independent unions. Post-democratisation, there has been more decentralisation and nego-tiation at enterprise level, although most unions remain federations at the national level as enterprise-level unions have met resistance.

Malaysia

Traditionally PM focused on work simplification, discipline, control and rule observance. However, change has come with shifts in economic development models and moves from labour-intensive, primary commodity and agro-based sectors towards more capital-intensive, manufacturing, hi-tech and service sectors. Since the late 1980s managers have increasingly used the term HRM and indeed there is even some evidence of the increasing strategic integration of the HR function (Todd and Peetz, 2001). Also, the government and the Ministry of HR play key roles in HRM policies and practices (Mellahi and Wood, 2004).

In terms of the four HRM areas we can note the following. In employee resourcing generally firms practise external resourcing (Mansor and Ali, 1998) and, while several large firms have taken the initiative to recruit graduates straight from university, managers still turn to specific ethnic groupings to fill certain jobs and use the countryside as a source of production workers (Mellahi and Wood, 2004). Employee development has been given a higher priority by government and firms, reflecting the desire to upgrade manufacturing. In terms of employee rewards, although the bulk is based on the wage for the occupation, tenure-related increments and contractual bonuses, some performance-related pay has spread (Todd and Peetz, 2001). In terms of employee relations the impact of ethnicity and anti-unionism is rife and low membership endemic (Rowley and Bhopal, 2005a,b; 2006).

Philippines

There has been a fairly long exposure to Western PM (with the practitioners' organisation founded back in 1956) under the influence of US education, culture and leading employers. PM was required to control and discipline and some practitioners had police/military backgrounds and most had legal training, reinforced by the country's large body of laws. Subsequently, non-lawyers, such as psychologists, MBAs and HR specialists and organisational experts, have come to dominate the field.

In terms of the HRM areas, employee resourcing is subject to a huge variety of practices due to form size, product/service, etc, including personal, informal and ad hoc methods. Employee development is often divided between core/professional workers, especially in capital/technology-intensive industries (receiving training), and semi-skilled and peripheral/casual workers (with the government trying to promote training through measures such as an agency and subsidies). Employee rewards are influenced by both market forces and laws, such as the minimum wage. Employee relations operates in the context of a well-developed body of laws and government promotion of tripartisim to help maintain industrial peace, and indeed there are few (fewer than fifty per year) strikes.

Thailand

Until the 1990s most firms still had traditional PM. The influx of FDI, MNCs and JVs, along with the shift in economic development from labour-intensive models, increased the spread of HRM.

In terms of employee resourcing, interviews were commonly used and involved both HR and line managers. In employee development there are differences between services (short-term plans) and manufacturing (long-term plans). In the area of employee rewards there has been some use of incentives. Employee relations has been dominated by the state and its laws. Unions were strong in the public sector pre-1997 Asian Crisis and in the private sector are usually at the operational level.

Singapore

Since the 1960s the PM function evolved from limited forms as in traditional family businesses due to the influence of MNCs and government. At the workplace there is HRM concern with labour flexibility in all its dimensions – functional, numerical and financial.

Of importance in employee resourcing is that in certain key occupations there are still shortages and retention problems. In terms of employee development most (about two-thirds) of the private sector companies train, spending 1.3 per cent of the payroll (2004). Interestingly, while business indicators improved post-training, pay and promotion did not. Of importance in employee rewards is the tripartite effort to develop pay flexibility via the 'monthly variable component' mechanism whereby companies can reduce overall rewards rather than cut basic salaries or employment. There has also been the spread of 'cafeteria' benefits. Employee relations is another area of a tripartite framework and various institutional structures and procedures along with the use of communications mechanisms, such as labour management councils and so forth.

Vietnam

Traditionally command-type PM was carried out in 'organisation departments'. This focused on administration and record keeping with little attention to employee resourcing and only dealing with promotion, rewards (centrally fixed and standardised) and training (on-the-job). Post-1990s a wide variation in people management between SOEs and the variety of foreign-owned companies (FOCs) emerged.

In employee resourcing more typical HRM methods have been more widely used, including links with colleges, using agencies and reliance on interviews as the selection device. Employee development was traditionally less important with reliance on cheap labour but now increasingly there are shortages of skilled staff. In employee rewards there is a minimum wage policy but also more flexibility in determining reward levels and pay differentials have increased, as has the percentage in reward packages taken by benefits and bonuses. Employee relations has a high coverage of firms by unions and membership density rates.

Globalisation, convergence and an Asian way?

These country backgrounds and contexts and HRM overview sketches indicate the impact of economic development and the role of FDI and MNCs in this. As such, globalisation has shaped contemporary Asian business, economic, political and social life (Rowley and Warner, 2005). Many such developments were linked to the large amounts of FDI going into the economies and the influx of MNCs from the US and Europe and other Asian counties, such as Japan and South Korea. MNCs became in turn the driving force behind much of the region's economic growth and expansion. One example is Malaysia where the role of FDI and MNCs was critical, especially in sectors such as electronics (Rowley and Bhopal, 2002).

Interestingly, small- and medium-sized enterprises (SMEs) also remained important (Rowley and Warner, 2005). First, in terms of their prevalence, for example the Philippines is dominated by micro/small firms: 77 per cent employ fewer than five workers, another 14 per cent have five to nine workers (Ofreneo, 2003). Second, in supply chains linking small 'downstream' firms to large 'upstream' enterprises (Rowley and Warner, 2006), SMEs are important.

Nevertheless, FDI and MNC trends are often taken as powerful integral drivers of globalisation and its impacts, such as in its more traditional guise of 'universalism'. What is the situation with regards to this? We may discount the development of a universal Western model (side-stepping what that may actually be) being taken up throughout Asia (Rowley, 1998; Rowley and Benson, 2002; 2004; Rowley *et al.*, 2004). This could be taken as 'hard' convergence. Research continues to find fundamental differences between Western and Eastern cultures in a range of aspects, including perceptions, logic and even models of reality 'with implications for business' (Mathews, 2005: 13). There is also continuing institutional variation across countries (Rowley, 1998; Rowley and Benson, 2002; 2004; Rowley *et al.*, 2004).

What about the development of a transferable, universal Asian model? This could be taken as 'soft' convergence. Is there an 'Asian way' to success or is it naive to assume that there would be a single formula for success that was an identifiable and transplantable recipe for business and HRM? One possible model was Japan. The Japanese model that dominated the way their large corporations were run was very popular, feeding the ideas of the 'Japanisation' of industry. It had implicit and explicit influence in Asian countries, such as Malaysia with its 1980s 'Look East' policy to deliberately copy Japanese practices (Rowley and Bhopal, 2002). Japanisation was also tied up with Malaysia's external loans and the eagerness to attract FDI from Japan. In the 1980s the country took huge amounts of soft loans from Japan, and again during the 1997 Asian Crisis. Indeed, perhaps it was the self-confidence of the period that such ideas of an 'Asian Way' could be promulgated. Japan was riding high with economic success and the notions of 'flying geese' and 'followers' promulgated (Rowley and Warner, 2006). Furthermore, the Asian model had been presented as an alternative to Western models that emerged in the post-war years.

However, the Japanese model has now become less de rigueur

(Rowley *et al.*, 2004). There is no other model as well known in Asia. There may be a number of common features across Asian economies in these respects, especially across the overseas Chinese locations (see Redding, 1990), even if the specific institutional forms vary between countries (see Hamilton, 1995). As such, there was no single management model shaping the way firms are organised, their HRM or how they manage their HR (Rowley, 1998; Rowley and Benson, 2002; 2004; Rowley *et al.*, 2004). The region, as we have seen, is a large and varied one, economically, politically and socially, so it is not surprising if it proved difficult to shape it into one mould.

Indeed, we can take this one step further. There seems to be less homogenous HRM even within countries given the impacts noted above and in the earlier sketches. The plethora of organisational forms, factors and political situations has increased – and with it the heterogeneity of HRM practices within countries.

Conclusion

This chapter has outlined the underpinning rationale of the book, its main structure, format, coverage and content. It has also provided overviews, albeit giving a very broad-brush picture, of the six South East Asian countries in terms of their evolving contexts and HRM. It has also outlined and made points about the debates on PM and HRM, globalisation, convergence and possible models.

The area of HRM remains full of contradictions. For example, the classic, Western model of HRM is inherently incoherent. For instance, ideas of trust, empowerment, skill enhancement and investment, etc. are often emphasised in HRM, but which in turn require long-term investments, returns and views. Yet at the same time organisations seek labour numerical flexibility and operate in short-term horizons. Similar problems exist with the notion of 'best practices' – what are they, even in the West? Also, some practices are mutually exclusive. Both these contradictions are difficult to resolve in the West, and in Asia they are exacerbated by institutions and cultures that underpin authoritarian regimes and management styles. Thus, there may be much written about the need for skill upgrading, knowledge work, etc but these then require commensurately different management, with more trust, empowerment, pluralist perspectives, etc, whereas many continue to focus on labour cost, tight control and unitary perspectives.

What is apparent is the diversity of practices between and within even geographically close countries. This restricts the use and application of 'classic' HRM with its Anglo-American roots and assumptions. Yet the lack of a simple, universal 'one best way' to manage HRs can be difficult and unpalatable to some who want 'the answer' which can then be simply applied. Yet HRM deals not with inanimate objects but people, who are complex social beings, making their management messy and not conducive to standard 'answers', but rather a contingent range of perspectives. What may be 'best' at one time may not be 'best' on the next occasion, even in exactly the same context. When the context changes as well, we see the chasm of contingency, a kaleidoscope of different possibilities, opening up before us (Rowley, 2003).

This collection now goes on to highlight similarities and differences in HRM. Our contributors provide some valuable observations, useful for researchers who wish to learn more about specific countries. Likewise, this collection contains an array of descriptive material which refers not only to practices in HRM departments, but also employment practices. Such documentation is essential for practitioners, especially managers of MNCs, who are interested to learn more about comparative differences set within each different political and cultural context. All in all, the book and its chapters show the continuingly changing face of HRM in South East Asia.

Bibliography

Ayudurai, D., Yahaya, S. R. and Zainuddin, S. (2002) 'Malaysia', in M. Zanko (ed.), *The Handbook of HRM Policies and Practices in Asia-Pacific Economies Volume 1*, Cheltenham: Edward Elgar.

Becker, B. and Gerhart, B. (1996) 'The impact of HRM on organizational performance: progress and prospects', *Academy of Management Journal*, 39, 4, 779–801.

Burton, J. (2005) 'Singapore labour law "fails to protect foreign maids"', *Financial Times*, 7 December, 13.

Burton, J. (2006a) 'Palm oil: Malaysia plans world's biggest listed producer', *Financial Times*, 24 November, 23.

Burton, J. (2006b) 'Stellar results mask a lack of flexibility', *Financial Times*, 18 October, 8.

Dyer, G. (2006) 'Proton in talks with Chery over manufacturing', *Financial Times*, 30 March, 30.

Economist, The (2005) 'The Malay way of business change', 20 August, 54.

Gullaprawit, C. (2002) 'Thailand', in M. Zanko (ed.), *The Handbook of HRM Policies and Practices in Asia-Pacific Economies Volume 1*, Cheltenham: Edward Elgar.

Hamilton, G. (1995) 'Overseas Chinese capitalism', in W. Tu (ed.), *The Confucian Dimensions of Industrial East Asia*, Cambridge, MA: Harvard University Press.

ICFTU (2006) 'Indonesia: Proposed labour laws would seriously weaken rights and conditions', *ICFTU Online*, 28 March.

Kazmin, A. (2006a) 'Thai retreat on equity controls after shares dive', *Financial Times*, 20 December, 1.

Kazmin, A. (2006b) 'Thailand to clarify its foreign ownership laws', *Financial Times*, 4 November, 8.

Kazmin, A. (2006c) 'Vietnam's tax cut deadline triggers listing stamped', *Financial Times*, 6 November, 25.

Kazmin, A. (2006d) 'Payment highlight's Vietnam risk', *Financial Times*, 28 November, 25.

Kazmin, A. (2006e) 'Vietnam seeks to resolve ABN case', *Financial Times*, 2 November, 28.

Kazmin, A. (2006f) 'Investors return to challenge Hanoi', *Financial Times*, 17 November, 9.

Kazmin, A. (2006g) 'Dressed for international success', *Financial Times*, 26 July, 8.

Kazmin, A. (2006h) 'Vietnamese banks face up to challenge', *Financial Times*, 20 September, 29.

Kazmin, A. and Daniel (2006) 'Vietnam's largest private bank to list', *Financial Times*, 21 November, 23.

Kostova, T. (1999) 'Transnational transfer of strategic organizational practices: A contextual perspective', *Academy of Management Review*, 24, 2, 403–28.

Krugman, P. (1996) *Pop Internationalism*, Cambridge, MA: MIT Press.

Landingin, R. (2006) 'Philippines growth stalls', *Financial Times (European Edition)*, 20 November, 9.

Leahy, J. (2006) 'Perodua shifts up a gear as Proton stalls', *Financial Times*, 16 June, 23.

Low, L. (2003) 'Singapore', in M. Zanko and M. Ngui (eds), *The Handbook of HRM Policies and Practices in Asia-Pacific Economies Volume 2*, Cheltenham: Edward Elgar.

Mansor, N. and Ali, H. (1998) 'An explanatory study of organizational flexibility in Malaysia: A research note', *International Journal of Human Resource Management*, 9, 3, 506–15.

Mathews, R. (2005) 'Where east can never meet west', *Financial Times*, 21 October, 13.

Mellahi, K. and Wood, G. (2004) 'HRM in Malaysia', in P. Budhwar (ed.), *Managing Human Resources in Asia-Pacific*, London: Routledge.

Ofreneo, R. (2003) 'Philippines', in M. Zanko and M. Ngui (eds), *The Handbook of HRM Policies and Practices in Asia-Pacific Economies Volume 2*, Cheltenham: Edward Elgar.

Ofreneo, R. and Samonte, I. (2002) 'Empowering Filipino Migrant Workers: Policy Issues and Challenges', Report submitted to the Department of Foreign Affairs, Manila.

Prijadi, R. and Rachmawati, R. (2002) 'Indonesia', in M. Zanko (ed.), *The Handbook of HRM Policies and Practices in Asia-Pacific Economies Volume 1*, Cheltenham: Edward Elgar.

Redding, G. (1990) *The Spirit of Chinese Capitalism*, Berlin: de Gruyter.

Rowley, C. (1998) *HRM in the Asia Pacific Region: Convergence Questioned*, London: Frank Cass.

Rowley, C. (2003) *The Management of People: HRM in Context*, London: Spiro Press.

Rowley, C. and Benson, J. (2002) 'Convergence and divergence in Asian HRM', *California Management Review*, 44, 2, 90–109.

Rowley, C. and Benson, J. (eds) (2004) *The Management of Human Resources in the Asia Pacific Region: Convergence Reconsidered*, London: Frank Cass.

Rowley, C. and Bhopal, M. (2002) 'The state in employment: The case of Malaysia electronics', *International Journal of Human Resource Management*, 13, 8, 1166–85.

Rowley, C. and Bhopal, M. (2005a) 'Ethnicity as a management issue and resource: Examples from Malaysia', *Asia Pacific Business Review*, 10, 1, 105–33.

Rowley, C. and Bhopal, M. (2005b) 'The role of ethnicity in employment relations', *Asia Pacific Journal of Human Resources*, 43, 3, 308–31.

Rowley, C. and Bhopal, M. (2006) 'The ethnic factor in state-labour relations: The case of Malaysia', *Capital and Class*, 88: 87–116.

Rowley, C. and Warner, M. (2004) 'The Asian financial crisis: The impact on HRM', *International Studies in Management and Organization*, 31, 1, 3–9.

Rowley, C. and Warner, M. (2005) *Globalisation and Competitiveness: Big Business in Asia*, London: Routledge.

Rowley, C. and Warner, M. (2006) 'Management in South East Asia: Studies in diversity and dynamism' *Asia Pacific Business Review*, 12, 4, 389–410.

Rowley, C., Benson, J. and Warner, M. (2004) 'Towards an Asian model of HRM', *International Journal of HRM*, 31, 1, 917–33.

Thao, P. Q., Tu, N. H. and Nguyen, N. X. (2003) 'Vietnam', in M. Zanko and M. Ngui (eds), *The Handbook of HRM Policies and Practices in Asia-Pacific Economies Volume 2*, Cheltenham: Edward Elgar.

Todd, P. and Peetz, D. (2001) 'Malaysian industrial relations at century's turn: Vision 2020 or a specter of the past?', *International Journal of Human Resource Management*, 12, 8, 1365–82.

2 The changing face of human resource management in Indonesia

Ahmad D. Habir and Krishnan Rajendran

- Political, economic and social/cultural background and context
- Key labour market features and developments
- Development of PM and HRM and the HR function and profession
- HRM practices
- Case studies of indigenous organisations
- Case studies of individual managers
- Challenges and prospects for HRM
- Conclusion

Introduction

Indonesia is a country with diverse HR and HRM challenges. The Asian Financial Crisis of 1997 had a profound political and economic impact on Indonesia. The country had a growth rate of 7 per cent per annum prior to the crisis. However, even though most of Asia has recovered from the crisis, Indonesia is still struggling to recover from unprecedented economic, political, social and natural environment problems. In the context of the recovery and the impact of globalisation on businesses in general, more attention is being paid to the need for effective HRM in Indonesia (Budihardjo, 1996; Ciptono, 1998; Kismono, 1999).

Historically, HRM did not play an important role in Indonesian management. Traditionally it is regarded as only an administrative personnel function. A survey conducted in 1995 showed that managers had negative perceptions of HR audits, HRD, HR planning, employee orientation and the salary system of their respective companies (Budihardjo, 1996). Nevertheless, since the 1997 crisis, business organisations have moved towards improvements in their

HRM systems; currently, personnel departments are known as HR departments and personnel managers are re-designated as HR managers. More companies are adopting strategic HR by highlighting the role of HR departments in their annual reports. Some companies have set up HR committees at the governance level, in line with good corporate governance practices. These developments indicate a growing realisation of the importance of HRM in Indonesia today.

Political, economic and social/ cultural background and context[1]

Political

Indonesia is the largest country in South East Asia and is the world's most populous Muslim state. It is the largest archipelago in the world, consisting of some 17,000 islands. However, only the five major islands of Sumatra, Java, Kalimantan, Sulawesi and Papua plus about 30 other smaller islands are populated. Indonesia is part of the 'ring of fire', a zone of frequent earthquakes and volcanic eruptions that encircle the basin of the Pacific Ocean.

The archipelago lies between the Pacific and Indian Oceans and the continents of Asia and Australia. This strategic geographic position has been a major factor influencing the cultural, social, political and economic life of the country. Historically the archipelago was a major trading crossroads and a source of valued trading commodities ranging from spices to minerals. Politically, Indonesia was ruled by Hindu–Buddhist kingdoms in the early centuries, followed by the establishment of Islam in the thirteenth century. By the eighteenth century the Dutch had become the major power, consolidating the archipelago into the colonial Netherlands East Indies that existed until the onset of the Second World War and the Japanese invasion in 1942. By the end of the war, led by Soekarno (the first president of the country), Indonesia declared its independence from the Dutch in 1945 (Cribb, 1999).

Since the late 1960s the country was ruled by President Soeharto for over 30 years. However, the 1997 Asian Crisis and its ensuing economic crash forced his resignation. Indonesia has since moved from a corrupt authoritarian regime dominated by a powerful president to a fledgling democracy struggling to recover from the excesses of the former government (Emmerson, 1999). Since the fall of Soeharto the country has experienced the rule of four presidents. Yet the transition has been a relatively democratic one and now Indonesia finds itself the third largest democracy located in a strategic area of the world. However, democracy is still precariously placed, as the public voice their previously unexpressed demands in terms of ethnic, regional, religious and labour aspirations, resulting in political instability.

Susilo Bambang Yudhoyono became the country's first democratically elected president in September 2004. While there has been some macro-economic progress and political stability, for example in the case of the peace treaty with the political separatist movement in Acheh, the slow pace of reform and the continuing failure to increase employment creates some disillusionment among citizens.

Economic

Indonesia experienced almost three decades of economic growth, but the economic contraction due to the 1997 Asian Financial Crisis plunged the country into a prolonged national crisis. In early 1998 the rupiah dropped to four times its pre-crisis rate, and consumer prices increased drastically. The number of people living below the poverty line had soared to 95.8 million (or about 48 per cent of the population) by the end of 1998 (Harsono, 1999).

The business sector, particularly the large conglomerates and state enterprises, shared some of the blame for the economic crisis (Habir, 1999). Companies that over-indulged in large foreign loans could not afford to service their loans due to the devaluation of the currency; hence international confidence in the country diminished and this led to the impoverishment of the economy (ibid.). Furthermore, there was a considerable exodus of capital and professionals, mainly ethnic Chinese Indonesians. Businesses remained stagnant as the implementation of many important reforms in areas such as the financial sector and the state sector were obstructed by nationalistic and patrimonial forces.

Within Indonesia, the press, parliament and non-governmental organisations (NGOs), especially the Indonesian Corruption Watch and the Indonesian Transparency Society, have become more active in overseeing the way business is conducted in the country. However, the weak legal structure remains an obstacle to the attempts at business reform. The law in Indonesia arises from numerous sources, is extremely complicated and somewhat vague, and much discretion is left to government authorities. Many 'safeguards' are provided in Indonesia's legal code, but 'in many important respects that protection is not available in practice . . . The legal system [is] unresponsive, corrupt, politicised and ineffective, [and] offers little recourse to the individual in righting perceived wrongs' (Schwartz, 1994: 245).

Social/cultural

The main language of the 207 million Indonesians is Bahasa Indonesia, although there are 250 other regional languages and dialects (Bishop and McNamara, 1997). While approximately 70 per cent of the population live in rural areas (Levinson, 1998), cities such as Jakarta, Surabaya and Medan continue to grow as rural residents seek work in urban areas. The population consists of at least 200 ethnic groups (*Straits Times*, 1997) but with only four considered to be significant numerically: Javanese (45 per cent), Sundanese (14 per cent), Madurese (7.5 per cent) and coastal Malays (7.5 per cent) (Levinson, 1998). Although less than 5 per cent of the population are ethnic Chinese, they are reported to control 60–80 per cent of Indonesia's economic activity (*Straits Times*, 1997). Muslims constitute 87 per cent of Indonesians, Protestants 6 per cent, Roman Catholics 3 per cent, Hindus 2 per cent and Buddhists 1 per cent (ibid.).

Based on his cultural dimensions survey, Hofstede (1982; 1983) characterised the Indonesian culture and its implications for HRM as follows: the relationship between employer and employee is seen as moral rather than calculative, implying mutual obligations of protection from the employer (irrespective of the employee's performance) and loyalty of the employee towards the employer. Relationship takes precedence over task. The society that is paternalistic in nature also recognises status differences. However, such cultural dimensions may not be static over time and there is some evidence that the paternalistic and status-orientated relationship at the workplace has eroded enough to allow for a more strategic and performance-oriented HRM (Habir and Larasati, 1999).

Key labour market features and developments

The labour force may be divided into the following categories: agriculture (46.7 per cent), industry (11.8 per cent) and services (41.7 per
cent) (Table 2.1). However, as nearly 70 per cent of the 'employed'
labour force are in the informal sector (Firdausy, 1995), readers are
cautioned that much of the discussion on the labour force and HRM
in this chapter applies only to the 30 per cent or so of the labour force
that are employed in the formal sector.

Table 2.1 Key employment and labour force indicators, 1996–2005

	1996–1997	2000–2001	2004–2005	Average growth rates (% per annum)	
				1996–2001	2001–2005
Working-aged population (millions)	133	143	155	1.7	2.0
Labour force	n/a	n/a	n/a	1.4	1.3
Employment by sector (% share)					
Agriculture	43	44	44	2.2	0.7
Manufacturing	13	13	12	1.9	−1.1
Other	45	42	44	−0.2	2.2
Total	100	100	100	1.1	1.1
Non-agricultural employment (%)					
Formal	52	51	48	−0.2	−0.1
Informal	48	49	52	0.8	3.0
Total	100	100	100	0.3	1.4
LFPR[a](%)	68.0	67.2	65.2	n/a	n/a
Unemployment (%)					
Pre-2001 definition	4.8	5.8	6.5	6.4	4.1
2001 definition[b]			8.1	10.1	n/a

Sources: BPS, National Labour Force Survey, various years; based on survey data collected in
August for all years except 2005; survey data for 2005 was collected in February as part of a new
biannual labour force survey (Manning and Roesyad, 2006).

Notes
a Labour force participation rate.
b The new definition of unemployment introduced in 2001 includes 'discouraged workers'.

The proportion of women in the labour force has increased to 39.2 per cent (Triaswati, 1996), but much of this increase is in low-skilled, labour-intensive industries where women are perceived to be more easily managed than men (Hadiz, 1997). For example, women dominate the workforce in industries such as tobacco, textiles, and food and beverages. According to White (1990) employers prefer them not only because of their perceived dexterity and patience, but also for their unassertiveness and deference to authority.

Prior to the economic contraction caused by the 1997 Asian Crisis, there were estimates that over one-third of the Indonesian labour force were either underemployed or unemployed (Hadiz, 1997). High-school and university graduates formed the bulk of the unemployed in the cities and towns (Manning, 1999), part of which was explained by selective job search behaviours (Manning and Junakar, 1998). In 2005 unemployment remained high at above 8 per cent, as shown in Table 2.1. The government has tried to address unemployment by formulating policy packages to improve the investment climate (Manning and Roesyad, 2006: 85). Yet the continuing high cost of conducting business in Indonesia, both in terms of regulations as well as the prevalent corruption, despite the ongoing anti-corruption campaigns, has slowed down new foreign investment in the country. Table 2.2 illustrates examples of the high cost of setting up business operations in relation to HR and labour regulations in selected Asian countries, and the data clearly show that Indonesia has one of the highest 'rigidity of employment indices' among the countries surveyed by the World Bank.

Development of PM and HRM and the HR function and profession

The personnel management (PM) function is still in transition. Most organisations consider PM as an administrative function within general administration, with the main responsibilities of organising company gatherings and outings, keeping records, complying with regulations, and administering leave and pay. To a large extent, the personnel administration function is considered necessary but not important to the organisation.

The transition from PM to HRM will not be easy for many

Table 2.2 Indices of employment flexibility and hiring and firing costs, selected Asian countries, 2005[a]

	Hiring		Firing			Average index (0–100)[b]
	Difficulty of hiring index (0–100)	Cost of hiring (% of salary)	Difficulty of firing index (0–100)	Cost of firing (weeks of wages)	Rigidity of hours index (0–100)	
More restrictive (rigidity of employment index >50)						
India	56	12	90	79	40	62
Cambodia	67	0	30	39	80	59
Indonesia	61	10	70	145	40	57
Brazil	67	27	20	165	80	56
Vietnam	44	17	70	98	40	51
Less restrictive (rigidity of employment index <50)						
Korea	44	17	30	90	60	45
Philippines	56	9	40	90	40	45
China	11	30	40	90	40	30
Chile	33	3	20	51	20	24
Thailand	33	5	0	47	20	18
Malaysia	0	13	10	65	20	10
Singapore	0	13	0	4	0	0
Mean for all countries	39	40	35	38	13	80

Source: adapted from World Bank/International Finance Corporation 2006, www.doing business.org (quoted in Manning and Roesyad, 2006).

Notes
a A higher index denotes greater difficulty.
b This is the 'rigidity of employment index', equivalent to the average of the three other indices.

organisations, as several major factors contribute to the difficulties of transition. First, the Soeharto regime of over 30 years in government kept tight control over all aspects of ER. Compliance with the HR rules and regulations of the country, as well as those formulated by organisations themselves, was the primary, and in many cases the only, task of personnel departments. Second, the task of monitoring and ensuring compliance created an administrative mind-set that remains entrenched among both senior management and personnel managers. Third, in the period of rapid economic growth during most of the Soeharto regime, the functions of production, marketing and finance gained status as strategic areas of business development while PM/HRM remained, with few exceptions, an administrative function. Fourth, the 1997 Asian Crisis that triggered the fall of the Soeharto regime led many companies to the brink of bankruptcy. Hence companies focused on cost reduction, downsizing and debt restructuring. The role of the personnel function was to ensure that redundancies were carried out smoothly and in line with labour rules and regulations. Fifth, the personnel function also schedules and organises training programmes, both in-house and external. Training activities are budgeted for yearly, and training is organised so as to utilise the training budget so that more allocation can be approved in the following budget cycle. However, in the general absence of proper evaluation of performance and assessment of competencies, training programmes tend not to be based on training needs analysis (Hess, 1995; Budihardjo, 1996; Ciptono, 1998; *SWA*, 2006).

Nonetheless, findings of a survey of forty-nine major companies comprising eleven state enterprises and thirty-eight private companies showed that there are companies that have made the transition towards HRM (*SWA*, 2006). These organisations do not consider employees as merely a factor of production but they believe that employees are human capital and ought to be developed to contribute their best and add value to the organisation (*SWA*, 2006: 35).

In the more professionally managed organisations, for example family or private businesses where professional managers play prominent roles, or partially privatised state enterprises beholden to their shareholders rather than wholly to the government, HRM is steadily gaining ground and obtaining an influential voice in boardrooms. Encouraged by their respective chief executive officers (CEOs) and managed by competent HR professionals, the HRM function in these companies is moving towards being recognised as a strategic function, with its role gradually shifting from merely securing compliance by employees to one of winning employees' commitment.

HRM practices[2]

Employee resourcing

Recruitment is a major HR activity in Indonesian organisations, particularly in the private sector. This is necessitated by fast and regular turnover of employees. Certain sectors in the service industry, such as telecommunications, are growing rapidly, thus placing a heavy demand on the recruitment function. In several organisations the policy statement on recruitment delineates the importance of having the right person in the right job. However, the process of recruitment and selection often does not fit with the stated policy.

Companies tend to use several methods of recruitment, ranging from advertising to 'headhunting' by consultants. Many organisations rely on recruitment consultants to furnish them with a list of suitable candidates while others rely primarily on advertisements in the media or over the internet. Referrals from employees, business partners, and other people known to the owners or management are still resorted to in the hope of obtaining employees who are trustworthy. It is assumed that personal contacts and referees would recommend only those they know well, and therefore could be trusted. Given the dearth of skills and talent, especially in the fast-growing sectors, poaching competent people has become an aspect of the recruitment of management and professional staff.

Some large organisations maintain their own recruitment centres where the primary focus is on external recruitment. These organisations carry out recruitment for management trainees on university campuses. However, this does not preclude recruitment from internal sources, which is often done through internal job postings. The practice of recruiting from the internal labour market is more common among state-owned enterprises (SOEs) where government policy of zero per cent recruitment growth prohibits recruitment from external sources in order to maintain control over the number of employees.

Selection practices vary across organisations. Personal interviews are a common practice. Most often, they are the only tools used in some of the smaller and medium-sized organisations. In others, especially larger organisations, interviews are combined with psychometric tests, with the hope that a better picture of the candidate's suitability can be obtained through the tests. Other tools like group discussions and presentations are often applied during the selection process, depending on the competency of the HR department and the time available. Time is a major constraint in the recruitment exercise, especially in companies facing a fast turnover of employees.

Multinational companies (MNCs) and large domestic companies are beginning to implement competency-based selection methods. Various tools, such as psychological tests, behavioural interviews, group discussions, roleplays, etc. are used in combination to select candidates with the right competencies. Some organisations have set up their own assessment centres to test candidates. These assessment centres are also used to test the potential of employees who are due for promotion. As assessment centres are costly, they are used mainly for the selection of candidates for senior positions.

A common practice in the government and the SOEs is the 'fit-and-proper' tests that are carried out to select senior management personnel. This method calls upon the candidate to make a presentation of their vision, mission and strategic plan for the organisation in front of a panel of experts. Clarity and depth of the presentation, along with the innovative ideas contained in it, would determine whether they would be selected to the position or not. Additionally, an in-depth review of applications, evaluation of a candidate's track record, and reference checks are also widely used.

Employee development

The important process of socialising a new entrant to the organisation is the most neglected area of HRM in Indonesia. While new employees are generally given company orientation programmes, these tend to be ritualistic rather than as a process that could have a long-term influence on the career of the individual concerned. Nevertheless, there are organisations that take this process seriously and build into it a learning experience that includes getting to know the business, its organisational structure, products and processes. The HR departments in these organisations monitor the induction process as it takes place, receiving and giving feedback. An evaluation of the training course is done at the end of the induction period. The induction process could vary from a couple of days to a week, depending on the training budgets of the companies.

Nevertheless, generally in Indonesia training is an activity that is carried out without a stated purpose or a defined plan. It is often perceived as a reward by employees sponsored for training, especially external training, and in such cases it is not based on predetermined training needs. In-house programmes are also organised and employees are sent for external programmes often just because HR departments have to ensure that the training budgets are expended so as to be able to get a new training budget approved the following year. Therefore, there is a tendency for training activities to take place towards the end of the year.

However, MNCs and large domestic organisations allocate substantial amounts for training, which is based on training needs analysis. In such organisations training managers are appointed to plan, coordinate and impart training to employees at various levels. Post-training evaluation is also carried out in these organisations. Both in-house and external training are planned and executed. In-house training is given either by a team of internal trainers or by external trainers. Sponsorship for training outside the organisation could include attendance at public workshops, conferences and seminars. To a large extent, training is used as a tool to enhance knowledge and skills at various levels within the organisation.

In organisations where training is properly planned, annual training schedules are drawn up based on a proper analysis of organisational and job needs, individual performance evaluations and competency assessments. Individual capability building plans are created for each employee. The design of training programmes follows the principles of adult learning. The emphasis is on interactive and experiential learning through the use of cases, exercises, games and role-plays. At the end of the training session an action plan is prepared by each participant, facilitated by the trainer, with the aim of implementing new work behaviour in the workplace. Such organisations, which are very few in number, use performance appraisal (PA) and competency assessment to gauge the attainment of new behaviours among its employees.

Employee rewards

The compensation structure in most Indonesian organisations is composed of basic pay and certain fixed allowances (transportation, meals, positional, etc.). Benefits include medical reimbursement for outpatient medical care, hospitalisation insurance and social security contributions. All employees are entitled to a thirteenth month pay, which is the sum of basic pay and fixed allowances. This is paid out in conjunction with the major festival holidays of either Idul Fitri or Christmas. Executives at senior levels are entitled to additional benefits, such as club membership subscription fees, provision of a car and a driver, and entertainment allowances. They may also be eligible for performance-based bonuses or profit sharing.

Certain organisations have implemented incentive schemes for their production and sales employees. The incentives are variable in nature, dependent on the production of a certain number of units or sales of a certain volume or value. These incentives are progressively scaled up in order to motivate the employee to stretch their effort and attain higher productivity levels. Incentive earners are also paid a base salary that is fixed in nature.

Some companies pay hiring bonuses to attract talented candidates. However, as a talent retention practice, organisations are known to carry out periodic market surveys, followed by adjustments of salaries to bring about market parity. This practice, though, is limited to organisations operating in competitive markets. Other organisations, constrained by budget considerations, do not consider market parity as an affordable exercise. They often choose to reward talent on an individual basis.

Market parity apart, internal equity is a predominant concern in many organisations. Some organisations, mostly MNCs, have evaluated and structured their jobs and pay. Yet other organisations continue to operate with internal inequities, without making an attempt to correct them. Companies are unwilling to adjust pay levels if it would also benefit those who do not perform. They would prefer, instead, to make salary adjustments for the performing few.

Legally there is a minimum wage level policy in Indonesia. However, minimum wage levels differ according to regions, although discussions by the relevant authorities are now focusing more on an 'appropriate' rather than a minimum wage. Manning (1993) and Hadiz (1997) argue that minimum wages have been set much lower than a level that would cover the minimum physical needs of a single person. The current belief is that minimum wage levels provide for about 95 per cent of the minimum physical requirements of a single person (*Jakarta Post*, 1997a), which is significantly lower compared with other Asian countries, such as Thailand, Philippines, South Korea, Taiwan, Hong Kong and Singapore (Tjiptoherijanto, 1998).

The minimum wage rate does not mean that all employees are actually paid according to this standard; employers pay less because they can defer minimum wage compliance for up to 12 months from the time of recruitment. By way of rationalisation some employers have complained that their businesses cannot afford increases in the minimum wage due to the very high prevalence of so-called 'invisible costs' of doing business, such as 'fees' (Lesmana, 1999). These 'fees' are sums of money paid by employers to various government agencies, which is seen as a normal practice in Indonesian bureaucrat-business relationships. The 'fees' facilitate employers in obtaining licences easily, as well as protecting them from any industrial action taken by their workers. The prevention of disputes at production facilities can be attributed to this collusion (Lesmana, 1999). This state of affairs pushes up costs borne by employers, varying from 2 to more than 30 per cent of total operating costs (Hadiz, 1997).

Although the constitution states that women are equal to, and have the same rights, obligations and opportunities as, men, in practice, women face some legal discrimination (BDHRLHR, 1999). Female workers in the manufacturing sector generally receive lower wages than men, and many jobs are gender stereotyped to the disadvantage of women (Cukier *et al.*, 1996). Apart from receiving lower wages, women are often hired as day labourers instead of as full-time permanent employees so that companies can avoid providing benefits, such as maternity leave; and in some cases women employees do not receive benefits, such as medical insurance.

Employee relations

There are three types of employment under the Employment Law: namely, fixed period employment, which requires a written contract in Bahasa Indonesia; indefinite period or 'permanent' employment, for which a written contract is not mandatory; and traditional employment in the informal sector, which is essentially unregulated (Surowidjojo, 1999). A 3-month probationary period applies to permanent appointments, and once this period has expired the termination of their employment is almost impossible; government approval is needed for the termination of employees (Surowidjojo, 1999). Indonesian labour legislation requires at least 30 days' notice for termination of an employment contract. Termination on grounds of labour union activities, religious activities, political activities, marriage, pregnancy, childbirth, or illness of less than 1 year is prohibited by law. Employers are required to pay compensation and severance pay, typically 1 month's salary plus 1 month's salary for each full year worked. Employees terminated after more than 3 years of service are also entitled to service pay of at least 1 month's salary per 3 years of service.

Legally, women are entitled to extra provisions under the Employment Law, such as 3 months' paid maternity leave and the monthly 2 days' paid menstruation leave. They are also protected from dismissal due to marriage, pregnancy or confinement (Bennington, 2001). Furthermore, special conditions are set for women regarding work at night; the employer is obliged to make a written request to the local office of the Department of Manpower, which sets out the kind of business and character of the job and the reasons why they want to employ women at night.

Notwithstanding the protective legislation for women in some areas, the regulations are reported to be commonly neglected (Grijns and van Velzen, 1993). For example, the government has acknowledged that pregnant women are often dismissed or are replaced while on leave; and some companies even require that women sign statements that they do not intend to become pregnant (BDHRLHR, 1999). Sexual exploitation of women in the workplace is not uncommon (Hill, 1996) and, even though only a small percentage of harassment incidents are reported, when they do reach the judicial court women generally lose their cases (Triaswati, 1996).

Apart from discrimination based on gender, other forms of discrimination based on ethnic and religious grounds also exist within the employment scenario. Sometimes it takes the form of 'positive' discrimination (such as preference for Chinese in certain positions like finance or marketing roles), but generally it is negative. The ethnic Chinese, who constitute less than 5 per cent of the population but are the major players in the economy, are often discriminated against in some jobs. The Chinese have been restricted from joining the civil service, state enterprises, the police and armed forces. At the same time, the large Chinese Indonesian business groups that dominate the private sector as well as *pribumi* (ethnic Malay) companies normally recruit out of their own ethnic pool.

ER in Indonesia is currently in a process of transition. A more decentralised system is being implemented where employers and employees negotiate the terms and conditions of employment at the enterprise level through Collective Labour Agreements (CLAs). This transition is in line with democratisation of the political system and the evolvement of more transparent decision-making. There are a number of labour organisations in Indonesia today.

These are mostly unions and federations at the national level. Formation of unions at the enterprise level has generally met with resistance from owners and the management, especially of small and medium enterprises. As it stands, most of these enterprises are without unions. Furthermore, research (SMERU, 2002) shows that owners and the management of enterprises, and even employees, are ignorant of the benefits of unionisation.

Besides, most disputes can be resolved through bipartite dialogue between employers and employees. Both employees (including enterprise unions) as well as employers argue that there are few serious indications of tension in employee–employer relations. Both parties are still undergoing a learning process; employees are learning to exercise the freedom to organise, articulate their demands and find better methods of negotiation, whereas employers are learning to regard employees as work partners (SMERU, 2003: 21). Thus, many cases of enterprise-level unionisation have taken place only after a period of strife.

In January 2006 Indonesia introduced a new law regarding termination of employment. In addition to labour rights and wage disputes, the new provisions established a labour court as a means of resolving labour disputes in a fair and efficient way, either by arbitration, mediation or conciliation. The new labour law also covers employment termination. Employers intending to terminate employees must first try to reach agreement over termination terms and submit the documentation to the local labour court. If an agreement cannot be reached, the dispute must move on to mediation with an outside mediator, and finally to the labour court. However, in a system where it is common for employees to be employed without labour contracts, this new system is not yet widely enforced by the authorities.

Existing labour unions in Indonesia can be categorised into two general types. The first type consists of unions formed by employees as a mode of expressing their grievances collectively. These unions have a clear mission, well-defined membership and good management. Second, there are unions which are organised on the basis of politics and political parties. Such unions are run by non-employees or people from outside the enterprise. Thus, generally they do not have a well-defined membership and may include non-enterprise workers. In short these unions more or less provide a political platform for their leaders. Indeed, studies found that the:

> overall effectiveness and professionalism of a labour union is dependent on how well they are able to organize and recruit their members, their level of understanding of their roles, functions and the regulations in place, as well as how well they can present their demands, negotiate, and resolve disputes.
>
> (SMERU, 2003: 9)

Organisations are also known to have initiated the formation of unions so as to facilitate organised discussion and negotiation on productivity and other improvements. Legally it is also possible for the formation of multiple unions within a given enterprise.

Case studies of indigenous organisations

The two companies we present in this section are one of the largest oil producers and one of the largest business groups in Indonesia. Both companies began as family-run businesses but have been transformed successfully into professionally run enterprises.

Organisation case study 1: PT Medco Energi

Medco Energi is an integrated energy company, with businesses ranging from the exploration and production of oil and gas on the upstream side to petrochemical and power generation on the downstream side. Founded in 1980 as one of the first Indonesian drilling contractors, it entered the oil and gas exploration and production business when it took over Tesoro's Kalimantan exploration and production contracts in 1992. In 1994 Medco had a successful Initial Public Offering at the Jakarta Stock Exchange, and subsequently purchased PT Stanvac Indonesia from ExxonMobil in 1995.

The corporate values that form the foundation of the company's corporate strategies are articulated as 'Professional, Ethical, Open and Innovative'. To realise the company's vision, the management drew up a HRM plan for 2002–2007. The plan encompassed the following issues: key HR processes, corporate culture and values enhancement, work condition enhancement and competencies and productivity improvement.

In 2003 an integrated performance management system (PMS) was initiated. The PMS cycle starts at the beginning of the year, at the same time corporate strategies and objectives for the year are announced to employees. A performance plan is formulated to encompass areas determined as the key performance indicators (KPIs). At the end of the year, performance evaluations based on the performance plans are conducted for individual employees. Finally, reward and compensation, as well as career development plans, are formulated based on the results of the performance evaluations.

So as to enhance corporate culture and values, in 2003 Medco initiated a training programme that institutionalised effective working behaviour. In addition, the company introduced a management assessment programme, which aims to improve competencies of senior executives and managers. Under the Individual Development Programme, employees formulate their own career plans, including the training requirements for achieving their plans. On the whole, the company spends rupiah 15.5 billion (US$1.87 million; £1.14 million) to enrol more than 2,900 employees in the company's domestic and international training programmes.

As part of its ER programme the company conducted an Employee Opinion Survey in May–September 2004. Findings of the survey showed that some 14 per cent of employees were unsatisfied with certain issues; however, the management took corrective action on those issues. In addition, since 2004 the company has started a 'working climate enhancement programme', which includes the 'Lunch Contact' and 'Tea Time' programmes, whereupon employees are given the opportunity to convey their concerns and expectations directly to the management team.

Sources: PT Medco Energi Internasional Tbk *Annual Report* (2003; 2004); interviews with company officers: P. M. Susbandono, Head of HR; Aviv Murtadho, Head of Information Services, MedcoEnergi Oil and Gas; and Budiarto Idries, Head of HSE and Management Audit, MedcoEnergi Chemicals.

Organisation case study 2: PT Astra International

PT Astra International, founded in 1957, is one of the largest business groups in Indonesia. The group is organised into six business divisions: automotive, financial services, heavy equipment, agribusiness, IT and infrastructure. It currently employs a total of 119,000 employees. Astra was initially a family business founded by William Soeryadjaya. In 1990 Astra became a publicly listed company with a diversified shareholder base that includes foreign shareholders with substantial shareholdings.

The Group has won recognition as the most well-managed and professionally run Indonesian business group. The modern management style at the Astra Group arose from the vision and philosophy of the founding family. William Soeryadjaya explained his management philosophy in 1975:

> From the founding of Astra International to the present we have always continued to adhere to one philosophy. That is, the company can grow and develop successfully if all personnel are diligent, cooperative, and have a sense of belonging to the company, and if all the personnel, the public, and the shareholders can perceive and enjoy the fruits of the company's success.
>
> (Sato, 1996: 263)

Astra has followed a non-discriminatory employment policy. Unlike many other Indonesian firms, Astra does not primarily recruit employees from one ethnic group only. Management and employees consist of both *pribumi* (indigenous Indonesians) and ethnic Chinese Indonesians.

The Astra Management Development Institute provides training support for the Group. A uniform training system ensures a strong quality-oriented work culture. Training modules at the institute focus on the development of three competencies, namely, basic, functional and leadership competencies. These training programmes are intertwined with on-the-job training, project assignments and mentoring by senior staff members.

Astra relies on its strong corporate base in order to command the loyalty of its employees and thus avoid labour disputes within the group. The HR department organises occasional forums which are attended by members of the Board of Directors and employees of the Astra group, with the aim of resolving any labour issues that are brought up by the employees.

Sources: Sato (1996); Habir and Larasati (1999); Susanto and Soelaeman (2006); Astra International (2006); *SWA* (2006).

Case studies of individual managers

In this section we focus on two managers, namely, Hilmi Panigoro of the Medco group of companies and George Tahija of the Austindo group of companies.

Manager case study 1: Hilmi Panigoro

In 2005 Hilmi Panigoro, CEO of the Medco Group, won the Ernst & Young Entrepreneur of the Year Award for managers in the industry and manufacturing category. He was cited as being instrumental in organisational restructuring and a series of debt restructuring negotiations during the 1997 Asian Crisis. Under his leadership Medco became the first private Indonesian company to own major oil and gas exploration and production blocks. He transformed the company from a drilling service provider to an integrated energy company operating in oil and gas exploration and production, drilling services, methanol production and power generation.

Production in the Indonesian oil and gas industry is declining. Hence Medco's key business strategy is to replace and add to reserves through acquisition and exploration of new oil wells and gas fields, as well as to diversify the business prudently. Hilmi has set up clear divisions of energy and non-energy business units. Growth is based on a three-stage strategy of expanding exploration, increasing productivity of existing fields, and strengthening the balance of the company's portfolio. For the next 5–10 years, the energy sector will be the backbone of the company. Yet the non-energy businesses (such as the food industry, hotels, and agro-business) would be prudently expanded in order to complement the energy division in the future. To guide these changes, Hilmi places paramount importance on developing core corporate values so as to facilitate adjustments to the business diversification exercise.

Medco has increased its workforce substantially through recruitment and by way of business acquisitions. Commenting on these acquisitions at a gathering of employees from a newly acquired operation in Kalimantan, Hilmi said:

> Medco also grew from different cultures. But even though we come from different environments, I hope we can all enter a new culture, the culture of ethics. Just recently we introduced four values which I hope every member of the Medco organisation would share as a way of life.

He expects all levels of Medco employees to be recognised as professional, ethical, open and innovative:

> Professional because we work at our best, ethical because we always have good governance, honest because we are never corrupt, and open because we can be trusted by everybody. We are innovative because we always do

continuous improvement. These are values that cannot be measured by money. This dream is much more important. With it our business aims can be reached.

Sources: Energise (2005: 10); BUMN Online (2005); Medco Group (2006).

Manager case study 2: George Tahija

George Tahija is the President of PT Austindo Nusantara Jaya (Austindo). He is responsible for planning, leading and developing the activities of the Austindo Group. Under George's leadership, in 1997 Austindo shifted its corporate strategy; hence, instead of being just a passive financial investor in the business sector, Austindo began to actively operate core businesses in areas such as oil palm plantations, gold exploration and the financial sector.

In describing the company's philosophy George Tahija stressed that:

We have a reason for believing in a family philosophy as to why we are in business and what our objectives are. It is our belief that the fortunes of the community that we live and work in are inextricably linked with the fortunes of our business. If the community does well, we will do well. If the community suffers, we too will suffer. The 1997 Asian Crisis and its effect in Indonesia was not a result of globalisation. For the most part, it was caused by irresponsible capitalism that thrived in a corrupt environment. Given the philosophy that we have, we set about establishing a set of values and a mission for the corporation to ensure that our philosophy is carried out in day-to-day operations.

The shift in business strategy and the acquisition of new business operations resulted in an increase in the number of employees within the Austindo Group. For George Tahija it is vital for his company to recruit and develop employees that would fit into a strong corporate culture based on honesty and transparency.

In 2005, so as to link the strategic objectives with operating parameters, George Tahija introduced the balanced scorecard approach to all operating business units in the Austindo group. A total performance scorecard was allocated for each business unit, while all employees were provided with personal scorecards so as to record their work progress in line with the company's objectives. This approach provided the basis of a pay-for-performance system for each individual's role in achieving the company's targets. George emphasised the importance of modelling the right behaviour in leading the company: 'You have to lead by example. People will follow what the boss does.'

Sources: McBeth and Tripathi (1998); Asian Business Dialogue (2003); interviews with company officers: George Tahija, President; A. Wahyuhadi, Commissioner; and Tommy Sudjarwadi, Director, PT Austindo Nusantara Jaya.

Challenges and prospects for HRM

The challenges facing HRM in Indonesia are considerable and are brought about by factors such as economic instability, poor corporate governance, rising competition and the need to develop competitiveness and the drive for productivity. Broadly the same set of challenges is faced by other countries in the region. While they were evident before the onset of the Asian Crisis (Heng and Low, 1994), the challenges have been highlighted by the crisis and its aftermath (Low, 2000). In addition, Indonesia has undergone major systemic changes in the political arena, specifically a shift from authoritarian government to democracy as well as regional autonomy, that have exacerbated the challenges facing HRM in Indonesia.

Consequently, more so than its neighbours, Indonesia is still recovering from the 1997 Asian Crisis. In order to improve financial performance, many companies are restructuring, mainly through downsizing. The restructuring programmes try to eliminate redundant labour and create a more competent workforce. The focus for business organisations is on improving their core processes and to resource these processes with their own workforce, while outsourcing employees for non-core processes. Working out a restructuring strategy and creating mechanisms for outsourcing have become major challenges for Indonesian HRM practitioners. In evolving these strategies and mechanisms and implementing them they need to work closely with the trade unions, which call for the need to build good bipartite ER. Simultaneously, HR managers need new skills and techniques in managing the shift from low skill and lower wage labour to high skill and higher wage labour. Given this situation, HRM practitioners are called upon to carefully plan their HR requirements, adopt competency-based HRM practices, and design and implement PMS and innovative reward mechanisms.

As part of their restructuring and rebuilding processes organisations are attempting to resort to better technologies and work processes which could not only drive productivity but also save on labour costs. The demand for skilled labour will increase and sourcing them will be another challenge for HR practitioners. In a situation where skills are scarce, organisations and their HR functions will have to formulate and implement new employee training programmes capable of developing the required knowledge and skills in a short period of time. At the same time there could be an increase in labour costs due to the higher pay requirements of skilled personnel. To counter this rise in costs, organisations would have to be more innovative and productive. Therefore, managing innovation and enhancing productivity would be another major concern of the HR function.

Talent in the country is spread thin, especially in the growth industries like telecommunications, financial services and IT. Locating talented individuals, attracting them to join the organisation and retaining them, as well as sourcing and recruiting employees with the right attitude to work, are some of the problems faced by HR practitioners. Formulating and implementing talent management and retention strategies is a primary concern not only of the HR practitioner but also of the top management of companies. To retain talent while at the same time remain competitive organisations will have to create terms and conditions of employment and rewards that cater to individual expectations, competencies and performance.

Employee commitment is another issue that causes concern to many organisations. The results of a survey on employee commitment conducted by the leading Indonesian business journal *Swasembada* (more commonly known as *SWA*), using the Hay Insight Model of Engaged Performance, revealed that employee commitment in Indonesia was driven by the following factors: external business focus (27 per cent), job enablement (17 per cent), internal effectiveness – communication (15 per cent), internal effectiveness – direction (8 per cent), and performance management (8 per cent) (*SWA*, 2006). Respondents to the survey felt that the reputation of a company and the quality of its products and services are important to the Indonesian employee as it provides them with social status (ibid.). Thus, it is essential for employers to formulate fair and equitable HR policies and practices that value and recognise employee involvement and contribution, and provide opportunities for them to gain more experience for their career development.

Many mergers and acquisitions occurred as a consequence of the 1997 Asian Crisis. Companies opting for slimmer and flatter organisational structures relied on cross-functional movements of people and more interactions between disciplines and functions. Thus, there is an increase in the need for multi-skilled employees, who are flexible and adaptable in carrying out their tasks. Consequently it is vital for the HR function to formulate policies for building and maintaining a cohesive organisation where teamwork could provide gains in productivity.

The challenges posed to HR practitioners have highlighted the need to relate work to performance as companies face increasing competition. The need to establish effective performance management has become important. Yet performance management is not practised by most organisations. Goal-setting is very often a ritualistic exercise and managers tend to shy away from reviewing and appraising performance. Performance coaching and feedback are rare occurrences. Also, more often than not, reward is provided irrespective of the level of performance. Therefore, a challenge to HR practitioners will be to design and implement a suitable PMS and drive performance in the Indonesian context.

Finally, a major challenge would be to ensure that training and development efforts are translated into action at work, and utilised by the employee to improve their performance. This would require thorough pre- and post-training planning, including ensuring the involvement of the trainee's manager in both the phases. It would be necessary to initiate a suitable competency model and assessment tool, and link the PMS to the competency development process.

The prospects for Indonesian companies to be able to handle the above HRM challenges may not be insurmountable. Given the constraints existing in the business sector, in many cases the degree of sophistication of HR practices in Indonesia is high, as in many MNCs and large national companies. Habir and Larasati (1999) found cases of a number of large Indonesian companies, including SOEs, that have successfully implemented international HRM practices such as empowerment, participation and incentive-oriented HR systems. Thoha *et al.* (2006) closely examined seven large Indonesian companies and found them to have complex patterns of HRM practices and systems that were characterised as being flexible, innovative, creative and adaptable. A leading business journal in conjunction with the University of Indonesia surveyed forty-nine companies for the journal's Human Resources Excellence Award 2006 in three categories, namely HRM, management performance, and training and development (*SWA*, 2006). The results confirmed indications of a transition towards the implementation of international HR practices by business organisations in Indonesia.

Conclusion

The impact of globalisation has forced companies to implement a range of measures in an attempt to increase efficiency and competitiveness. It is no longer sufficient for competitiveness to be based on low wages or natural resources. To be more precise, improving quality and reducing costs depend on innovation, skills, productivity and technology. The need for employees of quality in terms of knowledge, creativity, high motivation and skills has become paramount for ensuring the sustainability of companies.

Many companies that are successful in the new global context have moved away from rigid organisational structures to a more flexible, people-oriented organisational model. The characteristics of such a model, firstly, should place emphasis on building a rich and engaging corporate purpose. Secondly, the focus should be placed less on formal structural design and more on effective management processes. Finally, developing employees' capabilities and broadening their perspectives should take priority, in contrast to controlling their behaviour. In sum, organisations have moved beyond the old doctrine of strategy, structure and systems to a softer, more organic model built on the development of purpose, process and people (Bartlett and Ghoshal, 1994).

The demands of such an organisational focus places more importance on the capacity and strategic role of the HRM function. Not surprisingly, therefore, reports from practitioners in Indonesia indicate that HRM is seen to be important in Indonesia given the economic, political and social challenges it faces (Supriono, 1999; *SWA*, 2006). However, the perceived importance of HRM has not been translated into improvements in HRM practices at the company level on a general scale. Indeed, many national environmental factors slow down improvements in HRM; for example, constraints imposed by government regulations result in significant inefficiencies in areas such as a fair compensation and reward system, prevention of occupational health and safety problems and development of workers. Much Indonesian HRM practice therefore remains at the administrative personnel level.

Nevertheless, to an extent HR practices in Indonesia have evolved and are making advances, albeit in a highly uncertain environment.

As this chapter has discussed, many companies have experienced successes in implementing best practice HRM (Habir and Larasati, 1999). Thoha *et al.* (2006) emphasised that many large Indonesian companies are being flexible and adaptive as they face an uncertain environment to evolve appropriate and effective HRM systems.

In conclusion, we assert that HRM in Indonesia faces many challenges with respect to the cumbersome labour regulations, a confusing legal system, plus regional, ethnic and religious differences and the impact of globalisation. Yet there is heartening evidence that there are companies in Indonesia which are responding to these HRM challenges by increasingly practising internationally recognised HRM systems that could provide best practice examples for others to follow.

Notes

1 Much of this section was taken from Bennington and Habir (2003).
2 There is a dearth of published empirical research on HRM practices in Indonesia. Much of this section therefore depends on the extensive consulting experience of the second author in HRM in Indonesia and on both authors' supervision of many HRM consulting projects required of MBA students at the IPMI Business School, Jakarta.

Bibliography

Asian Business Dialogue on Corporate Governance (2003) 'Thinking Strategically about Governance', Conference Report, 16 October.

Astra International (2006) Available at www.astra.co.id.

Bartlett, C. A and Ghoshal, S. (1994) 'Changing the role of top management: Beyond strategy to purpose', *Harvard Business Review* 78, 80.

Beeson, M. and Hadiz, V. (1998) 'Labour and the politics of structural adjustment in Australia and Indonesia', *Journal of Contemporary Asia*, 28, 3, 291–309.

Bennington, L. (2001) 'Diversity management in Indonesia', in M. Patrickson and P. O'Brien (eds), *Diversity Management: An Asian and Pacific Focus*, Brisbane: John Wiley.

Bennington, L. and Habir, A. D. (2003) 'Human resource management in Indonesia', *Human Resources Management Review*, 13, 373–92.

Bishop, B. and McNamara, D. (1997) *The Asia-Australia Survey 1997–98*, South Melbourne: Macmillan Education Australia.

Budihardjo, A. (1996) 'Pendeketan sistematik strategi sumber daya manusia abad 21: program aksi bagi perusahaan Indonesia (A systematic HRM strategy for the 21st century: Action program for Indonesian companies)', *Forum Manajemen Prasetya Mulya*, 62, 7–11.

BUMN Online (2005) 'Investor Jangan di Peras Habis-habisan' (Don't Squeeze Investors So Much). Available at www.bumn-ri.com.

Bureau of Democracy, Human Rights, and Labour Human Rights (BDHRLHR) (1999, February) Indonesia Country Reports on Human Rights Practices – 1999, The US Department of State. Available at www.state.gov.

CIA (2006) *The World Factbook.* Available at https://www.cia.gov/library/publications/the-world-factbook.

Ciptono, W. S. (1998) 'The management reformation program: The total quality of Indonesian management', *Kelola,* 18, 7, 45–60.

Cribb, R. (1999) 'Nation: Making Indonesia', in D. K. Emmerson (ed.), *Indonesia Beyond Suharto: Polity, Economy, Society, Transition*, New York: M. E. Sharpe.

Cukier, J., Norris, J. and Wall, G. (1996) 'The involvement of women in the tourism industry of Bali, Indonesia', *Journal of Development Studies,* 33, 2, 248–71.

de Silva, S. (1997) 'The Changing Focus of Industrial Relations and Human Resource Management', International Labour Organisation, ACT/EMP Publications. Available at www.ilo.org/public/english/dialogue/actemp/papers/1998/srsirhrm.htm.

Deery, S. J. and Mitchell, R. J. (1993) *Labour Law and Industrial Relations in Asia,* Melbourne: Longman Cheshire.

Emmerson, D. K. (ed.) (1999) *Indonesia Beyond Suharto: Polity, Economy, Society, Transition,* New York: M. E. Sharpe.

Energise (2005) *Merajut Silaturahmi, Membangun Komunikasi* (Bonding Relationships, Developing Communication), Jakarta: Medco.

Fehring, I. (1999) 'Unionism and workers' rights in Indonesia', in T. Lindsay (ed.), *Indonesia: Law and Society*, Leichhardt: The Federation Press.

Firdausy, C. M. (1995) 'Role of the informal service sector to alleviate poverty in Indonesia', *The Indonesian Quarterly*, 23, 3, 278–87.

Grijns, M. and van Velzen, A. (1993) 'Working women: Differentiation and marginalisation', in C. Manning and J. Hardjono (eds), *Indonesia Assessment 1993, Political and Social Change Monograph 20*, Canberra: Australian National University.

Guerin, B. (2006) *Labour Pains in Indonesia.* Available at www.atimes.com.

Habir, A. D. (1999) 'Conglomerates: All in the family?', in D. K. Emmerson (ed.), *Indonesia Beyond Suharto: Polity, Economy, Society, Transition*, New York: M. E. Sharpe.

Habir, A. D. and Larasati, A. B. (1999) 'Human resource management as competitive advantage in the new millennium: An Indonesian perspective', *International Journal of Manpower*, 20, 8, 548–62.

Hadiz, V. R. (1993) 'Workers and working class politics in the 1990s', in C. Manning and J. Hardjono (eds), *Indonesia Assessment 1993 Labour: Sharing the Benefits of Growth*, Canberra: Australian National University.

Hadiz, V. R. (1997) *Workers and the State in New Order Indonesia*, London: Routledge.

Harsono, A. (1999) 'The markets: A fickle friend', *UNESCO Courier*, 23–24.

The Hay Group-SWA Survey on Employee Commitment (2002), *SWA* 02/XXII/26 January–8 February.

Heng, T. M. and Low, L. (1994) 'Human resource development in the Asia Pacific: Issues, challenges and responses, research and practice', *Human Resource Management*, 2, 1, 47–66.

Hess, M. (1995) 'Economic development and human resource management: A challenge for Indonesian managers', *The Indonesian Quarterly*, 23, 2, 49–58.

Heuer, M., Cummings, J. L. and Hutabarat, W. (1999) 'Cultural stability or change among managers in Indonesia', *Journal of International Business Studies*, 30, 3, 599–610.

Hill, G. (1996) 'Indonesia: Workers right to join a union', *Australian Nursing Journal*, 3, 7, 28–29.

Hofstede, G. (1982) 'Cultural pitfalls for Dutch expatriates in Asia', *Euro-Asia Business Review*, 1, 1.

Hofstede, G. (1983) 'Cultural pitfalls for Dutch expatriates in Asia', *Euro-Asia Business Review*, 2, 1.

Islam, I. (1989) 'Management and industrial relations in ASEAN', *Labour and Industry*, 2, 2, 282.

Jakarta Post (1997a) 'A worker killed every other day', 16 October.

Jakarta Post (1997b) 'A new labour law', 13 September.

Jakarta Post (1997c) 'Military involvement seen hurting labour protection', 11 December.

Jakarta Post (1998) 'President Habibie signs ILO convention on unions', 6 June.

Jakarta Post (2000) 'Corruption keeps money from wage earners: Official', 3 February.

Kismono, G. (1999) 'Perubahan lingkungan, transformasi organisasional dan reposisi peran fungsi sumberdaya manusia (Changing environment, organisational transformation and repositioning the role of the human resource function)', *Jurnal Ekonomi dan Bisnis Indonesia*, 14, 2, 62–76.

Lesmana, T. (1999) 'Workers need to better their bargaining power', *The Jakarta Post.com*, 9 December.

Levinson, J. (1998) 'Living dangerously: Indonesia and the reality of the global economic system', *Journal of International Law and Practice*, 7, 3, 425–64.

Lindsey, T. (1999) 'From rule of law to law of the rulers – to reformation?', in T. Lindsey (ed.), *Indonesia: Law and Society*, Leichhardt: The Federation Press.

Low, L. (2000) 'Political economy of human resource challenges and changes in the post-Asian financial crisis', *Research and Practice in Human Resource Management*, 8, 1, 23–40.

McBeth, J. and Tripathi, S. (1998) 'Ethics at work: Two pioneers of Indonesian business show how honesty and independence have stood them well through good times and bad', *Far Eastern Economic Review,* October 29.

Manning, C. (1993) 'Examining both sides of the ledger: Economic growth and labour welfare', in C. Manning and J. Hardjono (eds), *Indonesia Assessment 1993, Political and Social Change Monograph 20*, Canberra: Australian National University.

Manning, C. (1999) 'Poverty decline and labour market change in Indonesia', *The Indonesian Quarterly*, 27, 2, 122–45.

Manning, C. (1998) *Indonesian Labour in Transition*, Cambridge: University of Cambridge.

Manning, C. and Junankar, P. N. (1998) 'Choosy youth or unwanted youth? A survey of unemployment', *Bulletin of Indonesian Economic Studies,* 34, 1, 55–93.

Manning, C. and Roesyad, K. (2006) 'Survey of recent developments', *Bulletin of Indonesian Economic Studies,* 42, 143–70.

Medco Group (2006) *CEO Medco Group: Hilmi Panigoro*. Available at www.medcogroup.co.id/en/sekilasMedco/CEO.php.

PT Austindo Nusantara Jaya, *Annual Report* 2002, 2003, 2004.

PT Medco Energi Internasional Tbk, *Annual Report* 2003, 2004.

Sato, Y. (1996) 'The Astra Group: A pioneer of management modernization in Indonesia', *The Developing Economies*, 34, 3, 248–80.

Schwartz, A. (1994) *A Nation in Waiting: Indonesia in the 1990s*, St Leonards: Allen and Unwin.

Sharma, B (2000) 'Stateness and changing contours of industrial relations in ASEAN', *Research and Practice in Human Resource Management*, 8, 1, 41–62.

The SMERU Research Institute (2002) *Industrial Relations during the Freedom to Organize Era*, Newsletter No. 3: July–September.

The SMERU Research Institute (2003) *The Practice of Industrial Relations in Indonesia SMERU Working Paper*, SMERU Research Team.

Stening, B. W. and Ngan, E. F. (1997) 'The cultural context of human resource management in East Asia', *Asia Pacific Journal of Human Resources*, 35, 2, 3–15.

Straits Times (1997) 'Ban ethnic Chinese from some industries in Indonesia', 25 October.

Supriono, G. (1999), 'Organisational restructuring (from human resources viewpoints)', paper submitted to the Sekolah Tinggi Manajemen, Bandung.

Surowidjojo, A. T. (1999) 'Employment law in Asia: Indonesia' *Asia Business Law Review*, 25, 24–39.

Susanto, A. and Soelaeman, H. (2006) 'Astra: Pengembangan SDM adalah Komitmen (Astra: The development of HRM is a commitment)', *SWA*, 15 November, 44–5.

SWA (2006) 'Para Kampiun SDM (The HRM champions)', 15 November, 30–38.

Tahija, J. (1993) 'Swapping business skills for oil', *Harvard Business Review*, September.

Tambunan, T. (1995) 'Poverty and human resource development in Indonesia: A brief survey', *The Indonesian Quarterly*, 23, 2, 159–74.

Thoha, N., Bickley, M. and Whitely, A. (2006) 'HRM transition in Indonesian companies: Linear and non-linear approaches', *International Review of Business Research Papers*, 2, 1, 1–5.

Tjiptoherijanto, P. (1998) 'Social and economic consequences of international labour migration: Indonesian case', *The Indonesian Quarterly*, 26, 3, 282–95.

Tjiptoherijanto, P. (1999) 'Economic crisis and recovery: The Indonesian case', *Gadjah Mada International Journal of Business*, 1, 1, 1–10.

Triaswati, N. (1996) 'Women and children labour force in Indonesia', *The Indonesian Quarterly*, 14, 1, 19–30.

van Diermen, P. (1997) 'Labour remuneration in Jakarta's small enterprises: Exploitative or equitable?', *World Development*, 25, 12, 2129–41.

White, M. C. (1990) 'Improving the welfare of women factory workers: Lessons from Indonesia', *International Labour Review*, 129, 1, 121–33.

3 The changing face of human resource management in Malaysia

Saaidah Abdul-Rahman and Chris Rowley

- Political, economic and social/cultural background and context
- Key labour market features and developments
- Development of PM and HRM and the HR function and profession
- HRM practices
- Case studies of indigenous organisations
- Case studies of individual managers
- Challenges and prospects for HRM
- Conclusion

Introduction

HRM in Malaysia is strongly influenced by its context of colonialism, ethnic relations and economic development models. Thus, in order to foster a better insight into HRM as practised in Malaysia this chapter begins with a brief geo-political summary of the country, followed by an examination of its economic and social as well as cultural conditions. All of these factors affect HRM style in Malaysia. While much has been written about the politics and economy of the country, less is known about Malaysian-style HRM. Although HRM practices have been well entrenched in the country there is a paucity of research that focuses on a thorough examination of HRM practices in Malaysian firms. The extant literature mainly discusses HRM policies in foreign-owned firms and comparisons of management practices between Malaysian subsidiaries and the parent companies (see Abdullah, 1994; Adnan and Ali, 1990; Raduan, 2002).

There is no clearly defined indigenous Malaysian management style, as is more the case for a Japanese management style, for example. The reader has to understand this situation of cultural and values pluralism in the country, although 'the practice of HRM continues to exhibit a number of distinctive features' (Mellahi and Wood, 2004: 201) including targeted affirmative action policies, paternalism at both government and firm level and government efforts to promote selected sectors. Throughout our discussion we will examine how cultural as well as socio-economic advancement help shape HRM practices in Malaysia. Indeed, 'A range of authority mechanisms prevail at community, national and international level, strongly shaping economic and social outcomes' (Mellahi and Wood, 2004: 210), including in HRM. Malaysian firms have begun to focus significant attention towards HRM, innovation and productivity as Malaysian managers realise that people are capable of generating competitive advantages. As will be seen from the various studies cited in this chapter, managers in Malaysia are more aware of the integral role of HRM in organisations. HRM should be seen as a device for transforming the Malaysian work culture from one of some complacency to one of greater competitiveness.

In this chapter we present a contemporary picture of HRM. The chapter looks at the emergence, development and future of HR, personnel management (PM) and HRM in Malaysia. It also locates and highlights these with case studies of organisations and managers. However, the authors received limited cooperation from the private sector, effectively precluding the collection of data from a wide range of firms. Thus, the conclusions are, at best, provisional in nature and we do not claim the case study companies are representative of the total HRM style in the country. Nevertheless, we believe our data shows some indicative trends as to how Malaysian firms are adjusting to globalisation from the perspective of HRM.

Political, economic and social/ cultural background and context

Political

The federation of Malaysia was formed in 1963, a political unification of four former British colonies in South East Asia, i.e. the Federation of Malaya (which gained independence from Britain in 1957), Singapore, North Borneo and Sarawak. Singapore ceded to become a separate sovereign country in 1965. Malaysia is divided into two regions separated by the South China Sea. Peninsular Malaysia occupies the southernmost land mass in Asia, bordering Thailand in the north and Singapore in the south. Sabah and Sarawak occupy one-third of the island of Borneo, sharing common borders with the Indonesian Kalimantan region and Brunei. In total, Malaysia encompasses an area of some 328,550 square kilometres (Malaysia EPU, 2006).

Contemporary Malaysia is a democratic federation with an elected parliamentary system of government. The elected assembly lasts for a maximum of 5 years. Thus, general elections are held normally once in about every 5 years, or earlier if the King decides to dissolve Parliament before its maximum period. Malaysia consists of thirteen states and the Federal Territory. Eleven states are located in Peninsular Malaysia; i.e. Johor, Kedah, Kelantan, Melaka, Negri Sembilan, Pahang, Perlis, Perak, Pulau Pinang (Penang), Selangor and Trengganu. Sabah and Sarawak are on the island of Borneo. The Federal Territory comprises Kuala Lumpur (the federal capital), Putrajaya (the federal administrative headquarters) and Labuan (an island off the coast of Sabah, which has been designated as an international offshore financial centre).

Malaysia has a unique constitutional monarchy system. The King, who is the federal head of state, is elected from among the nine Malay Sultans on a rotational basis for a five-year term. The Conference of Malay Rulers, comprising the Sultans of Johor, Kedah, Kelantan, Negri Sembilan, Perlis, Perak, Selangor and Trengganu have the power to elect the King. Melaka and Penang were former British colonies known as the Straits Settlements, while Sabah and Sarawak were former British Crown colonies, and thus these four states do not possess their own Malay royal courts. Individual states have their own sultans (whose line of succession is hereditary) or *Yang Di Pertua Negeri* (citizens of distinction, whom the federal government appoints as heads of state for a specific period of time) as the constitutional heads of state. Each state also has its own state legislative assembly whose members are elected at the same time as the parliamentary general elections. While the federal government decides on overall policies for finance, education, defence, development and other matters of national interest, state governments have exclusive control over access to, and use of, natural resources, such as land, water and minerals.

From the time of the first general election in 1955 the federal government has been continuously ruled by the National Front coalition, which is a political alliance consisting of mainly communally based political parties. The United Malays National Organisation (UMNO) plays the dominant role in the coalition government. Soon after home rule was granted in 1955 the country embarked on an ambitious socio-economic development programme.

Economic

Although Malaysia inherited a good basic physical infrastructure system, a well-organised civil service (modelled on the British system) and established primary export sector, colonial economic expansion and immigration policies had deliberately turned the country into an unbalanced multi-racial society of economic, social and political polarisation. The stratification of ethnic groups according to occupations and spatial distribution became a trademark of Malaysian plural society in the 1960s. The Malays were engaged primarily in the subsistence economy, cultivating mainly rice and some rubber in rural areas; the Chinese were active in commerce and business, especially in the urban areas; while the Indians formed the wage labour class in the rubber and oil-palm plantations. The transformation of the economy along a capitalist path deliberately excluded the participation of the Malay population from the modern economic sector. Thus, colonial economic developments in relation to liberal colonial immigration fostered the emerging social structure of inequality in the population and created different strata of society that experienced particular socio-economic disadvantages. As a result, independent Malaysia inherited the distribution or 'structure' of poverty that was laid down by the colonial rulers (Saaidah, 1991), in which the Chinese had economic power, unlike the Malays, who had political power (Mellahi and Wood, 2004).

The multi-ethnic differentiations formed the basis of ethnic-based political tensions. In 1969 these tensions erupted in violent racial riots. Subsequently, the National Operations Council was set up to examine the root causes of economic disparity and the unequal development of the different racial groups. A new policy was formulated to restructure the economy in order to achieve a more equal distribution of wealth. In view of the ethnic stratification, the crucial concern of the Malay-dominated federal government was the achievement of national unity and maintenance of a balanced relationship between the main ethnic groups, the consequence being the cautious approach adopted in the formulation of political, economic and social policies, especially those concerning economic and social integration.

The focus of economic restructuring policy was to draw Malays into the mainstream of economic activities. The intention was to 'enrich the Malays through expanding the "economic cake" and apportioning a larger slice to them' (Mahathir, 1999: 34). Thus, no ethnic group should suffer from economic or social deprivation. This goal was pursued through the New Economic Policy (NEP) of 1971–90 (Malaysia, 1971). The NEP was a policy tool with a two-pronged approach to eradicate poverty and restructure society so as to eliminate the identification of race with economic function and geo-graphical location. The policy included affirmative action for Malays, extended by the NEP's replacement, the 1990 National Development Plan (NDP). Thus, 'the need to maintain a satisfactory relationship between the three main ethnic groups has dominated political, eco-nomic and social policies' (Mellahi and Wood, 2004: 202).

Malaysia also embarked on the 'Look East Policy' in 1982. A year later the government announced the 'Malaysia Inc.' policy (revived in 2005). Together these formed the basis of Malaysia's attempt to emulate the factors that contributed towards Japan's economic suc-cess. These factors are patriotism, discipline and good work ethics, competent management systems and above all close cooperation between government and the private sector, also referred to as 'Japan Inc.'. Indeed, the economic output of Japanese corporations in Malaysia was crucial, contributing some 23 per cent of Malaysia's GDP (Mahathir, 1999). The fastest pace of Malaysia's progress and development took place in the 1980s and 1990s, coinciding with these policies.

At the same time the government attempted to transform the economy from labour-intensive and agro-based sectors towards capital-intensive and high technology industries through a large-scale public investment programme. Accordingly, in 1985 the Industrial Master Plan (IMP) was drawn up as a blueprint to accelerate industri-alisation. The IMP stressed a shift from primary commodity-intensive industries to manufacturing and service-intensive industries. It also meant giving high priority to education and training and devising and implementing effective HRM policies and strategies. However, it was not until 1987 that manufacturing overtook agriculture in terms of value added to GDP (Lucas and Verry, 1999).

In response to the recession of the mid-1980s, when real GDP rates fell to –1 per cent and unemployment rose to 6.9 per cent in 1985 (Malaysia, *Economic Report*, 1985), Malaysia again revised its economic management philosophy. The public sector was downsized and public finances were consolidated, while the private sector was recognised as a primary catalyst of growth. The state embarked on a privatisation programme, announced as a national policy in 1983. Guidelines on privatisation of state enterprises were introduced in 1985 and subsequently the Privatization Master Plan was adopted in 1991. Initially, the state allowed the privatisation of non-financial public enterprises, such as those in the telecommunications, energy and power-generating sectors. Subsequently, privatisation was extended to include new projects proposed by the private sector, such as highways, ports, water supply and waste management. As a result of the shift in government policies and economic restructuring, rapid growth occurred during 1986–97, with the economy growing at an average annual rate of 8.5 per cent, the longest period of sustained high growth in the country's history (Malaysia, 2001a).

In 1990 Malaysia launched Vision 2020 as a long-term vision for the country's further development. Its two pillars state that Malaysia must modernise and become a developed country in its own mould; and develop in economic, political, social, spiritual, psychological and cultural dimensions. To facilitate developed nation status Malaysia would have to create a 'scientific and progressive society, a society that is innovative and forward-looking, one that is not only a consumer of technology but also a contributor to the scientific and technological civilization of the future' (Malaysia, 1990: 3).

The policies and strategies for the first phase of Vision 2020 were spelt out in the Second Outline Perspective Plan 1991–2000 (OPP2). It embodied the NDP, which replaced the NEP, and contained several shifts in policy to provide new dimensions to development efforts in bringing about more balanced development while maintaining the basic policies of the NEP. The main thrust of the NDP was the attainment of balanced development and growth with equity, thereby enabling all citizens to participate in the mainstream of economic activities. In doing so, political stability and national unity could be ensured. The NDP placed greater emphasis than its predecessor on the goal of rapid industrialisation and stressed the importance of human resource development (HRD) (Malaysia, 1991).

Although the 1997 Asian Financial Crisis ended the impressive economic growth, the economy had rebounded by 1999. This was partly due to the setting up of the National Economic Action Council in January 1998, which in turn launched the National Economic Recovery Plan. Consequently, the government imposed tight exchange controls and in September 1998 the currency (ringgit Malaysia or RM) was pegged at a rate of 3.8 per US$ (lifted in 2005). The successful instituting of a series of policies to address the issues of the crisis, in particular fiscal and monetary policies, resulted in the economy recovering after a negative growth rate of –7.5 per cent in 1998.

Malaysia's structural economic transformation is the outcome of social and economic priorities which are normally revised to meet the needs and circumstances of the different 5-year development cycles. In 1970 the *laissez-faire* economic management of the 1960s was replaced by active government intervention; emphasis was placed on poverty reduction. This was pursued largely through physical and infrastructure development, especially in rural areas, the expansion of education and employment creation. One of the most salient features of government intervention in socio-economic restructuring is the significant decline in the incidence of poverty and income inequality. The incidence of poverty declined from 49 per cent in 1970 to 4.3 per cent in 2004 (Table 3.1). Between 1970 and 2002 income

Table 3.1 Peninsular Malaysia: incidence of poverty (%), 1970–2005

	1970	1976	1984	1989	1995	1999	2002	2004
Peninsular Malaysia	49.3	39.6	18.4	15.0	8.7	7.5	5.1	4.3
Rural	58.7	47.8	24.7	19.3	14.9	12.4	11.4	9.6
Urban	21.3	17.9	8.2	7.3	3.6	3.4	2.9	1.6

Sources: various Malaysia development plans; *Review of the Eighth Malaysia Plan; Economic Report* (2000).

inequality, as measured by the Gini coefficient, fell from 0.537 to 0.4607 (Malaysia, 1971; 2003), indicating that a large proportion of the population derived benefits from economic growth.

Industrialisation in Peninsular Malaysia began with the pioneer industries programme in 1958, with the subsequent setting up of import substitution industries (ISI) producing manufactured goods from primary products, mainly tin, rubber and timber, as well as consumer goods, such as household detergents, toiletries and edible oil. The relatively small domestic market was exploited fairly quickly and from 1968, with the inception of the Investment Incentive Act, the government offered incentives to encourage production of manu-factured goods for export markets.

With the inception of the NEP in 1971 foreign direct investment (FDI) incentives were designed to achieve both economic and social objectives. Employment creation was seen as a preferred option in the attainment of poverty reduction. What followed in the early 1970s was the formation of export processing zones or free trade zones (FTZ), reinforced by the introduction of the Industrial Coordination Act in 1975, which strengthened the power of the Ministry of Trade and Industry. In principle, the FTZs were designed to attract FDI to the export production sectors by offering a package of incentives that included duty-free import of raw materials and capital equipment, company tax concessions and provision of good infrastructure. The subsequent Promotion of Investment Act of 1986 introduced more generous packages and incentives for foreign investors. The critical success factors of FDI lay in Malaysia's economic policy. FDI incen-tives, such as taxable income deductions linked to domestic perform-ance and local content, other tax allowances, liberal custom controls, location incentives, double deduction for promotion of exports and political and economic stability, all contributed to the massive influx of FDI and increased exports.

The radical transformation of the economy also affected Malaysia's output patterns. In the 1960s agriculture contributed more than one-third of domestic output and more than half of the country's labour was employed in this sector. Currently the manufacturing sector contributes one-third of GDP, while the services sector, including government services, contributes more than half (Table 3.2).

As an open economy Malaysia is susceptible to impacts from the

Table 3.2 Malaysia: share of GDP by sector (%), 1961–2005

Sector	1961	1980	1995	2000	2003	2004	2005
Agriculture	38.5	22.9	13.6	8.7	8.7	8.5	8.4
Mining	6.1	10.1	7.4	6.6	7.2	7.0	7.0
Manufacturing	8.5	19.6	33.1	33.4	30.6	31.6	31.5
Construction	4.6	6.0	6.7	3.3	3.2	2.9	2.8
Services	42.5	41.4	39.2	52.4	57.4	57.4	57.8

Source: compiled from various 5-year development plans.

global economy. The total external trade of goods and services to GDP ratio is very high, at 208 per cent in 2003 (Malaysia, Ministry of Finance, 2004). In general, growth was almost exclusively driven by exports, especially electronics (Table 3.3). The electrical and electronics sub-sector contribute significantly to the country's manufacturing output, accounting for 64 per cent of total manufactured exports. Employment in this sub-sector accounts for 36.6 per cent of total employment in the manufacturing sector. Malaysia is a leading exporter of electronic semiconductor devices among developing countries, accounting for some 7 per cent of global semiconductor exports. Likewise, manufacturing activities in the electrical industry

Table 3.3 Exports of manufactured goods (%), 1998–2005

	1998	2000	2001	2004	2005
Electronics, electrical machinery and appliances	67.5	71.1	69.4	65.5	64.9
Textiles, apparel and footwear	3.9	3.3	2.5	2.7	2.4
Wood products	3.7	4.0	3.3	3.1	3.1
Rubber products	2.4	1.4	1.5	1.6	1.6
Food, beverages and tobacco	2.3	1.7	2.3	2.2	2.3
Petroleum products	1.5	3.0	3.0	3.6	4.3
Chemicals, chemical and plastic products	4.9	5.3	6.5	7.8	7.8
Non-metallic mineral products	0.8	0.8	0.9	0.8	0.7
Iron, steel and metal products	3.5	2.7	3.0	4.1	4.1
Transport equipment	3.4	0.9	1.0	1.2	1.3
Other manufactured goods	6.1	5.8	6.8	7.5	7.5
Total (RM million)	237,810	323,998	301,658	222,154	242,421

Sources: compiled from *Economic Report* (2000/2001, 2004/2005, 2005/2006); Table 3.6.

have evolved from mere assembly of electrical components and household appliances of foreign brands (mainly import substitution fabrication) to higher value-added activities, including research and development, and design and marketing of 'local' brands for regional and global markets.

Malaysia is dependent on continued sustainable growth in its leading trading partners and sources of FDI (US, Japan and China). Malaysia's export-driven growth is dependent upon foreign capital, thus attention needs to be focused on its competition with China for FDI.[1] Table 3.4 shows a decreasing trend in the amount of FDI received by Malaysia since 2001. On the other hand, foreign investors may disperse their investments in Asia due to risk diversification. In view of its political and social stability, past investment record, good infrastructure and skilled workforce, Malaysia is in a position to command a considerable portion of FDI in Asia.

Social/cultural

Malaysia is a plural, multi-ethnic, multi-cultural and multi-religious society and a considerable proportion, 64 per cent, of the population live in urban areas (Malaysia, DOS, August 2005). Total population

Table 3.4 Foreign investment in approved projects by countries (%), 1999–2005

Country	1999	2000	2001	2002	2003	2004	2005[a]
Australia	0.1	0.0	0.4	0.6	0.7	0.8	0.4
Japan	8.2	14.5	17.8	5.1	8.3	7.7	31.1
Singapore	7.4	9	11.8	8.8	7.8	11.5	27.5
Taiwan	2.2	4.6	6.0	2.2	4.0	3.4	3.0
UK	1.6	3.9	0.7	1.5	24.7	1.0	0.7
USA	42.1	37.8	18.0	23.0	13.9	8.1	13.8
Germany	1.5	8.3	13.8	43.7	1.1	36.0	0.7
Others	36.9	21.9	31.5	15.1	39.5	31.5	22.8
Total[b]	12,273.8	19,848.5	18,907.2	11,578.0	15,640.4	13,112.3	7,900.6

Sources: *Economic Report* (2004/2005, 2005/2006); Table 8.1.

Note
a January to July.
b RM million.

in 2005 was 26.1 million, consisting of: 65.1 per cent *bumiputera* (a Malay word literally meaning 'sons of the soil', which is used to refer to Malays and other indigenous ethnic groups); 26.0 per cent Chinese; 7.7 per cent Indians; and 1.2 per cent others (numerous small groups). The social formation of the population was the result of British colonial capitalist economic activities and expansion, particularly in tin mining and rubber cultivation, which relied on labour from outside the peninsular, namely China and India, while the Malays were not incorporated directly into the colonial economic system. This has important implications for the role of the state and management (Rowley and Bhopal, 2002; 2005a; 2005b; 2006).

The Malays are Muslims and Islam is the official religion of the country. In 2005 the Prime Minister introduced the term *Islam Hadhari* or 'progressive Islam'. This concept of Islam emphasises wisdom, practicality and harmony, and encourages moderation or a balanced approach to life, yet without straying from the fundamentals of the Quran and examples/sayings of the Prophet Mohammad.[2] The Malays play a dominant role politically and the Malay language is the official language of the country. The Chinese are mostly Buddhist and the Indians are largely Hindus. A very small percentage of the population term themselves Eurasians and these are the descendants of Portuguese, Dutch and British colonisers, who ruled the Malay peninsular during varying periods from the sixteenth century. The Eurasians and indigenous ethnic groups in Sabah and Sarawak are mainly Christians.

In general, there is a mix of indigenous management systems in Malaysia. Initially, organisational culture was influenced by the former British colonial power. In the 1970s some Americanisation of organisations was apparent, due to US dominance in the management science field and aid in the form of training, for example via the Ford Foundation. The 'Look East Policy' of the 1980s led to the possible adoption of Japanese values in workplace organisations.

An interesting and useful overview of the social and cultural impacts on Malaysian management is provided by Mellahi and Wood (2004). This includes the following points. Malaysian management practices should be understood in the context of the mixture of local Confucian, Islamic and Western values (Mansor and Ali, 1998). Malaysia is a collectivist society, for example social relations, self-sacrifice and family integrity are very strong (Noordin *et al.*, 2002). Hofstede (1991) noted that high power distance in Malaysia was reflected in the unwillingness to make any decisions without reference to the most senior executive and the high ratio of supervisory to non-supervisory personnel, and strong uncertainty avoidance as well as low individualism.

Indeed, Malay culture is essentially a cooperative society based on *kampong* (village) and *gotong royong* (mutual help) values (Taib and Ismail, 1982). Importantly, 'The *gotong royong* is underpinned by the Islamic concept of the *ummah* (Islamic religious community) where each muslim is responsible for fellow muslims' (Mellahi and Wood, 2004: 202). Mellahi and Wood go on to argue that Malay culture puts a strong emphasis on the importance of having and maintaining 'face' (an emphasis shared by many Asian cultures). Furthermore, Islamic values and teaching put a strong emphasis on obedience to leaders. Thus, 'The authority of the leader and manager is thus accepted as right and proper and subordinates are expected to show respect and obedience to superiors' (ibid.: 208). Some argue there is 'dynamic followership' (Beekum and Badawi, 1999), noting the onus on leaders to convince subordinates that their orders are worth obeying rather than just being imposed upon them. Thus, leaders should consult before decisions are made. Also, there is an emphasis on forgiveness, kindheartedness and compassion, harmony, cooperation and avoidance of conflicts. 'The business leader, in turn, is expected to show responsibility for the quality of work life of employees and concern for their families and surrounding society' (Mellahi and Wood, 2004: 208). Also, 'Further, the Malays are socialized to be non-assertive and compliant, and humility, courtesy and tactfulness are strongly held values. The latter have a strong impact on HRM policies and practices' (ibid.: 208). For example, Malay values make direct discipline at work unacceptable because it leads to the loss of face.

Concepts of Islamic work ethics and work values have origins in the Quran (Alhabshi and Ghazali, 1994). Others note that such Islamic work ethics advocate work to give meaning to life and economic activity to be an obligation, dedication to work a virtue, with an emphasis on cooperation and consultation (Darwish, 2000). Thus, 'the new business environment has slightly shifted management culture from collectivist towards individualist practices. This has led to the erosion of some of the old HRM practices' (Mellahi and Wood, 2004: 209). For example, there are attempts, especially by foreign MNCs, to modernise management via Western best practices. Indeed, 'overall Malaysian companies pick and mix Japanese and Western HRM practices to suit their needs' (ibid.: 210).

The Chinese Malaysian cultural values are to a large extent similar to Malay values, for example collectivist and high power distance. However, 'the sharp difference between the two values is entrepreneurial drive' (ibid.: 210), for example, which has strong traditions in the Chinese.

Key labour market features and developments

Population growth has been declining, as shown in average annual rates (Table 3.5); i.e. 2.4 per cent for 1996–2000 and 2.3 per cent for 2000–05. This is expected to slow further with declining fertility rates. In 2000 the median age for the population was 23.9, reflecting Malaysia's young age structure. Likewise, the dependency ratio dropped from 62.7 per cent in 1995 to 59.1 per cent in 2000, mainly due to the increase in the proportion of the working age (15–64 years) population, a decrease in the population below 15 and a slower growth of those 65 and above. Population forecasts estimate that from 2000–10 the proportion of the working age group will increase from 62.9 to 65.8 per cent, while those under 15 will decrease from 33 to 29.7 per cent.

Structural transformation and economic growth brought about extensive implications for employment opportunities. Subsequently, significant changes occurred in the distribution of the labour force by sector (Table 3.6). From 1970 to 2005 the employment share of the primary sector decreased drastically from 53.5 to 13 per cent while manufacturing doubled from 14 to 28 per cent and services increased from 32 to 51 per cent (Malaysia, 1971; Malaysia, Economic Report, 2005). Furthermore, since the mid-1980s trade liberalisation and FDI-friendly policies led to rapid employment creation directly in export-oriented sectors, and indirectly, owing to the multiplier effect, in domestic market-oriented industries. Table 3.6 shows the trends in employment by sector for 1996–2005, of which the leading sector is services, followed by manufacturing.

Table 3.5 Malaysia: population size and age structure (million persons), 1995–2005

	1995	%	2000	%	2005	%	2010[a]	%	Average annual growth rate (%)		
									1996–2000	2000–2005	2001–2010
Total population	20.7	100	23.3	100	26.1	100	28.9	100	2.4	2.3	2.2
Citizens	19.7	95.2	22.0	94.4	24.7	94.6	27.3	94.5	2.3	2.3	2.2
Non-citizens	1.0	4.8	1.2	5.6	1.4	5.4	1.6	5.5	4.3	2.4	2.4
Age structure											
0–14	7.25	35.0	7.71	33.1	8.2	31.4	8.6	29.7	1.2	1.1	1.1
15–64	12.7	61.5	14.6	62.9	16.8	64.4	19.0	65.8	2.8	2.8	2.9
65+	0.72	3.5	0.93	4.0	1.1	4.2	1.3	4.5	5.3	3.6	3.4
Dependency ratio (%)	62.7		61.4		59.0		52.2		n/a	n/a	n/a
Median age	22.8		23.9		25.3		n/a		n/a	n/a	n/a

Sources: Malaysia (2001a,b); *Economic Report* (2005).

Note
a Estimate.

Table 3.6 Malaysia: employment by sector (%), 1996–2005

Sector	1996	1998	2000	2002	2005
Agriculture, forestry and fishing	17.7	18.8	17.5	14.3	13.1
Mining and quarrying	0.5	0.4	0.4	0.4	0.4
Manufacturing	26.5	23.2	25.1	27.2	28.3
Construction	9.4	8.6	8.1	7.9	7.3
Services[a]	46.9	49.0	48.9	50.2	50.9
Total (million)	8.4	8.6	9.3	9.5	10.5

Sources: compiled from Ministry of Finance: *Economic Report* (1999/2000, 2000/2001, 2004/2005, 2005/2006); Table 6.1.

Note
a Government and private sector services.

Malaysia's key labour market indicators for the period 1995–2005 are show in Table 3.7. With the rise in employment opportunities in more modern sectors the unemployment rate contracted to 2.6 per cent by 1996 and 1997. The labour market became so tight in the 1990s that it caused some sectors, especially the plantation, manufacturing and construction industries, to resort to employing foreign labour. However, the country was badly affected by the 1997 Asian Financial Crisis. The crisis hit the urban areas more than the rural areas. Economic slowdown led to retrenchments, mainly in the form of voluntary separation schemes. Out of a total of 83,865 workers laid off in 1998, more than half or some 54 per cent were from the manufacturing sector and another 12 per cent from services and 9 per cent from construction – thus creating a growing problem of urban poverty. In the later stage of the crisis, pay cuts rather than voluntary separation or layoff schemes were more common, thus reducing the number of laid-off workers (Malaysia, *Labour Market Report*, 1998).

The global downturn and the slump in the IT sector in 2001–2 also had adverse effects on the economy, subsequently causing an estimated 11 per cent contraction in exports. The rate of employment growth decreased to 2.8 per cent in 2001, and 3.1 per cent in 2002, as compared with 4.5 per cent in 2000, resulting in a 3.6 per cent unemployment rate. Nonetheless, a substantial fiscal stimulus package of RM 7.22 billion (US$1.9 billion) alleviated the worst of

Table 3.7 Malaysia: key labour market indicators (%), selected years, 1996–2005

	1996	1998	2000	2001	2002	2004	2005
Real GDP growth	8.6	−7.5	0.3	4.1	5.3	7.1	5.0
Employment (million)	8.4	8.6	9.2	9.3	9.5	10.2	10.5
Employment growth	5.3	−2.5	4.5	2.8	3.2	3.6	3.2
Unemployment rate	2.6	3.2	3.1	3.6	3.5	3.5	3.5
LFPR[a]							
Total	65.8	64.3	65.7	66.1	66.3	68.2	66.0
Males	84.4	83.4	85.7	86.1	86.1	88.7	85.2
Females	45.8	44.2	44.8	45.0	45.0	46.7	45.8
Productivity and labour wages in manufacturing sector (% growth)							
Real productivity	4.9	−6.3	22.7	6.9	8.9	10.4	2.6
Unit labour cost	2.8	−5.0	−12.0	11.1	1.2	−12.0	−9.9
Real average wage	4.4	−2.7	12.9	3.4	10.1	−2.8	−7.5

Sources: compiled from Ministry of Finance: *Economic Report* (1999/2000; 2000/2001; 2004/2005; 2005/2006); and Tables 1.2 and 6.1.

Note
a Labour force participation rate.

the recession, so much so that the economy rebounded with a growth rate of 5.3 per cent in 2002. In 2003 the economy grew substantially: the GDP growth rate was 7 per cent, despite external pressures from the Iraq War and the severe acute respiratory syndrome (SARS) epidemic. The economy recorded growth of 7.1 per cent in 2004 and 5 per cent in 2005, although the unemployment rate rose slightly to 3.5 per cent in 2005 (Malaysia, Economic Report, 2005). Accordingly, ever since 2002 the unemployment rate has levelled off at 3.5 per cent (Malaysia, Economic Report, 2005/2006).

The total labour force grew steadily during the 1990s, decreasing slightly in 1999, but has since increased beyond 10.5 million. In the 1990s the overall labour force participation rate (LFPR) fluctuated around 65–66 per cent. The male LFPR is much higher than the female rate, the former fluctuating around 85 per cent while the latter is half that (see Table 3.7).

Malaysia has an educated labour force. According to the Labour Force Survey 2003, the proportion of the local labour force with tertiary education increased from 15.2 per cent in 2000 to 19 per cent in 2003, including 12 per cent having technical and vocational education qualifications (Malaysia, Ministry of Finance, 2003: 94). The proportion possessing secondary school education increased from 52 per cent in 2000 to 56 per cent in 2003 (ibid.).

Table 3.7 also illustrates a correlation between real average wages and unit labour costs and labour productivity in the manufacturing sector for the period 1995–2005. In general, the manufacturing sector has been able to maintain an increasing level of productivity versus a decreasing trend of unit labour costs. At the same time, except for 1997 and 2002, real average wage growth rates have remained lower than labour productivity growth rates. This signifies that labour competitiveness improved, although reasons for this could include the utilisation of high technology and the employment of foreign workers at a lower cost as compared with local workers (not least as there is no legal minimum wage except for workers in the hotel industry). The National Labour Advisory Council, a tripartite forum, has introduced a set of guidelines for a productivity-linked wage system to facilitate collective negotiations of wage agreements.

Even so, output fluctuates according to global demands, particularly in the manufacturing sub-sector of electrical and electronics goods,

which in turn affect the volume of exports in the manufacturing
sector (see Table 3.6). In view of the potential of China and India
the government is concerned about future labour competitiveness.
For that reason employers need to stress productivity enhancement
programmes, such as training and skill upgrading for all levels
of their workforce. In 1992 the government established the HRD
Corporation (HRDC) as an agent to manage the HRD Fund (HRDF).
This is a fund set up primarily for the training and retraining of
workers in manufacturing and services sectors; the objective is to
avoid redundancy and skill deficiency. Moreover, Malaysia no longer
seeks labour-intensive industries and reserves its fiscal incentives for
high technology and high value-added projects, including those in
biotechnology.

Development of PM and HRM
and the HR function and profession[3]

HRM as a specialised and specific business function is a relatively
new area of interest in Malaysia. Traditionally there was concentration mainly on work simplification and methods for increasing
output. In the 1970s personnel issues were still given low priority
by employers, often operating only as sub-units of General Affairs
departments. PM was still more concerned about discipline, control
and rule observance. Since independence, the government has had
a key role in the design and implementation of personnel practices
(one reason being that it is the largest employer). The Ministry of HR
developed labour administration and welfare policies, HR planning,
and training for the private sector. The main laws affecting employment and labour are the Employment Act 1955 (and subsequent
amendments), Trade Unions Act 1959 and the Industrial Relations
Act 1967. These laws apply fundamentally to the private sector only.
Since the 1980s managers have increasingly used the term HRM
instead of PM. HR departments are usually staffed by people with
general qualifications but much working experience in the field and
there is evidence of increasing strategic integration of the HR function (Todd and Peetz, 2001). The Ministry of HR plays a key role in
HRM policies and practices (Mellahi and Wood, 2004).

It was not until the 1990s that companies began to reassess their corporate philosophy in favour of regarding people not as 'costs' but as 'assets', thus assenting to one of the key underpinnings of HRM. Managers in Malaysia realised that HRM had to be effective in order to bring about organisational stability and harmony, particularly in an ethnically diverse society. Multinational companies (MNCs) and Malaysian companies that operate at the global level set the pace for progress in the field of HRM. Nonetheless, in the absence of an indigenous management style (ethnic diversity is a contributing factor towards this), profit maximisation becomes the underlying core ideology of organisations, a feature analogous to the market-oriented system.

The key features of work systems in firms operating in Malaysia are the job grade system, broadly defined jobs and the dualistic nature of the system. The standard job grade system is based upon the post and rank of an employee. The grades are thus determined by job analysis and evaluation, which in turn require certain levels of skills and knowledge on the part of the employee. Detailed job analysis was not a common feature until the end of the 1990s, a time when private companies and government agencies started to apply for the International Organization for Standardization (ISO) certification.

Another common feature of the job grade system is its dual characteristic. There is one scale for managerial and administrative staff, usually eleven to twelve grades, and a separate scale with fewer grades for production workers. Thus, production workers have fewer opportunities for promotion. Furthermore, foreign-owned plants, characterised by standardised mass production, employ mainly semi-skilled production line workers and a limited number of maintenance workers. There is little scope for innovation. Although quality circles were widely introduced in the early 1980s, they have done little to broaden work roles or responsibilities.

HRM practices

Many companies in Malaysia adopt various new practices in their HRM functions, particularly in employee resourcing, employee development and rewards.

Employee resourcing

Generally, Malaysian firms practise external recruitment (Mansor and Ali, 1998). Several large companies have taken the initiative to recruit new graduates straight from universities and managers still turn to ethnic groupings to fill certain jobs, and 'even if *bumiputra* managers are employed, Chinese are still favoured for supervisory roles' and production workers recruited from the countryside (Mellahi and Wood, 2004: 216).

The practice of positive discrimination is enshrined, including in the area of employee resourcing. This section contains data obtained through interviews with HR personnel and surveys. The author conducted a small random survey in June 2005 to identify recruitment methods frequently used by firms in manufacturing and services sectors. Some 62 firms responded to the telephone survey. Telephone numbers were chosen from a list obtained from the website of the Federation of Manufacturers, Malaysia and the KL Chamber of Commerce. Only firms in Peninsula Malaysia, mainly in Kuala Lumpur and Selangor, were included in the survey. Results showed that 98 per cent tend to rely more on the use of advertisements in recruiting at all levels. Approximately 6 per cent rely on the services of web-based recruitment agencies. Recruitment by non-web-based employment agencies is widely used for recruiting non-management workers. Other methods of recruitment include referrals by employees, personal application, and to a lesser extent direct recruitment from schools and institutes of higher learning.

In general, selection is conducted in two stages – by curricula vitae and interviews. Curricula vitae are used to select and narrow down the applicants who have the basic qualifications necessary for the job. The HR manager and the heads of the respective divisions usually interview the shortlisted candidates. In selecting applicants who are appropriate for the job, there is a tendency for employers to stress problem solving, communication and teamwork skills. Speaking and writing proficiency in English is essential for administrative and managerial jobs. It is common for firms to recruit mid-career workers who are ready to perform in their specialised field immediately.[4]

Employee development

Mellahi and Wood (2004: 217) remind us of the important contradictions as:

> much industrial production centres low-value-added activity on Fordist lines, dependent on cheap labour supplies. However, Malaysia has long since lost any competitive advantage in the sweatshop stakes . . . whilst official HRD initiatives have had some success . . . chronic skills shortages persist in certain sectors. Moreover, the kind of products, and components therefore do not always readily lend themselves to a more value-added production paradigm. Further institutional barriers to a high-wage skill scenario include an autocratic managerial tradition, with geographic, ethnic and regional barriers being deliberately erected between managers and workforces.

Also,

> the diffusion of a culture of autocracy from the political centre would seem to mitigate against the emergence of a genuine culture of involvement and participation, unlocking the fullest potential of the country's human capital . . . In other words, HRM can only be developed if corporate and societal governance systems have the ability to support and follow through the necessary investments in physical resources and trust.

To cope with the demands of the changing work environment, companies usually provide training programmes for continued growth in areas pertaining to knowledge, skills and attitudes of their employees.[5] MNCs, such as Panasonic and Nestlé, have set up their own HRD centres with the aim of providing in-house training programmes to cater to each company's internal learning requirements. The training budget usually takes up between 2 and 3 per cent of total salary budget. Annual training calendars are circulated to all employees. In general, four key areas of focus can be identified:

1 management training, which emphasises administrative excellence and the enhancement of HR in the work organisation;
2 functional training, which stresses the use of IT and business-specific issues such as logistics, procurement and supply chain management;
3 engineering and operations management training, especially for new engineers, often provided by instructors from the MNCs' headquarters;

4 e-learning programmes through the intranet (see also Wan, 2006).

In order to encourage training for employees in small and medium companies, in 1992 the government set up the HRDF, primarily for the training and retraining of workers in the manufacturing and services sectors. Employers are required to register with the HRDC and contribute 1 per cent of their monthly wage bill as a levy. Registered employers are able to apply for training assistance. Generally, HRDC-sponsored training programmes are conducted by the private sector. The electronics and the electrical sectors constitute the largest membership group and accordingly receive the biggest share of training and finances.

Employee rewards

Although the bulk of pay is based on the wage for the occupation, tenure-related increments and contractual bonuses, Malaysian companies include performance-related bonuses in pay packages (Todd and Peetz, 2001). Again, due to a paucity of extant literature, this section uses primarily data and information collected through interviews with HR personnel (see note 5). The structure of rewards in Malaysian firms is fairly simple. The basic components of pay are basic salary, allowances and bonuses. Usually, basic salary is the largest portion of the remuneration package and is determined by educational qualifications and experience. Annual salary increases are given according to length of service and performance. Nevertheless, the National Labour Advisory Council, a tripartite forum, has introduced a set of guidelines for a productivity-linked wage system to facilitate collective negotiations of wage agreements.

Allowances form a lesser component of pay packages and are usually categorised as job-related and variable. Job-related allowances vary according to the duties of certain posts, difficulty level of the tasks and expenses incurred in certain posts (such as mobile phone bills for top management and employees in sales and marketing). Variable allowances are given in some cases, such as for night shift work, payment for the entertainment of clients and off-the-job training. Employees usually receive year-end bonuses, the amount depending upon the firm's as well as the individual's performance for that particular year (Table 3.8).

Table 3.8 The components of rewards in Malaysian firms

Component	Type	Example
Basic salary (salary step by job grade)	Single-factor type	Job, ability/competence
Allowances	Job-related	Service, housing, transport, communications, work environment allowances
	Variable	Overtime, night shift, entertainment and training allowances
Bonuses	Regular (but not fixed amount)	Year-end bonus

In the private sector there is considerable mobility of employment. In a market-based wage and salary system employees are inclined towards self-designed mobile, rather than regulated, careers. Career development is largely left to the responsibility of the individual. Employees at all job grades have to find their own ways to develop their careers, through internal and external opportunities.

Employee relations

Early post-independence ER reflected the colonial legacy, with legislation providing for collective bargaining and minimum standards while the focus of government policy was to contain conflict in the interest of economic development (Kuruvilla and Arundsothy, 1995). ER can be characterised by extensive state control, guaranteeing a high level of managerial prerogatives, minimal overt conflict and weak bargaining power of labour (Mellahi and Wood, 2004: 211). In 1980 some 13 per cent of workers were unionised, and in 2000 trade unions registered some 734,037 members, a constant rise from 680,007 in 1992 with the number of unions also up from 479 to 563 over the same period (ibid.). At the firm level, the ability to strike is restricted and had little influence on management. Despite extensive power to control union activities, little is needed to invoke them (ibid.). The second phase of development of ER came in the early 1970s when the economy moved to an export strategy based on manufacturing via FDI. ER rules and regulations were extended to restrict union activities, exemptions from labour protection laws, alteration

of wages and working conditions, and affiliation of unions (ibid.).
The third shift occurred in the 1980s, a result of the Look East Policy.
Export sector unions were banned until 1988 and then only 'in-house'
unions were allowed at the plant but not national level (ibid.).

In general, Malaysia has a paternalistic ER system. Malaysia is a
member of the International Labour Organization (ILO). There are
three main pieces of legislation governing labour matters such as ER
and trade unionism in Malaysia (Ayadurai, 2004). The Employment
Act 1955 (which applies only to the private sector in Peninsular
Malaysia) regulates ER, as well as terms and conditions of employment, such as hours and wages. The Trade Unions Act 1959 regulates
trade unions and union federations per se by defining trade unions
and describing their rights and responsibilities. The Industrial
Relations Act 1967 regulates the relations between employers and
employees. This Act upholds four principles:

1 trade unionism: employees and employers are entitled to basic
   union rights;
2 union recognition: unions must be recognised by employers
   before they represent employees;
3 collective bargaining: unions may negotiate with employers the
   terms and conditions of employment and produce enforceable
   written agreements incorporating the terms and agreements
   agreed upon;
4 dispute resolution: disputes between employers and employees
   ought to be prevented through a grievance mechanism or settled
   through conciliation and arbitration rather than industrial action.

The 1955 and 1967 Acts apply to the private sector only, while the
1959 Act applies to both the public and private sectors.

Hence, in a system of restrictive laws which strongly discourages
strikes, some labour disputes are settled through arbitration by the
Industrial Court. Thus, labour relations in Malaysia are generally
non-confrontational. At the end of 2005 the Department of Trade
Union Affairs registered a total of 496 trade unions, with a membership of 761,160, equivalent to 7 per cent of the total workforce.[6]

In addition, there is other legislation concerning the welfare aspects
of employees. For example, the Employee Social Security Act 1969

stipulates that employees in the private sector who earn less than RM 2,000 monthly are required to contribute towards a social insurance scheme for employment injury and invalidity pension. Employees and employers share the total costs of contributions, equivalent to 2.25 per cent of monthly earnings. The fund is administered by the Social Security Organization (SOCSO), a central government corporate agency. Malaysia lacks an unemployment insurance scheme. Hence, no unemployment welfare benefits programmes exist for retrenched workers. However, under the Employees' Provident Fund (EPF) Act 1951, the government set up a provident fund scheme that provides retirement benefits for employees primarily in the private sector. The EPF scheme consists of individual and entirely separate accounts for each employee. Employers and employees contribute 12 per cent and 11 per cent, respectively, of each individual employee's monthly earnings.

Case studies of indigenous organisations

In the following sections we provide case studies of two indigenous organisations, followed by two case studies of individual managers. Our primary objective here is to illustrate further and add 'voice' to our previous analysis.

Organisation case study 1: UMW Corporation

Operating in partnership with leading global companies, UMW, which is registered as a private limited company, has established business ventures in Malaysia and the Asia-Pacific region. It is a leading Malaysian-based industrial enterprise which is also the country's assembler of Toyota vehicles. The corporation consists of four core divisions: automotive, equipment, manufacturing and engineering, and oil and gas. The UMW group employs about 8,500 workers, of which around 2,700 are in the non-motor sector. From 2003 to 2004 there was an increase of 24 per cent in its total workforce.

HRM department

UMW can be considered as an innovative role model in terms of its sophisticated HRM and non-confrontational ER. The Group's HRM is divided into two categories: motor and non-motor sectors. The motor sector has its own HRM team, while the three non-motor sectors are combined under one HR General Manager who is also the General Manager of the Group's HR division. Thus, all policies relating to HR matters and both HRM teams come under the responsibility of the Group's General Manager for the HR division.

The HR Avenue is an interactive HR payroll and time attendance system which has been installed for the non-motor division. Also included in the set-up is the interactive Employee Self Service system, which enables employees to view and update personal details and apply for leave online and also to access information relating to training and benefits. In 2005 the UMW's non-motor HR division was awarded ISO9001: 2000 certification for the provision of HR services. By getting the ISO recognition it means that UMW has to document all policies and standard operating procedures pertaining to HRM.

The company practises good corporate governance in line with the government's effort of establishing transparency in all its dealings. Performance of the company is reviewed at monthly management meetings. Further performance reviews are plotted at quarterly and half-yearly intervals. The company adopts a 'best practices' approach by combining some Western as well as Japanese management practices in its HRM, thus its management style, in the words of the HR Director, 'is a combination of both Eastern and Western methods'.

Employee resourcing

New employees are recruited as and when the need arises through employment agencies and 'headhunting' companies, media advertisements and the internal labour market. The company places importance on recruiting employees who already have skills to start work immediately; thus, mid-career workers have a higher chance of being selected compared with new graduates. However, the company also considers the significance of 'good community relations' in its efforts to help the poor and increase the *bumiputra* content of the highly skilled-category workforce through direct recruitment. Hence it has embarked upon a scheme in which the company provides scholarships to students of a university situated within the same locality as the company's headquarters. Some twenty scholarships are offered at any one time, primarily in the fields of engineering and accountancy. When they graduate, these scholarship holders will be absorbed into the company's workforce, either as engineers or management executives. Additionally, new graduates from other universities in Malaysia are recruited under the Trainee Executive Programme. These trainees undergo on-the-job training at various divisions and subsidiaries within the non-motor sector before they are assigned permanent posts within the same sector.

Overall employee turnover rate is very small. Resignation is more common among engineers in the automobile sector as they are able to command higher rewards as well as career advancement in other automobile companies. Hence it is the company's policy to recruit graduates who scored second best (as compared with those who scored top) in examination results as they are more likely to be loyal to the company and stay in service longer. Sudden layoffs and restructuring have not been practised by UMW. If employees do not perform as required they are informed of their weaknesses and are required to tackle them accordingly in order to achieve improvements.

Employee rewards

Base pay is determined through comparisons with market standards. Figures are derived from a salary-related survey of about fifteen local and international companies operating in Malaysia. The company then sets a pay scale that is equivalent to the top 80–90 percentile of those surveyed. A standard pay system based on job grades is applied to all workers. Job grades correspond to job descriptions and ranks. There are twelve grades in the managerial and administrative group, of which the top three grades are for top management, such as general managers.

Pay reviews are based on annual PAs and are performance-based. Appraisals are conducted on the basis of results achieved by individual employees as well as the process individuals take to achieve them. For example, the company takes into account cases of individuals who gain some extra skill or qualification through their own expenses, by attending classes in the evenings or weekends, and who subsequently apply the knowledge to further enhance their work. In other words, the appraisal is results as well as individual driven. Bonuses are rewarded once a year and are mainly performance driven. It is customary for the company to pay out bonuses totalling up to 6 or 7 months of an employee's basic pay.

Employee development

The company has a culture of encouraging personal growth in the medium and long run. The training budget forms 2.5 per cent of the total salary budget. Staff development programmes are coordinated and organised by the UMW Training Centre. Additionally, the company has schemes that enable employees to engage in external training programmes to enhance their skills and abilities. For example, during the course of their career employees are granted educational financial assistance to acquire further professional competence and skills necessary for performing their jobs or undertake part-time study for a higher degree. The company has devised an employee retention scheme whereby it reimburses educational fees incurred by employees who have obtained an additional qualification two years later and this is seen as a self-regulating bond that compels employees not to leave the company.

Employee relations

Employees are members of the UMW enterprise union. The management organises regular dialogue sessions and seminars with union representatives with the aim of increasing the understanding and realisation of the role of the union at the workplace. Union leaders are viewed as partners by the management in sharing the responsibility of working as a team with the objective of achieving corporate goals.

Hence, seminars are conducted for union leaders to understand the importance of cost management, increased productivity and improved quality. In essence, ER in UMW is paternalistic in nature, with the management maintaining a harmonious relationship with the union; an example of a Japanese-style ER system.

Sources: Mr Madzlan Mansor, General Manager, Group Human Resource Division, UMW Corporation, Malaysia (interviewed by the author on 10 November 2005); UMW Corporation, Annual Report (2004).

Organisation case study 2: Ajinomoto Malaysia

Ajinomoto Malaysia, established in 1961 as a pioneer Japanese–Malaysian JV, is a public-listed company formed between Malaysian shareholders and the Japanese Ajinomoto Group. The Malaysian plant is part of a global corporation specialising primarily in the manufacture of monosodium glutamate and other food seasonings. As an established brand, the company commands a sound market position nationally. The company employs some 400 personnel, of whom about ninety are at the executive level.

HRM department

Matters pertaining to local employees are the responsibility of the General Affairs manager. Given that Ajinomoto is a JV with Ajinomoto Corporation of Japan, the company practises certain aspects of Japanese-style HRM.

Employee resourcing

The company recruits new employees as and when necessary, especially when a vacancy arises due to resignation or retirement. Staff turnover is small while expansion in HR is minimal; thus, it is uncommon for the company to conduct annual recruitment exercises, as is the case of the parent company in Japan.

Employee rewards

Prior to the Asian Crisis the company practised HR policies that had been implemented since it was first established in Malaysia and which were more or less similar in principle to policies practised by its parent company in Japan. During the crisis the company did not resort to retrenchment. Yet management used the crisis as a rationale for creating a new classification and compensation system for managers and executives which was implemented in 2001. As shown in Table 3.9, job grades for executives were expanded from six to nine, thus opening up more opportunities for promotion. Pay increments are merit based; thus, the basic notion of the new compensation scheme is to reward good performers and prevent resignations among employees with high potential. In the production section job ranks are divided into five main divisions. Pay increments are based on the Collective Agreement agreed once every 3 years between management and employees. The new remuneration scheme is a major transformation from the old system, which was based on the Japanese seniority-based pay and promotion scheme. Ajinomoto Malaysia's adoption of the new system could also be seen as a move towards localisation, not only in terms of the component of its managerial staff, but also in terms of its HR policies.

Employee development

The training budget constitutes about 2.5 per cent of the total salary budget. Training sessions are conducted both in-house and outside the company's premises. Two topics are emphasised: team-building and good inter-departmental communications; so as to reduce intra-organisational conflict. Additionally, several executives have been identified as 'high-potential employees' (there are about 300 high-potential employees in the Ajinomoto Corporation worldwide) who are deemed to be promotable to the posts of director, senior manager, manager or section head in the future. These employees attend further training at the corporation's Ajinomoto International Management Seminars (AIMS), conducted periodically in Tokyo.

Employee relations

Local employees are permitted to organise themselves into a trade union. Some 200 or so employees are members of the Food Industry Employees Union, which is affiliated to the Malaysian Trade Union Congress. Currently, the leader of the Ajinomoto union is the president of the national level union.

Sources: Mr Shariff Abdullah Shariff Along, General Affairs Manager, Ajinomoto Malaysia (interviewed by the author on 17 January 2006); Ajinomoto Malaysia, Annual Report (2004).

Table 3.9 Ajinomoto Malaysia – job grades for executives

Job grades	Position
1	Senior Manager
2–3	Manager
4	Deputy Manager
5–7	Executive/Section Head
8–9	Executive

Case studies of individual managers

We now present two case studies of individual managers. To reflect the indigenous nature of our case studies, we focus our attention on two local managers.

Manager case study 1: Shariff Abdullah Shariff Along

Mr Shariff Abdullah Shariff Along[7] is the General Affairs Manager of Ajinomoto Malaysia. With an MBA qualification plus diplomas in industrial relations and Japanese management, Shariff began his career as an assistant unit chief and presently he is a senior manager. He is currently responsible for the company's HR, corporate affairs and administration. With some 16 years' experience as an employee of Ajinomoto Malaysia he considers himself as one who has worked himself up the promotion ladder of the company and further anticipates being in the service of the company until his retirement. Focusing on long-term goals rather than short-term gains, Shariff agrees that loyalty to the company is one of the pillars of the Japanese employment system. He has benefited substantially from company-sponsored training in knowledge building and skills enhancement, including AIMS (see Employee development, in Ajinomoto Malaysia case study).

As a result of his education and training in the US and Japan, Shariff applies a combination of Japanese and Western management principles in carrying out his duties. Management by objectives, consensus decision-making and teamwork are some of his guiding principles. Training and skills enhancement are two crucial aspects of employee development that are stressed by Shariff. In particular, he believes there is much scope for developing team building and good inter-departmental communications among employees. He strives to ensure a comfortable work environment in which employees are self-motivated and take the initiative for their own advancement. Employees are given recognition for their efforts, even though it may not result in immediate gain.

Ajinomoto Malaysia's management team has maintained acquiescent relations with employees. As the chief negotiator between management and trade union leaders, Shariff has secured the rapport of the company's union leaders. Furthermore, he has adopted a Japanese approach when dealing with ER, thus avoiding any conflict that might arise due to differences of opinion between management and employees. Shariff firmly believes in the spirit of *nemawashi*, which is a typical Japanese company culture. It involves an informal process of quietly laying the foundation for some proposed change or project by talking to all the people concerned and gathering support and feedback. This is considered an important element in any major change and it enables changes to be carried out formally with the consent of all sides. One specific example upon which *nemawashi* is applied concerns matters relating to the Collective Agreement, which determines pay increases and work conditions and is endorsed between management and union every 3 years. The clauses that are included in the agreement are usually agreed in advance before a decision is made at the formal management–union meeting. To Shariff the spirit of *nemawashi* forms the basis of maintaining a harmonious relationship between management and employees and so far it has proven successful in Ajinomoto Malaysia. Shariff sees Ajinomoto Malaysia as a role model in terms of a harmonious management–union relationship in the local food industry.

Sources: Mr Shariff Abdullah Shariff Along, General Affairs Manager, Ajinomoto Malaysia (interviewed by the author on 17 January 2006); Ajinomoto Malaysia, Annual Report (2004).

Manager case study 2: Dato Zuraidah Atan

Madam Dato Zuraidah Atan is a respected corporate figure in Malaysia. A lawyer by training, she worked in the banking industry for 10 years prior to her appointment as President and Chief Executive Officer (CEO) of a major local investment bank, Affin Investment Bank Malaysia (AIBM), in 1999, at a time when the bank had suffered heavy losses due to the Asian Crisis. Prior to her appointment, the bank's Chief Operating Officer acted as custodian of the corporation for one and a half years. Through a headhunter, Zuraidah's expertise was sought after by AIBM, chiefly for the purpose of reviving the finances of the corporation. Zuraidah's philosophy was simple: take care of the employees and they will work hard. She adopted what she referred to as the 'buy-in' concept whereby she retained the existing management team and put her trust in them rather than procuring her own management team from outside the bank (in Malaysia it is the common practice of CEOs and Managing Directors (MDs) who are recruited from outside the organisation to bring in their own management team, usually their close aides at the old workplace, and appoint them as part of the top management team at their new workplace.) As the CEO of the corporation, and in the absence of an HR Director, Zuraidah recommended to the Board of Directors several ways of streamlining the corporation.

Particular emphasis was placed on the improvement of the HR system, primarily by introducing a HR handbook listing the employee code of ethics and employee benefits. Zuraidah initiated increased welfare benefits, including medical and dental entitlements. Realising the importance of good communications and its link to successful performance, Zuraidah implemented major advancements with regards to the employees' tools of the trade – concentrating on two important aspects, namely the internet and mobile technology, and transportation. The internet and an e-mail system were implemented in the company, while sales and marketing employees were allocated a substantial allowance for their mobile phones. In the absence of a reliable public transport system heads of units were provided with cars so as to avoid delays in meeting clients. Second, Zuraidah saw teamwork as imperative in the management of knowledge. Hence, sales and marketing employees worked in teams so that in the event of unavoidable circumstances, such as the sudden death of an employee, other members of the team would be knowledgeable about his/her business dealings. Third, she created a setting which would be more conducive for work, particularly overtime work. The tiny pantry was renovated into a boutique-style coffee lounge. Employees were provided with free coffee all day long and breakfast was provided for those who came in early. In a way this instilled a sense of belongingness among the employees, which led to loyalty in the long run.

Zuraidah succeeded immensely in recouping profits for the bank. From a loss of RM 2 billion (then, RM 3.8 = 1 US$) in 1999, the CEO turned around the corporation and brought in profits of RM 24 million in 2001, RM 32 million in the following year, and over RM 20 million at the end of her tenure in September 2003. The bank's rating, as endorsed by the Rating Agency of Malaysia, rose from BBB to A3. During that time shareholders received 10 per cent dividends, while the employees enjoyed bonus payments of up to 6 months of their basic salaries.

Source: Dato Zuraidah Atan (interviewed by the author on 10 October 2005).

Challenges and prospects for HRM

Malaysia was one of the countries critically affected by the 1997 Asian Financial Crisis. Smith and Abdullah (2004: 418) examined changes in HRM practices in a number of selected Malaysian companies and MNCs in Malaysia. They affirmed that Malaysia's comparatively successful response to the crisis was not just based on stringent currency policy, but also on 'the implementation of successful HRM practices in the midst of uncertainly' (ibid.).

It is interesting to note that the crisis presented HR managers with the opportunity to innovate new strategies for the survival of their respective business organisations. For example, HR managers were given the responsibility to innovate promptly in terms of implementing successful 'Voluntary Separation Schemes'. In a way the crisis presented the HRM function with added strategic importance in the corporation and strengthened the status of HR departments within organisations. Accordingly, some companies began to implement the concept of strategic HRM and incorporating the HR Director as a member of the Board of Directors, for example the National Savings Bank.

Companies continue to give emphasis to workplace innovations. Generally, manufacturing plants organise their production workforce along the assembly line concept. In the late 1990s manufacturing companies began to introduce a combination of assembly tasks organised into small cells. The cell system involves a cross-trained and multi-skilled production workforce. By optimising the utilisation of labour and reducing line-balance loss, the cell system also shortened the delivery time of the product. This system generated a 20 per cent increase in production in a TV assembly plant.[8]

The Six Sigma concept is another form of workplace innovation that is being practised by several companies. For example, Malaysian Airlines had the business support of the US-based General Electric Company, which provided training for the Six Sigma team members. The aim is to improve work processes and reduce costs. A specific project is the Airline's 'Internal Recruitment Process Improvement'. In this case the HR Recruitment and Selection Unit must process any request for additional general employees who are recruited through the 'Staff Vacancy Notice' (recruitment through the internal labour market) within 45 days; otherwise the recruitment exercise would be considered a defect.

Samsung SDI Malaysia is a company operating under the ownership of the South Korean MNC that specialises in the manufacture of electronics display products. The Malaysian plant applies Six Sigma with the aim of reducing the company's operating costs and increasing the efficiency of the business processes. A case in point is the Six Sigma team that monitors the creation of a 'paperless office'. The objective of this project is to reduce the usage of paper in all the company's divisions. The project produced a positive result. By taking advantage of the developments of the digital era, all hard copies (printed documents) are converted into soft copies stored in the computer system.

Conclusion

The fact that Malaysia is a multi-ethnic society has created diversity in existing management patterns (Rowley and Bhopal, 2006). At the same time private firms need to operate in accordance with government policies. For example, the government recognises that the pattern of HRM practices must be consistent with the country's development policies and Vision 2020 (Malaysia, 1990).

During the past 30 years or so, as a consequence of proactive government policies, HRM functions have advanced in comparison to global standards. Prior to the influx of FDI into the country, most of the large firms that operated in Malaysia were those whose foundations were laid by the colonial rulers, and who were inclined to adopt Western management practices. Since the 1980s in particular, through influencing factors such as the Look East policy and liberal FDI policy, Western concepts of HRM have been blended to include Japanese-style management practices. Management concepts such as quality control, total quality management and performance-related pay were readily absorbed into the management system. For example, our two case study companies show high influences of the Japanese management style, seeing that these firms incorporate features such as the enterprise union and *nemawashi*. This is due to the fact that both companies were established in partnership with leading Japanese companies.

Furthermore, globalisation has altered the focus and form of many industries. In the early 1990s Malaysia was considered as a preferred low-cost manufacturing site (Teagarden *et al.*, 1992). However, many MNCs and locally owned companies (LOCs) have begun to shift operations to China, primarily with cost-related factors in mind. Hence, under the Ninth Malaysia Plan 2006–2010, the government is preparing the country's human capital for a shift in industry requirements. Industries will become more capital-, technology- and knowledge-intensive as well as service-oriented. Hence, in order to increase worker productivity new forms of training may be required to enhance learning at the organisational level (Malaysia, 2006a).

The evolution of management practices is influenced by developments pursued by the parent company of foreign subsidiaries. Large firms, including MNCs, are more at ease in adopting new HR practices, although local socio-cultural values may slow down their acceptance. It is common for companies to conduct seminars and training sessions on quality accountability and positive work values for their employees. However, it may not work out well if HR managers simply implant Western-style or even Japanese-style management practices in their organisations' work culture. In this sense, new 'hybrid' forms of HRM policy can be devised that match corporate goals along with the cultural expectations of local employees. This is a key challenge and will continue to contribute to the changing face of management in Malaysia.

Notes

1 Recent data show that in 2003 China received 17.5 per cent of Japanese FDI, while the corresponding figure for South East Asia was 23.6 per cent (Toyo Keizai, 2004). Moreover, in the first half of the 2004 financial year, Japanese investment in China rose by 89.2 per cent as compared with the same period in the preceding financial year, even surpassing Japan's investment in the US, which decreased by 73 per cent during the same periods of comparison. The availability of cheap labour is the main reason why Japanese corporations chose to increase their investment in China (JILPT, 2005).
2 By doing so Malaysia hopes to correct the prevailing misconceptions of Islam, especially at this time when the West views Islam as a religion that gives approval to terrorism.
3 The authors would like to remind readers that research in HRM is a relatively new field in Malaysia and there is a paucity of research material on this subject. The extant literature mainly discusses HRM policies in foreign-owned firms and comparison of management practices between Malaysian subsidiaries and the parent company. Examples of such publications are: Abdullah (1994), Adnan and Ali (1990) and Raduan (2002). Thus, this section relies mainly on the authors' interviews with several HR personnel of large firms.
4 Information obtained from the authors' interviews with managers who are featured in the case study section of this chapter and other HR personnel/ consultants who are named in the acknowledgements.
5 Information for this paragraph was collected by the writer from interviews with HR personnel in MNCs and local corporations, conducted in 2002, 2003, 2005 and 2006.
6 Calculations based on data from the following sources: *Ninth Malaysia Plan 2006–2010* (Table 11–2, p. 239) and http://jheks.mohr.gov.my (4 May 2006).
7 In accordance with the practice in Malaysia of addressing persons by their first names, henceforth he is referred as Shariff.
8 Information related by Mr Azman, Production Manager, Panasonic TV Malaysia.

Bibliography

Abdullah, Hj. F. (1997) 'Affirmative action policy in Malaysia: To restructure society, to eradicate poverty', *Ethnic Studies Report*, 15, 2, 189–221.
Abdullah, W. A. W. (1994) 'Transnational corporations and human resource development: Some evidence from the Malaysian manufacturing industries', *Personnel Review*, 23, 5, 4–20.
Adnan, M. A. and Ali, A. (1990) 'Technological acquisition and absorption via multinational companies: The Malaysian experience', *Jurnal Ekonomi Malaysia*, 21–22, 151–71.
Ajinomoto Malaysia Berhad, Annual Report 2004.
Alhabshi, S. O. and Ghazali, A. H. (1994) *Islamic Values and Management*, Kuala Lumpur: Institute of Islamic Understanding Malaysia.

Anand, S. (1983) *Inequality and Poverty in Malaysia: Measurement and Decomposition*, New York: Oxford University Press.

Ayadurai, D. (2004) *Industrial Relations in Malaysia,* 3rd edn, Kuala Lumpur: Malayan Law Journal.

Balaisegaram, M. and Pillai, S. (1999) 'Looking beneath the surface', *Sunday Star*, 29 September.

Beekum, R. and Badawi, J. (1999) *Leadership: An Islamic Perspective*, Beltsville: Amana Publications.

Bhopal, M. and Todd, P. (2000) 'Multinational companies and trade union development in Malaysia', in C. Rowley and J. Benson (eds), *Globalization and Labour in the Asia Pacific Region*, London: Frank Cass.

Chapra, M. U. (1992) *Islam and the Economic Challenge*, Herndon, VA: International Institute of Islamic Thought.

Darwish, A. Y. (2000) 'Organizational commitment as a mediator of the relationship between Islamic work ethic and attitudes toward organizational change', *Human Relations*, 45, 4, 513–37.

Esman, M. J. (1972) *Administration and Development in Malaysia: Institution Building and Reform in a Plural Society*, Ithaca: Cornell University Press.

Hofstede, G. (1991) *Culture's Consequences: Software of the Mind*, London: McGraw-Hill.

Japan Institute for Labour Policy and Training (JILPT) (2005) *Labour Situation and Analysis 2005/2006*, Tokyo: JILPT.

Kuruvilla, S. and Arundsothy, P. (1995) 'Economic development, national industrial relations policies and workplace IR practices in Malaysia', in A. Varma, T. Kochan and R. Lansbury (eds), *Employment Relations in the Growing Asian Economies*, London: Routledge.

Lin, L. (1998) 'Cultural attributes of Malays and Malaysia Chinese: Implications for research and practice', *Malaysian Management Review*, 33, 2, 81–8.

Lucas, R. E. B. and Verry, D. (1996) 'Growth and income distribution in Malaysia', *International Labour Review*, 135, 5, 553–75.

Lucas, R. E. B. and Verry, D. (1999) *Re-structuring the Malaysian Economy – Development and Human Resource*, New York: St. Martin's Press Inc.

Mahathir M. (1999). *A New Deal for Asia*, Kuala Lumpur: Pelanduk Publications.

Malaysia, Department of Statistics (DOS), Monthly Bulletin (various issues).

Malaysia, Department of Trade Union Affairs, http://jheks.mohr.gov.my (4 May 2006).

Malaysia, Economic Planning Unit (EPU), *Malaysian Economy in Figures* 1996.

Malaysia, Economic Planning Unit (EPU), *Malaysian Economy in Figures* 2006.

Malaysia, Ministry of Finance, *Economic Report* (yearly; various issues).

Malaysia, Ministry of Finance (2003), *The Budget 2004*.

Malaysia, Ministry of Human Resources, *Labour Market Report* (various issues).

Malaysia, *Five-Year Development Plans* (various issues).

Malaysia (1971) *Second Malaysia Plan 1971–1975*.

Malaysia (1973) *Mid-Term Review of the Second Malaysia Plan, 1973*.

Malaysia (1990) *Vision 2020*.

Malaysia (1991) *Second Outline Perspective Plan 1991–2000*.

Malaysia (2001a) *Third Outline Perspective Plan 2001–2010*.

Malaysia (2001b) *Eighth Malaysia Plan 2001–2005*.

Malaysia, Ministry of Finance (2003) *Economic Report, 2003/2004*.

Malaysia (2006a) *Ninth Malaysia Plan, 2006–2010*.

Malaysia (2006b) *Economic Report, 2006/2007*.

Mansor, N. and Ali, M. (1998) 'An exploratory study of organizational flexibility in Malaysia: A research note', *International Journal of Human Resource Management*, 9, 3, 506–15.

Mellahi, K. and Wood, G. (2004) 'HRM in Malaysia', in P. Budhwar (ed.), *Managing Human Resources in Asia-Pacific*, London: Routledge.

Naqvi, S. N. H. (1981) *Ethics and Economics: An Islamic Synthesis*, Leicester: The Islamic Foundation.

Noordin, F., Williams, T. and Zimmer, C. (2002) 'Career commitment in collectivist and individualist cultures: A comparative study', *International Journal of Human Resource Management*, 13, 1, 35–54.

Raduan, C. R. (2002) *Japanese-Style Management Abroad: The Case of Malaysian Subsidiaries*. Kuala Lumpur: Prentice Hall/Pearson Education.

Rowley, C. and Bhopal, M. (2002) 'The state in employment: The case of Malaysian electronics', *International Journal of Human Resource Management*, 13, 8, 1166–85.

Rowley, C. and Bhopal, M. (2005a) 'Ethnicity as a management issue and resource: Examples from Malaysia', *Asia Pacific Business Review*, 10, 1, 105–33.

Rowley, C. and Bhopal, M. (2005b) 'The role of ethnicity in employment relations', *Asia Pacific Journal of Human Resources*, 43, 3, 308–31.

Rowley, C. and Bhopal, M. (2006) 'The ethnic factor in state-labour relations: The case of Malaysia', *Capital and Class*, 88, 87–116.

Rowley, C. and Warner, M. (eds) (2007) *Business and Management in South East Asia: Studies in Diversity and Dynamism*, London: Routledge.

Saaidah, A. R. (1991) 'Poverty and Social Security in Malaysia: Major Themes in Economic and Social Development', unpublished PhD thesis, University of Bristol, UK.

Sarji, T. S. A. (1995) *Perkhidmatan Awam Malaysia Ke Arah Kecekapan dan Keberkesanan*, Kuala Lumpur: Government Printers.

Siddiqi, M. N. (1982) 'Muslim economic thinking: A survey of contemporary literature', in Kurshid Ahmad (ed.), *Studies in Islamic Economics*, Leicester: The Islamic Foundation.

Smith, W. and Abdullah, A. (2004) 'The impact of the Asian financial crisis on human resource management in Malaysia', *Asia Pacific Business Review*, 10, 3/4, 402–21.

Taib, A. and Ismail, M. Y. (1982) 'The social structure', in E. K. Fisk and H. Osman-Rani (eds), *The Political Economy of Malaysia*, Kuala Lumpur: Oxford University Press.

Teagarden, M. B., Butler, M. C. and Von Glinow, M. A. (1992) 'Mexico's Maquilador industry: Where strategic human resource makes a difference', *Organizational Dynamics*, Winter, 34–47.

The Star (2001) 4 December.

The Star (2006) 9 September.

Todd, P. and Peetz, D. (2001) 'Malaysia industrial relations at century's turn: Vision 2020 or a specter of the past?', *International Journal of Human Resource Management*, 12, 8, 1365–82.

Toyo Keizai (2004) *Japanese Overseas Investment 2004*, Tokyo: Toyo Keizai.

UMW Holdings, Annual Report 2004.

Wan, H. L. (2006) 'Implementing E-HRM: The readiness of small and medium sized manufacturing companies in Malaysia', *Asia Pacific Business Review*, 12, 4.

4 The changing face of human resource management in the Philippines

Rene E. Ofreneo

- Political, economic and social/cultural background and context
- Key labour market features and developments
- Development of PM and HRM and the HR function and profession
- HRM practices
- Case studies of indigenous organisations
- Case studies of individual managers
- Challenges and prospects for HRM
- Conclusion

Introduction

Relative to other Asian countries the Philippines has a fairly long history of promoting industrialisation and HRM in industries. In the 1950s the policy of import-substitution industrialisation (ISI) paved the way for the rapid rise of light industries assembling varied products, from toiletries to vehicles, out of imported semi-processed materials or knocked-down packages. In the 1970s ISI was replaced with the policy of export-oriented industrialisation (EOI), initially known as labour-intensive export-oriented industrialisation (LIEO). LIEO/EOI is anchored on the promotion of FDI in enterprises based in export processing zones (EPZs) or housed in bonded warehouses engaged in re-export manufacturing (Ofreneo, 1993). In the 1980s a World Bank-supported structural adjustment programme (SAP) sought to deepen EOI by opening up the economy through the privatisation of government enterprises, deregulation of key sectors of the economy, i.e. finance, agriculture, transport, distribution and telecommunication, and the adoption of varied trade and investment liberalisation measures (Balisacan and Hill, 2003; Lim and Montes, 1997).

Nonetheless, the Philippines has had a fairly long exposure to the discipline of PM as developed by the American school of PM. In fact, the Personnel Management Association of the Philippines (PMAP) was founded as early as 1956 for the express purpose of advancing 'the profession, the science and the art' of PM, which covers the traditional functions of recruitment, selection, placement, ER and varied employee support programmes. However, beginning in the l970s and following trends among corporations in giving importance to behavioural concerns as well as skills, HR and the human resource development (HRD) needs of the work force, the term PM has been eclipsed by the broader HRM concept (Sison, 2003).

In recent years, economic globalisation and the emergence of corporate investors and managers of different cultural backgrounds such as Japanese, European and Asian have led to changes in the theory and practice of HRM. Globalisation, too, has resulted in the blending of different models of HRM and corporate cultures (Amante *et al.*, 1992; Ofreneo, 1996). This chapter seeks to give an overview of this changing 'face' of Philippine HRM. The chapter consists of the following sections: political, economic and socio-cultural background; key labour market features and developments; development of PM and HRM; key HRM practices (employee resourcing, employee development, employee rewards and ER); case studies of Filipino organisations and managers; challenges and prospects for HRM; and conclusions.

Political, economic and social/cultural background and context

Political

The Philippines, with a population estimated at 84.2 million in 2005, is an archipelago of more than 7,000 islands, clustered into three island groups – Luzon, Visayas and Mindanao. There are seventeen administrative regions covering seventy-nine provinces, 116 cities, 1,500 municipalities and 41,974 *barangays* or villages (NSO, 2005).

The Philippines has a liberal-democratic system of government, originally established in 1946 when the country formally acquired independence from the US at the end of the Second World War. The two-party presidential system was interrupted in 1972–85 when President Ferdinand Marcos put the country under martial rule and exercised decree-making powers. In 1986, the military–civilian uprising known as 'EDSA[1] People Power Revolt' resulted in the election of Corazon Aquino as President. Subsequently, President Aquino revived the pre-1972 tripartite system of government featuring a strong executive branch, an independent judiciary and a bicameral congress (NSO, 2005). However, the Lower House now includes representatives from social movements and civil society organisations elected through a party system. This government structure has remained in place despite another EDSA uprising in 2001, dubbed EDSA II, which catapulted Gloria Macapagal-Arroyo to the Presidency.

The Philippines has had one of the longest-running communist insurgencies in Asia. In addition, the government has to contend with other armed threats such as those posed by the Muslim separatist movements in Mindanao.

Economic

A major source of political instability is the huge national debt. The Marcos regime left behind a US$24 billion foreign debt, which in 2006 had risen to over US$56 billion, even after the government has paid over US$100 billion in debt service. Together with the domestic debt of over US$56 billion sourced from the local banking system, the consolidated national debt represents over 130 per cent of GNP. The debt burden effectively limits the government's capacity to deliver basic services, maintain and expand the nation's eroding infrastructure, and spend on education and technical–vocational education/training (TVET). According to Social Watch Philippines (2005), interest payments account for more than 30 per cent of the annual national budget.

On the industrial front, there has been a shift in policy from the ISI regime of the 1950s and 1960s to the EOI strategy of the succeeding decades. In the ISI period a nascent industrialising elite, composed mainly of politically well-connected and the rich Filipino Chinese business people, emerged and provided competition to the US corporations engaged in light industrial assembly. In the 1970s the LIEO programme of the martial-law government liberalised the entry of Japanese, European and other foreign investors. In the 1980s, the SAP deepened the thrust towards export orientation via a whole range of economic liberalisation measures (Ofreneo, 1993). In the 1990s EOI was consolidated further by the policy of integrating the economy regionally, through the ASEAN Free Trade Agreement (AFTA), and globally, through the WTO. Today the Philippines, with its regime of low tariffs (0–7 per cent for manufactured goods) and free-market orientation on trade and investment, is one of the most open economies in Asia (Lim and Montes, 1997).

Yet one of the bitter ironies for the Philippines is that the LIEO-SAP programme, after over three decades of implementation, has failed to strengthen and expand the industrial sector. As shown in Table 4.1, since 1980 the share of the industrial sector in GDP has been declining, along with its most important sub-sector, manufacturing. In 1980 the share of manufacturing in total GDP was 25.7 per cent, declining to 22.8 per cent in 2001. With agriculture stagnating even more, it is the service sector that has expanded, accounting for more than half (53.3 per cent) of GDP by 2001.

Industrial growth in the Philippines has been uneven, with the economy experiencing cycles of mild recoveries in between prolonged stagnations. The Philippines' economy has been left behind by other more dynamic Asian economies. Josef Yap, President of the quasi-government Philippine Institute for Development Studies, wrote that SAP has failed to achieve industrial transformation, pointing out that while the share of manufacturing in the total Philippine national output went down between 1980 and 2002, those of Indonesia and Malaysia increased by 10–11 per cent for the same period and that of Thailand by a remarkable 14 per cent (Yap, 2003).

Table 4.1 Share of major sectors in GDP (%), 1980, 1990, 2001

Sector	1980	1990	2001
Agriculture	25.1	21.9	15.1
Industry	38.8	34.5	31.6
Manufacturing	25.7	24.8	22.8
Services	36.1	43.6	53.3

Source: Asian Development Bank (2002).

A solution to the economic malaise is for the country to generate more productive investments. Yet, despite the general economic liberalisation under SAP, the Philippines is still seen in the region as a poor investment destination compared with China, Malaysia, Thailand and now Vietnam (Table 4.2). After the 1997 Asian Financial Crisis, the flow of FDI has been very uneven.

As a result of weak and uneven economic growth patterns, GNP per capita in the Philippines has barely increased in the last three decades, fluctuating around US$1,000. In turn, weak and uneven growth is the main explanation why poverty has remained endemic and persistent. In its Second Progress Report on the country's millennium development goals (MDGs), the National Economic Development Authority (NEDA) reported that national poverty was recorded at 30.4 per cent in 2003, a moderate improvement from 33 per cent in 2000 and still far below the 2015 MDG target of 9.6 per cent (NEDA, 2005).

The poverty situation has dire implications for children of the poor, especially in terms of nutrition and education. Both moderately and severely malnourished children constituted 30.6 per cent of the total number of children for 2001 compared with 34.5 per cent in 1990 and the MDG target of 17.25 per cent by 2015 (NEDA, 2005). As for education, the percentage of those who managed to finish elementary education totalled 69.84 per cent for school year (SY) 2002–03, a slight improvement compared with 67.21 per cent for SY 2000–01, but below the MDG target of 100 per cent by 2015 (ibid.).

Table 4.2 Comparative net foreign direct investment (US$ billion), 1970–2003

Country	1970–79	1980–89	1990–97	1998–2002	2003
China	0.00008	16.2	200.6	224.4	53.5
Indonesia	2.0	3.3	23.7	−12.4	−0.6
Malaysia	3.3	2.6	35.2	14.1	2.5
Philippines	0.8	2.1	8.4	7.4	0.32
Thailand	0.8	2.8	17.2	21.8	2.0
Vietnam	0.008	0.1	10.1	7.0	1.45

Sources: World Bank, World Development Indicators Database (2004) and UNCTAD Database (2004).

Note
Malaysia's 2000 FDI net inflows were US$3.8 billion.

Nevertheless, most Filipinos who live in poverty have remained stoic amidst the generally lacklustre growth of the economy and the limited job and income opportunities in the country.

Social/cultural

The findings of a task force on values and culture, formed by the Philippine Senate in 1987–8, pointed out that due to historical circumstances the average Filipino possesses a strong belief in religion, which enables them to accept calmly the twists and turns in life (Ramos-Shahani, 1993). The task force also identified other positive and negative sides of the Filipino 'character'. On the positive side it listed, among others, the following: deep empathy with others (*pakikipagkapwa-tao*), manifested in the Filipino's emphasis on interpersonal relationships; a high sense of family orientation, which sustains the extended family system; a cheerful disposition in life; great ability to adapt to changing circumstances, including unanticipated events; and strong capacity for hard work given appropriate working conditions, which explains the success of the Filipinos as overseas migrant workers. On the negative side are the following: extreme personalism, which causes Filipinos to give undue importance to personal contacts in any transaction; extreme family-centredness, which puts priority on the interests of the family above all else; casual and relaxed attitudes towards time and space, which results in work inefficiencies; a tendency to be complacent, which means there is rarely a sense of urgency about any problem; colonial mentality, manifested in a strong preference for things foreign; and a selfish and self-serving attitude, which makes Filipinos vulnerable to intrigues and divisions.

Against the socio-cultural backdrop mentioned in the preceding paragraph, and given the historical development of the Filipino nation, it is difficult to define Philippine culture in terms of race. This difficulty is further complicated by the fact that there are numerous ethno-linguistic groups. Most of the pre-colonial natives belong to the Malay race, which is also predominant in Indonesia and Malaysia. The Philippines is a predominantly Catholic nation, a legacy of three and a half centuries of Spanish colonial rule (1550s–1890s). However, there is a high concentration of Muslims in some areas of Mindanao and a sprinkling of other Christian denominations active in various parts of the country. The strong Islamic influence in Mindanao can be explained by the fierce resistance of the Filipino Muslims in the island against the Spanish and the succeeding American colonial invaders as well as the proximity of Mindanao to Indonesia and Malaysia, which are predominantly Muslim countries (Constantino, 1975). However, the Philippine Constitution provides for a secular state by enshrining the principle of separation of church and state.

Nevertheless, over three centuries of 'Hispanisation', decades of 'American tutelage' and waves of Chinese immigration, mainly from the Fukien province in China, have set the Filipinos apart from their Asian kin, not to mention the differentiating impact of other value-creating factors, such as language, insular life and long history of resistance to Spanish, American and Japanese occupation (Constantino, 1975). Overall, therefore, there is a complex intertwining of values imbibed from the indigenous Filipino, Chinese, Spanish and American cultures (Selmer and de Leon, 2003).

Key labour market features and developments

The Philippines' failure to develop an economy with a strong industrial base is reflected in the patterns of employment. The share of the industrial sector in the total employment hardly changed in three decades, from 16.5 per cent in 1970 to 16.2 per cent in 2000, with the share of its manufacturing sub-sector declining from 11.9 per cent to 10 per cent for the same period (Congress of the Philippines, 2001; Balisacan and Hill, 2003). Instead, it is the service sector which has grown rapidly, displacing the agricultural sector as the leading generator of jobs.

The sluggish growth of the economy and the large number of labour entrants are the main explanations for the high rates of unemployment and underemployment. There were nearly 5 million unemployed and 8.5 million underemployed in 2005 (Table 4.3). This means virtually one out of three in a labour force of 37 million is either unemployed or underemployed. The gravity of the employment problem is the reason why the Macapagal-Arroyo administration declared that the creation of 6–10 million jobs by 2010 is one of the programme thrusts under the government's medium-term development plan (NEDA, 2004).

Table 4.3 Labour force, employment and unemployment, 2003–2005

	Population ('000)		
	April 2005	April 2004	April 2003
Total population aged 15 years+	54,194	52,971	51,596
Labour force	37,003	36,509	34,635
Participation rate (%)	68.3	68.9	67.1
Employment	32,217	31,520	30,418
Rate (%)	87.1	86.3	87.8
Unemployment	4,786	4,989	4,217
Rate (%)	12.9	13.7	12.2
Underemployment	8,422	5,831	4,733
Rate (%)	26.1	18.5	15.6

Source: National Statistics Office, www.census.gov.ph.

Furthermore, the working age population (WAP) is projected to increase by 15 million from 2005 to 2015 and the number of entrants to the labour force to rise to over two million by 2015 (Table 4.4). Demographic projections indicate some changes in the WAP composition from 2005 to 2015 – the share of the 15–24 age group in the total WAP declining from 30.5 per cent in 2005 to 29.4 per cent in 2010 and 27.5 per cent in 2015, and the share of the 25–54 age bracket slightly rising from 55.5 per cent in 2005 to 56 per cent in 2015. The dependency ratio (total population below 15 plus those above 65 and divided by the WAP) is predicted to fall to 57.7 per cent by 2015 (from 64.4 per cent in 2005). Life expectancy for the average Filipino for the period 2005–15 is forecast to increase by 3 years – from 64.11 to 67.61 years for the Filipino male, and from 70.14 to 73.14 years for the Filipino female.

The crisis in employment can readily be seen in the long queues of job-seekers in the various recruitment agencies applying for local or overseas placements. Underemployment is reflected further in the fact that the labour force statistics classify around 12–15 per cent of the employed as unpaid family workers (UFWs) (Ofreneo, 2005). UFWs contribute to the upkeep of the family by becoming part of the extended workforce of micro family businesses, such as farming or home-based economic activity.

Table 4.4 Projected demographics of the Philippine workforce, 2000–2015

	2000	2005	2010	2015
Population ('000)	79,946	85,259	94,012	102,965
Working age population (WAP), 15–65 years ('000)	48,400	55,357	62,855	70,284
Percentage of WAP				
15–24 years old	31.3	30.5	29.4	27.5
25–54 years old	55.3	55.5	55.6	56.0
Entrants to the labour force ('000)	–	1,929	1,960	2,068
Dependency ratio	69.3	64.4	59.9	57.7
Life expectancy				
Male	–	64.11	66.11	67.61
Female	–	70.14	71.64	73.14

Source: Bureau of Labor and Employment Statistics, www.bles.dole.gov.ph.

The Philippine labour force is greatly dependent on the overseas labour market. As estimated by the Department of Foreign Affairs, in 2001 there were over 5 million overseas Filipino workers (OFWs) and over 3 million Filipino immigrants in over 120 countries (Ofreneo and Samonte, 2002). These figures symbolise the lifeline of the economy, with their remittances supporting the economic requirements of nearly one-quarter of the population. The remittances, totalling US$8.5 billion in 2004 and US$10.7 billion in 2005, are considered as the 'oil wells' of the country (Bureau of Labor and Employment Statistics, 2006).

Thus, consumption spending by OFW families is one explanation for the continuous growth of the service sector. There has been a proliferation of shopping malls and service establishments, such as restaurants, internet cafes, cinemas, resorts, and so on. In recent years, the growth in the service sector has been boosted further by the rapid expansion of the global business process outsourcing (BPO) industry, particularly the establishment of call centres by international corporations. Call centres are centralised offices handling large volumes of telephone requests from customers of international corporations, providing product support and dealing with complaints. As telecommunication becomes cheaper, many corporations are now saving money by outsourcing call centre services to countries with lower labour costs. Call centres created nearly 100,000 jobs for the Filipinos in the relatively short period of 2000–04 (Ofreneo, 2005).

However, the informal sector forms the largest sub-sector of the expanding service sector. The limited number of jobs available in the formal sector means the majority of workers, especially those who have no secondary or tertiary education, have no choice but to join the informal sector where jobs are generally precarious and are not covered by labour laws or labour standards. The Employers Confederation of the Philippines (ECOP) estimates that informal sector workers constitute 60 per cent of the labour force. Informal sector workers have been multiplying because the formal sector has been shrinking. As proof, Rene Soriano, ECOP President, pointed out that between 1999 and 2003 some 107,439 registered companies did not renew their registration (Table 4.5), resulting in the displacement of some 900,000 formal sector workers. Yet, in the same period, the number of informal sector workers was estimated to have increased by at least 2 million.

Most of the formal sector job losses cited by ECOP occurred in the industrial sector. However, even some EOI industries have downsized their workforce. For example, in the 1980s the leading EOI employer, the garments industry, employed almost a million workers under a complicated factory-cum-subcontracting system. Jobs in this industry have decreased to less than half a million (Ofreneo, 2006). This is due largely to the closure of a number of garment factories as a result of the removal of the quotas under the Multi-Fibre Arrangement, phased out under the WTO. The electronics industry experienced rapid growth in the 1990s; however, growth has been anaemic since 2000. Nevertheless, the electronics sub-sector still accounts for

Table 4.5 Growth of employment, 1999–2003

	1999	2003	Difference
Formal sector workers (millions)	6.0	5.1	0.9
Informal sector workers (millions)	18.0	20.0	2.0
Public sector workers (millions)	1.6	1.6	0
Number of registered firms	826,769	719,420	107,439

Source: Soriano (2005).

two-thirds of the country's exports and employs around 300,000 workers. The industry involves over 700 foreign subsidiary firms, JVs, subcontractors and local companies engaged in the assembly of electronic devices, parts manufacture and other electronic-related jobs (Ofreneo, 2005).

The growing informal sector and the trend towards increasing flexibility in the formal sector is reflected in the widespread use of non-regular staff and the stagnant growth of unionism and collective bargaining in the Philippines. Although competing unions in the country claim millions of members, official statistics on registered collective bargaining agreements (CBAs) and the number of workers covered under CBAs indicate a weakening union movement.

As shown in Table 4.6, in the 1990s the number of CBAs decreased by almost half, plummeting from 4,982 in 1990 to 2,678 in 2000. At the same time the number of workers covered by CBAs declined by 133,000 between 1990 and 1995. The CBA decline stopped in 2002 and the number of workers covered increased to over half a million. However, the number of CBAs in the years 2002 to 2005 was still below the 1990 figure, although the larger number of CBA-covered workers in the present decade implies some success of the union movement in organising in bigger enterprises. Overall, the number of workers covered by CBAs in 2003 (556,000) accounted for less than 10 per cent of the 7.7 million formal sector workers (public and private), and the 2,842 CBAs were small in number compared with the total of 719,420 registered enterprises (see Table 4.6).

Table 4.6 CBAs and workers covered by CBAs, 1990–2005

Year	CBAs	Workers covered by CBAs ('000)
1990	4,982	497
1995	3,264	364
2000	2,687	484
2001	2,518	462
2002	2,700	528
2003	2,842	556
2004	2,798	555
2005	2,793	556

Source: Bureau of Labor and Employment Statistics, DOLE.

Development of PM and HRM
and the HR function and profession

Despite the weak and uneven development of the economy, the art
and science of HRM is well developed and has a fairly long history
in the Philippines. HRM is practised in the bigger corporations,
employing 100 or more employees, which happen to dominate the
formal sector of the economy. In general, firms are classified as follows: micro establishments are firms with fewer than ten employees;
small firms are those which employ ten to ninety-nine employees;
medium-sized corporations are firms employing between 100 and 199
employees; and large enterprises are those firms with 200 or more
employees (Ofreneo et al., 2001).

Medium and large manufacturing enterprises emerged in the 1950s
during the ISI period. These enterprises required the services of
personnel managers, whose primary tasks were of controlling and
disciplining employees. Thus, some of the PM recruits during that
time had either police or military backgrounds, or, in most cases, had
training in the discipline of law (Sison, 2003). The demand for the
services of lawyers was reinforced by the huge body of labour laws
enacted in the 1950s such as the Minimum Wage Law (1951), the
Industrial Peace Act (1953), and the Social Security Law (1954). Also,
it should be noted that the 1950s witnessed a surge in unionisation
in the manufacturing sector (Ofreneo, 1993). Later, the mining and
wood industries and the sugar and banana plantations became a fertile
field for the recruitment of members by the resurgent unions.

The original 'bible' of Filipino HR managers, *Personnel Management*
by Perfecto Sison, was first published in 1965 as a handbook for
the PMAP (its seventh edition was published in 2003). Most of the
training materials used by the PMAP, as well as the topics covered
by the earlier editions of *Personnel Management,* were inspired by
those produced by the PMAP's counterpart in the US. This was due
not only to the strong American influence on education and culture
in the Philippines but also to the fact that Americans were among
the leading corporate employers in the 1950s–60s; they were the
only foreigners allowed to invest in manufacturing, mining and land
development under the special 'parity rights' agreement of 1946
(Ofreneo, 1993). Gradually, PM became accepted as a discipline
under the broader concept of general management, focused on the

traditional functions of planning, organising, directing, coordinating and controlling activities of the enterprise. It was in support of these functions that PM tasks were defined, specifically in recruitment, hiring, deployment, training, motivation, compensation and handling of ER (Sison, 2003).

However, PM as a professional requirement in managing an enterprise was observed more fully in the medium and large manufacturing corporations, commercial banks and the subsidiaries of US firms. In family-run companies there was a great deal of unevenness in the application of the principles of PM. Then and even now, there are all kinds of PM patterns, even among firms of similar sizes and products/ services. For example, a company may have a number of managers (recruitment, HR planning, compensation and benefits, legal and ER, training and development, health and safety and community relations) under a PM department, while another company may have only a HR manager attending to all these concerns, backed up by just a few staff. Furthermore, observations made by the author revealed the fact that there has also been a confusing use of terms, e.g. an 'admin manager' can mean a HR manager too, while a 'legal director' may actually refer to the HR manager of the company.

Today, non-lawyers such as psychologists, Master of Business Administration (MBA) graduates, HR specialists and organisation experts dominate the HR field (Sison, 2003). The more profitable companies have also learned to accept job evaluations conducted by external consultants as important aspects of HRM. In the 1980s and 1990s, HRD became a popular term for training and skills upgrading. Because of the positive subliminal meaning of HRD, HR managers began to identify themselves as 'HRD managers', which is sometimes confusing because some companies have their own training managers who are also called 'HRD managers'. For the bigger corporations with professional management teams the preferred term is simply 'HR manager', whose subordinates include a personnel manager in charge of mainly administrative work and a HRD manager specialising in training.

In the EOI decades there had been an influx of new HRM ideas and approaches as a result of the emergence of managers of different nationalities and management cultures. The Japanese introduced a number of efficiency-raising programmes such as *kaizen* (continuous improvement), quality circles and labour–management cooperation schemes. On the other hand, globalisation has also promoted some HRM practices, such as the Japanese 5S rules on good housekeeping, the Korean modular approach to manufacturing and Motorola's Six Sigma art of management (Ofreneo, 1995).

However, globalisation also creates some problems. For example, the resulting 'cultural shock' experienced by expatriate managers and local staff can lead to tensions. Some strikes in the EPZs are the result of the absence of open labour–management communication (especially among foreign managers and supervisors who do not speak English) and the inability of Filipino staff and the expatriate managers to understand and relate to each other. In some cases, some expatriate managers and supervisors insist on doing things 'their way' even if this contravenes local labour laws and cultural practices (Ofreneo, 2004).

On the whole it is extremely difficult to generalise the patterns and practices of HRM in the Philippines given the evolution of HRM, the unevenness of the economy, and the varying HRM adjustments made by firms and industries in response to the changing economic environment. Perhaps two assertions are possible. First, there is no single Filipino HRM model. In fact, there is literally a variety of HRM practices, most of which are developed in reaction or adjustment to the changing economic environment. Second, there has been no complete transfer of a foreign-based HRM scheme by a foreign investor or manager. One way or the other there has to be a process of adaptation to the local culture and practices, or a 'hybridisation' of HRM practices (Ofreneo, 1994; Takahashi, 1998).

HRM practices

Employee resourcing

Hiring practices by corporations vary depending on size, product or service, technology and work organisation. There are no clear employee resourcing guidelines being observed in the small enterprises, medium-sized firms and family-owned corporations with limited technology. Hiring is often conducted on an informal ad hoc basis. Nevertheless, the trend towards increased external labour market flexibility is discernible in almost all industries. Unions are against labour market flexibility, which is practised through the short-term hiring of non-regular casual workers and the intensification of work through the re-engineering of the work process and the introduction of labour-displacing productivity-enhancing measures (Asper, 2006; APL, 2001). This is the reason why labour federations rejected the Report of the Congressional Commission on Labor (2001) when the Commission recommended easing the rules on subcontracting.

In the past recruitment was done through notices on company gates, media, schools and the public employment service office (PESO) of the local government unit (LGU). In the case of small firms with ongoing operations, recruitment was conducted through employees' relatives, circles of friends and the local community (WINT-NMYC, 1992). Today, many organisations such as the PMAP, ECOP, LGUs, and schools are organising and utilising job fairs held on campuses, malls, community halls and LGU offices. The most active participants at these job fairs are the private recruitment agencies engaged in labour contracting or in supplying companies with temporary short-term staff and who, therefore, need to maintain a standby HR pool. These agencies usually go from company to company offering their services under a system of 'proposal marketing' targeted to individual employers or HR managers. Thus, the intermediary recruitment industry for semi-skilled workers is hidden from the public as they do not resort to open media advertising.

For the high-end labour market characterised by the search for talent and special skills, large companies resort to media advertising or rely on executive headhunters, such as John Clements, who utilise extensively the internet, executive directories and special contacts in large corporations. There are complaints about the 'poaching' of skilled professionals. The problem is that there are no clear rules and code of conduct governing poaching; for instance, foreign recruiters advertise through the internet and thus are invisible to the Filipino public regulatory bodies (Ziga, 2006).

Of course companies try to look for a good fit – matching the right people with the right skills for the right jobs. In doing so large corporations translate, through their strategic HR managers, the business plans into HR plans, identifying activities which can be outsourced and those requiring a regular employee. Some companies even have experiments in promoting enterprise competitiveness by transforming employees into highly motivated and highly skilled workers (ECOP, 2006). This naturally implies a rigorous system of employee recruitment.

Employee development

HRM practitioners are generally appreciative of the importance of investments in employee development (Amante *et al.*, 1999). However, budgetary spending on employee development is subject to strict scrutiny in the large corporations, which may decide to outsource or undertake in-house training. Core and professional workers are generally the ones given a variety of training to enhance their productivity and skills. Training is conducted regularly in capital- and technology-intensive industries such as those in the electronics, banking, pharmaceuticals, and gas and fuel sectors. Similarly, firms within the information communication technology (ICT), such as call centres and BPO firms, also conduct regular training for their employees. Lately a popular term in HRM circles is 'core competencies'. In the larger and more professional enterprises HR managers are given greater freedom to plan and build up the firm's core competencies, partly through the development of strategic training programmes to enhance the 'hard' and 'soft' skills of those directly involved in value-creating aspects of the business (Sison, 2003).

The government tries to promote training for semi-skilled, casual and peripheral workers through the TVET system led by the Technical Education and Skills Development Authority (TESDA). TESDA, which provides subsidies for training, encourages the use of apprentices and learners to promote training. Some electronic and automotive companies utilise more and more of these trainees and have concluded cooperation programmes with a number of technical–vocational schools (Amante *et al.*, 1999).

A complicating factor in the company-initiated skills training programmes is poaching, especially by foreign poachers who recruit through the internet (Ziga, 2006). In the call centre industry employees have no qualms about leaving their companies after only several months or even weeks of work for higher pay and benefits.

Some companies retain their valued HR by sending their managers and professionals to institutions providing both short-term certificate courses and academic degrees in business and management. Some of these institutions are well known in the Asian region, such as the College of Business Administration of the University of the Philippines, the De La Salle University, the Ateneo de Manila University, the University of Asia and the Pacific and the Asian Institute of Management. The Philippines also has a Development Academy which provides courses in development for both government and private sector managers. In labour and industrial relations, the School of Labor and Industrial Relations of the University of the Philippines is considered one of the few such institutions in the region (Kaufman, 2004).

Employee rewards

In organising their wage and salary structures companies usually undertake wage and benefit benchmarking within and across industries as well as within and across geographical communities (Sison, 2003). The pay system is subject to the forces of competition as well as to legislative fiats (ibid.). The legislated minimum wage is used as a reference for wage levels by companies, particularly for newly recruited semi-skilled and unskilled workers. Unions in labour-intensive enterprises often complain that wages hardly differ from minimum wage rates. This is because labour-intensive enterprises, such as the garments factories, often benchmark Philippine wages with those in other Asian countries, a number of which offer lower minimum wages. Furthermore there are various laws governing overtime pay (usually an additional premium of 25 per cent of regular pay), holiday pay and rest days, as well as deductions for income tax and social security contributions. The most conflict-laden wage and benefit issues are those arising from collective bargaining deadlocks and formulas on how to correct wage distortions as a result of minimum wage increases.

However, the Philippines is generally considered competitive in the skilled and professional category, based on global competitiveness surveys (Macaranas, 2003). In companies where employees are guaranteed a career path and promotions the reward system is based on a graduated salary and compensation system. Rewards correspond to the functions, responsibility and seniority; however, the levels of rewards are determined by performance and job evaluation. Some companies utilise the services of companies specialising in the survey of international wage levels, such as Wyatt Watson. Unionised firms usually rely on CBA wages and benefit surveys which are conducted by ECOP in order to determine general wage levels across industries.

The Philippines is an employers' market for low-skilled and unskilled workers. This is why the legislated minimum wage level has become the reference wage level in most industries. However, in the call centre industry the shortage of employees who can speak good conversational English and handle the ICT interactive technological package well is pushing wages to rise rapidly. In 2000, when the industry was relatively new, minimum wages for new employees were 50 per cent higher than the minimum wages in other industries; in 2005 the wage differentials increased by 100 per cent (Ofreneo, 2005). Then again, employers are naturally forced to keep wages competitive for professionals and skilled workers who are liable to be poached for overseas placements, such as pilots, nurses and engineers.

Appraising employee performance for the 'regularisation' of an employee, promotion in rank and salary or granting of merit awards is a fairly routine exercise among various enterprises (Martires, 1988). However, the frequency of appraisals and the complexity and formality of the methods used vary between companies. In large corporations, such as commercial banks, HR managers employ multirating systems involving evaluation by supervisors and managers, peers and customers (Aganon, 1994). In highly competitive companies a system of continuous appraisal puts middle managers continuously on their toes. In recent years a number of companies have been experimenting with the promotion of productivity by compensating performance. Yet many HR managers find the process exhausting because it entails stringent monitoring, evaluation and recording of output per employee (author's interviews with HR managers).

Employee relations

PMAP's counterpart for the employers, ECOP, was established in 1975 and has been representing the business community in national tripartite deliberations on wages, labour and related social policy issues. It has been active in promoting the UNDP's Global Compact Initiative, the ILO's Decent Work programme and the global campaign against the use of child labour. ECOP also works closely with the Philippine Chamber of Commerce and Industry and the various industry associations and business chambers on labour-related issues such as benchmarking on best practices in HRM and the propagation of corporate social responsibility (CSR) among employers and investors (ECOP, 2006; Soriano, 2005).

The Philippines has a fairly developed body of labour laws and labour jurisprudence. These laws have been codified into a Labor Code of the Philippines, with Books III and IV (working conditions) and Books V and VI (labour relations) attracting the most interest among employers. Being a member of the ILO the Philippines has ratified most core ILO Conventions dealing with freedom of association, collective bargaining and labour standards. So as to maintain industrial peace, tripartism is also widely promoted by the government.

There are four major types of employees under the law: regular employee – doing a regular and necessary job and who is placed in the regular rolls; probationary employee – hired to occupy a permanent or regular position in a company but subjected to a trial period of around 6 months; casual or contractual employee – hired to do non-regular activities; and project employee – whose employment has been fixed for a specific project or undertaking (Azucena, 2006).

However, unions at present are in a defensive position. A substantial number of the unionised ISI companies, including the EOI garments firms, have either closed down or downsized their operations. On the other hand, unions face difficulties in trying to organise workers in most of the stable EOI firms, including the burgeoning call centre and BPO sector. Currently, workers covered by CBAs number around half a million or so and they constitute a minority of the labour force (see Table 4.6); in contrast, the total labour force is 37 million and there are at least 5 million formal private sector workers and 1.6 million government workers who are yet to be organised to form labour unions (see Tables 4.3 and 4.5).

Overall, the number of industrial strikes has gone down dramatically, from over 500 a year in the mid-1980s to fewer than fifty in 2006.

This is due partly to the weakened state of the trade union movement. However, an added explanation is the increased ability of companies to transform relations with the unions into cooperative ones through better communication and other positive ER practices such as initiating grievance and consultation mechanisms on various issues and concerns at the firm level. In fact, in the large non-unionised sector, such as electronics assembly, management is able to keep the unions at bay not necessarily through an active anti-union policy but mainly through a proactive ER policy. The instruments for such a policy, based on the management's commitment to the principle of fairness, include open communications, non-confrontational employer–employee relations, better training of middle managers in handling people's concerns, establishment of grievance machinery, consistent application of the code of discipline, stringent employee selection procedure, training and the formation of labour-management councils (LMCs) (Sison, 2003).

The concept of management prerogative or the right of an investor to manage businesses freely subject only to the limitations imposed by law, contract and fair play is well established under Philippine jurisprudence (Azucena, 2006). Yet so are the various rights of workers (wages, occupational health and safety) as defined by the Labor Code. Industrial disputes can be settled at the plant level through the grievance machinery and at adjudicatory level involving the Department of Labor and Employment (DOLE) and the National Labor Relations Commission (NLRC). DOLE provides conciliation–mediation services while the NLRC conducts compulsory arbitration. Most of the NLRC cases are termination cases, reflecting widespread downsizing of business enterprises. Around 25,000 new cases are filed annually with the NLRC (Ofreneo, 2004).

Thus, in general, ER in the Philippines today appear stable compared with the situation in the mid-1980s at the height of the economic crisis under the Marcos administration, and during the 1997 crisis. One explanation for the stability is the growing maturity in the relations between unions and management. Another is the increased ability of many companies to pursue a proactive ER policy. Nevertheless, industrial stability is partly due to the relatively weak position of unions in a labour-surplus economy and the ability of many employers to undertake various labour flexibility measures.

Case studies of indigenous organisations

Joachim von Amsberg, the World Bank country representative, observed that the Philippines is a paradox. He said: 'As a country with world-class companies, it should be among the fastest-growing countries in the world but it is not' (Legaspi, 24 July 2006). Indeed, it is a paradox. As outlined earlier, the Philippines economy, one of the more dynamic in the region in the 1950s–1960s, has been overtaken in recent decades by the Asian NICs (newly industrialising countries) and other South East Asian countries. Yet, as demonstrated in the following case studies, the country is host to a number of world-class companies led by home-grown Filipino managers. The following case studies present two Filipino companies and two Filipino managers spearheading varying innovations in the HRM area.[2]

Organisation case study 1: Jollibee Foods Corporation

Jollibee is the country's most successful fast-food chain. It controls the Philippine market for hamburgers, quick meals and snacks. The name 'Jollibee' signifies a hard but happy worker. The phenomenal success of Jollibee is credited to the firm's efforts to make every customer delighted with the store's layout, friendliness, cleanliness, fast service, reasonable price and food quality. Every Jollibee store has a children's play area. The Jollibee mascot appeals to Filipino children.

The company was established in the 1970s as a neighbourhood ice cream parlour. Initially the founders, Tony Tan Caktiong and his younger brothers, could only raise Php350,000 (US$50,000, at the exchange rate of Php7 to US$1). Today it grosses annual sales worth over Php25 billion (US$490 million at the current exchange rate of Php51 to US$1) from around 500 stores nationwide and twenty stores overseas. Owing to its rapid and continuous growth in the last two decades, Jollibee is now in the top 100 Filipino corporations, ranking fifty-first in 2004.

Jollibee has a well-run food provisioning system. In its advertisements Jollibee reminds Filipinos that its food is cooked in the Filipino way. However, another explanation for Jollibee's success is in the area of HRM and the propagation of Jollibee's core values – always customer first, spirit of family fun and excellence in team organisation – among the firm's managers, supervisors and rank-and-file employees. These values are cascaded at all layers of the organisation and are extended to the numerous Jollibee franchisees and their workers.

Jollibee has been meticulous in selecting its employees, who are normally absorbed as regular workers after the standard probationary period. Jollibee also offers college students part-time work of 4–6 hours daily, mainly as part of the service crew. Thousands of Jollibee part-timers, paid on an hourly minimum wage basis, have been able to finish their college education; many of these graduates have even applied to the firm for regular employment.

The company also organises monthly social gatherings to strengthen the spirit of 'Jollibee family' oneness among its employees. Jollibee takes pride in its harmonious relations with the union of rank-and-file employees (excluding those of the franchisees). Tan Caktiong is also known for his great capacity to listen to and learn from subordinates, a trait which is emulated by Jollibee managers.

Sources: Business World (2005); ECOP's corporate files; interview with Nenette Fernando, Employee Relations Manager, Jollibee, 26 September 2006.

Organisation case study 2: Central Azucarera de Don Pedro

Central Azucarera de Don Pedro (CADP) is the country's leading sugar mill. The company was established by the Roxas family in 1912. Initially the company was set up to take advantage of the then growing sugar market in America. However, CADP went through a difficult phase in the 1970s and 1980s due to several factors, including controls on sugar trading imposed by the Philippines National Sugar Trading and Regulatory Agency, depressed world sugar prices and the liberalisation of sugar trading under the country's structural adjustment programme. Nevertheless ,CADP survived the crisis; subsequently the company pursued a modernisation programme in the 1990s, and today it is the Philippines' leading sugar mill.

CADP's HRM practices could be regarded as notable in an industry that is often described as feudal and antiquated because of its colonial background. Employee turnover is relatively low, while the majority of the employees are in the middle-age range of 35–55 years old. The company has comprehensive training programmes for all levels of employees. In particular CADP has also developed a skills training programme especially for the youth in the residential areas within the plant's locality; these youths are the potential workforce for the company. Furthermore, despite the seasonal nature of sugar milling, CADP exerts extra efforts to maintain its workers in the company's regular payroll by assigning them repair and maintenance work as well as by conducting employee training during off-season periods.

The wages of the lowest-paid workers are generally above the legislated national minimum wage and are supplemented by a variety of non-statutory bonuses plus monetary incentives for meritorious performance. CADP also has numerous programmes on environmental management, customer service, good housekeeping, gender equality, family welfare, and health and safety.

From the 1930s to the 1970s, ER in CADP were adversarial and chaotic. The situation began to change in the mid-1980s. In the midst of the national crisis under former President Marcos' regime, CADP's President, Don Eduardo Roxas, encouraged his management team to look for new approaches to transform adversarial ER. Roxas told the head of the personnel department to 'stop being a lawyer' and to reach out to the workers. Subsequently the personnel department introduced a number of innovative programmes: *balikatan* (an attitudinal and awareness programme for rank-and-file employees), the setting up of a Community Development Office; and the establishment in 1983 of a LMC (when it was still unheard of in many parts of the country) to discuss employee problems and concerns. The LMC developed a Code of Industrial Harmony and helped transform the litigious system of collective bargaining into a win-win process characterised, for instance, by a joint study between management and employees on an industry-wide survey of CBAs, joint reflections on common problems and joint prayers before and after every bargaining session. Thus, in a way the company's employee relations could be regarded as progressive and non-authoritarian in nature.

In the second half of the 1990s CADP underwent a series of potentially divisive personnel reduction plans, which was a natural consequence of its modernisation programme. However, employees were prepared for such plans. For instance, in 1998 CADP organised workshops on *Talakayan sa Krisis* (Dialogue on the Crisis) and *Oplan Sagip-Buhay* (Operation Save Lives) to reduce costs of production with minimal labour displacement. As a result of improvements in ER, these downsizing exercises were undertaken in an orderly and humane manner.

Sources: Lloyd and Salter (1999); ECOP's corporate files; author's interview with Rafael Francisco, VP for HR, 1 September 2006.

Case studies of individual managers

We now present two case studies of Filipino managers who have achieved success in their careers.

Manager case study 1: Feliciano Torres

Feliciano Torres is the CEO of Yazaki-Torres Manufacturing Inc. (YTMI), a Filipino Japanese JV company specialising in producing wire harness. Feliciano Torres has demonstrated the capacity of Filipinos to manage a large manufacturing enterprise that rivals or even surpasses similar foreign enterprises in terms of productivity. The success of YTMI owes a lot to the steadfast consistency of Torres to impress his business partners, managers and workers on the importance of positive values in sustaining a business enterprise – together – in good times and bad. He has been quoted as saying that 'the best values that serve a company are those that are person-centred, values that put man and his welfare at the core'. By putting this philosophy into practice, Torres has succeeded in building a productive YTMI and in convincing the YTMI employees and union to agree to difficult adjustment measures needed for YTMI to survive.

The company experienced its first major test in the mid-1970s when the fledgling YTMI lost its market for its initial auto part products (auto gauges and PVC tapes) because of the oil crisis. Torres negotiated with his employees for a radical downsizing exercise, with the promise that the affected employees would be rehired once YTMI was able to recover through the marketing of its new wire harness products. The second test came from the mid-1980s up to the 1997 Asian Crisis, a period which saw almost all major enterprises in the industrial area (Laguna province) where YTMI was located being hit by debilitating strikes and industrial disputes. YTMI survived the decade-long industrial unrest strike-free through the proactive efforts of Torres to hold regular dialogues and consultations with the union and the communities around it.

The third and most difficult test came in 2005 when it became clear that YTMI's wage and benefits package, developed in three decades of productive partnership between YTMI's managerial and rank-and-file workforce, was too high compared with those of other wire harness producers in the Philippines and other South East Asian countries. Torres personally led the negotiations, not only with the union but also with the managerial and supervisory staff, on the necessity of cutting wages across the board, including his pay. A 30 per cent wage cut was agreed, an unprecedented development in the Philippines where the principle of 'non-diminution' of wages and benefits is considered sacrosanct.

Torres and his HR team have adopted the best HRM and manufacturing practices developed by their Japanese partners and have modified them to suit the Filipino culture. Above all, they have animated the HRM programme with Torres' own vision of the 'Yazaki-Torres Man', a Filipino employee working for the prosperity of his family, community and country. This explains why YTMI has numerous outreach programmes aimed at reducing poverty in the towns around it and why it is the employer of choice in Southern Luzon.

Sources: ECOP corporate files; interview with Renato Almeda, Director for HR, 13 February 2006.

Manager case study 2: Pacita Juan

Pacita Juan, born to a family engaged in the auto business, stumbled into the coffee business in 1993 when she and her friends thought of a good Filipino coffee shop which serves 'the perfect coffee' and has 'all the necessary accoutrements for coffee making'. Figaro Coffee Company has since expanded rapidly and has now over fifty stores, including franchisees.

This Filipino company is giving tough competition to Starbucks and Seattle's Best coffee chains in the Philippine market. Figaro now boasts more than fifty stores in the country and several branches in Hong Kong, Shanghai and Dubai, UAE. More interestingly, Figaro, through the Figaro Foundation Corporation, is active in the rehabilitation of the ailing domestic coffee industry by promoting good coffee farming practices among coffee farmers in Luzon and Mindanao. Up to the 1980s the Philippines was a major coffee exporter but today it has become a major coffee importer due to falling coffee production (Nuguid-Anden, 2003).

Figaro's phenomenal success in the highly competitive high-end coffee market is due primarily to the passion with which its President-CEO Pacita Juan pursues the development of Figaro's coffee business. Figaro does 'things with passion', from the way it prepares every cup of coffee to the satisfaction of every customer up to the way it maintains profitable relations with coffee farmers cooperating with Figaro's programme to rehabilitate the Philippine coffee industry. Asked what this passion means in terms of HRM, CEO Juan declares it as how Figaro focuses on the overall development of the employees, who are considered members of the 'Figaro family'.

In fact, recruitment for the growing chain of Figaro stores is increasingly dependent on referrals by happy and contented employees. Figaro has a system of direct hiring, which means qualified workers are put on a regular status and that hiring through a third-party recruitment agency is avoided. The entry wage is based on the statutory minimum wage rate; however, regular workers receive higher compensation and benefits depending on their skills, positions and years of service. Juan also proclaims that Figaro is 'an equal opportunity company', meaning male and female applicants have equal chances of being accepted in the firm and, once accepted, in rising up the corporate ladder.

Figaro has low employee turnover. It has a training centre which provides employees with an array of training programmes, including refresher courses and cross-training for multi-skilling purposes. A major thrust of the training module is to instil Figaro's values of professionalism, people-oriented service and teamwork. It also offers qualified employees a career path in terms of promotions and possibilities of being posted in branches abroad. Figaro also organises exciting coffee farm trips for employees and their families, a programme which strengthens the identification of these employees with the coffee farmers and with Figaro itself.

Labour disputes are virtually unheard of. Figaro management maintains an open-door policy in dealing with employee concerns. Pacita Juan herself organises a monthly lunch with all the birthday celebrants for the month; this enables her to interact directly with the employees for at least 1 hour, a time when employees have the chance to voice their sentiments about Figaro and their jobs. Additionally, Juan has established a project providing technical and marketing assistance to coffee farmers, and this forms part of the company's CSR programme.

Sources: ECOP's corporate files; Nuguid-Anden (2003); author's interview with Pacita Juan, President and CEO, 26 September 2006.

Challenges and prospects for HRM

The development and management of Philippine HR both at the national and enterprise levels face daunting challenges. Such tasks require a deeper understanding of the changing labour market in the context of economic liberalisation and global integration. As pointed out, economic growth has been uneven and punctuated by cycles of downturns. As a result both the unemployment and underemployment rates have remained in double digits since the early 1990s. The main job generator is the informal sector where jobs are precarious and unprotected. The small formal sector is shrinking, as indicated in the trend towards short-term hiring of semi-skilled minimum wage earners. The job crisis is a sad testimony to the failure of the three-decade SAP programme, whose overall objective was to transform the economy into a vibrant and more industrially developed one with a great capacity to create meaningful jobs for the growing labour force.

Yet, ironically, there are severe personnel shortages in emerging industries, such as the BPO industry and the call centre service. There are also shortages of critical personnel in certain industries, for example in the health and aviation industry, which are losing talent and skills to the overseas labour market. In an economy with a relatively open labour market the poaching of professionals, such as doctors, nurses, pilots, and engineers, is not difficult.

There are continuing and seemingly endless debates in the Philippines in relation to the overseas labour market and on the social and economic costs of migration. However, for some Filipinos the overseas labour market is the saviour of the economy and constitutes the economic lifeline for at least a quarter of the national population. At the same time, the country has been losing trained HRs to the overseas labour market. This has serious ramifications for HRD and HRM at the national and enterprise levels. For example, at the national level, should higher education be geared towards the training of students for the overseas job market? At the enterprise level can industries be enticed to invest into higher skills training for employees who may leave the company at any time? Yet given the larger picture of the economy and the labour market, what is the best way to approach the development of HR in the Philippines? It is obvious that there are no easy answers to these questions – unless the Filipino government and companies adopt a holistic and strategic approach to HR planning and development. HR and education planning which is based merely on the requirements of protected home industries no longer work.

For workers and entrepreneurs in the informal sector, many of whom have not reached college or received any TVET, HR intervention may come in the forms of skills and entrepreneurship enhancement programmes. For those pursuing higher education, signals from the labour market and from industry are important guides to education planning. However, the government should play a facilitating role to insure that industries do get the right graduates they need and that the graduates are able to develop a career worth pursuing, so as to reduce poaching and ensure industry sustainability. Of course, in the medium and long run it is imperative that both industries and the government are able to find a way to scale up and sustain job creation and industry development. What is clear is that there is a need for a serious re-thinking of the job creation strategy by re-examining the existing agro-industrial strategy in the context of the realities of economic liberalisation and globalisation.

In the meantime various enterprises belonging to the three economic sectors of industry, agriculture and services have to undertake their own economic, organisational and HRM adjustments if they are to survive, expand or stay competitive. Some companies are able to do it well, as illustrated in the case studies cited in this chapter. Part of their adjustment arsenal is the adoption of proactive HRM practices. Unfortunately, many enterprises, especially the small and family-owned firms, are unable to make the right adjustment choices. On hiring, the most common approach is to take the easy way out; that is, to resort to external labour market flexibility, meaning to utilise more short-term staff in order to save on labour costs and avoid the prospect of unionism. This gives companies short-term competitiveness but also limits the opportunity to invest in sustainable competitive measures such as the acquisition of new technology, upgrading of skills and the adoption of more modern and productive techniques. Thus, within the export-oriented garments industry, many firms which relied on external labour market measures have now closed down while those which have taken the route of innovation, creativity, a focus on higher value creation and skills development are continuing their production (Ofreneo, 2006).

Overall, a lot has to be done to promote better adjustment measures necessary to insure the preservation and creation of industries and decent jobs. There should be more studies and documentation of 'win-win' HR and organisational adjustments to the changing business environment, including employee–employer dialogues. Furthermore, organisations need better techniques in monitoring changes in industry and business competition and assessing how such changes will affect HRM and employment. Business organisations should be able to come up with proactive, not just reactive and remedial, programmes such as the retraining, reskilling and redeployment of affected or vulnerable employees.

Conclusion

There are contradictory images about the Philippine economy and its implications for HRM. However, the foregoing outline of the economy and HRM practices shows that the country has great economic potential which can be achieved at a higher level through a more forward-looking programme of active industrial policy and proactive HRM practices. In fact, the latter can serve as an incentive for gaining greater competitiveness for the economy, as illustrated by the cases summarised in this chapter. This is why increased awareness among managers on the importance of investing time and resources in ways to upgrade the skills of the workforce, improve ER and develop a world-class company is a welcome development. This increased awareness is in response partly to the labour unrest which swept the country in the 1980s and partly to the challenge of global competition and economic liberalisation, which have forced many ISI and even EOI companies to undertake painful restructuring programmes, mostly leading to downsizing.

Yet, much has still to be done. On the economic front it is the responsibility of the government to re-think the programmes of growth and industrialisation which have not worked and to undertake deeper and holistic economic strategies. In HRM the role of the government should be to become a partner of industry in attaining growth and competitiveness. One good way of doing this is through the documentation and propagation of best HRM practices. Each company, big and small, local or foreign-owned, should be challenged to develop its regime of best HRM practices in accordance with the company's history, corporate culture and business vision and mission. There is no single model of the most appropriate HRM scheme; it is the job of every company to develop its own.

Notes

1 EDSA refers to the busy Epifanio de los Santos Avenue, an area in Manila which became the centre of the political insurgence due to its proximity to the two military camps of Fort Aguinaldo and Camp Crame.
2 Data on the companies were obtained from sources compiled by the ECOP. ECOP's compilation is based on its 'Kapatid Awards' programme, which selects outstanding Philippine companies in the field of industrial relations every other year. In addition, ECOP, in its annual National Conference of Employers, invites the CEOs of these outstanding companies to give a presentation of their corporate and HRM practices. The author has visited all the companies cited in the paper and interviewed the following: Rafael Francisco, Vice-President for HR of CADP; Pacita Juan, President and CEO of Figaro; Nenette Fernando, Employee Relations Manager of Jollibee; and Renato Almeda, Director for HR of YTMI.

Bibliography

Aganon, M. E. (1994) 'HRM: A comparative analysis of Japanese, Chinese and Western models in the Philippines', in M. S. V. Amante (ed.) *Human Resource Approaches in the Philippines*. Quezon City: UP School of Labor and Industrial Relations.

Alliance of Progressive Labor (2001) *Fighting Back with Social Movement Unionism*, Manila: APL.

Amante, M., Ofreneo, R. and Ortiz, I. (1999) *Philippines: Skills Training and Policy Reforms*, Makati City: ILO SEAPAT.

Amante, M. S. V. (ed.) (1994) *Human Resource Approaches in the Philippines*, Quezon City: UP School of Labor and Industrial Relations.

Amante, M., Aganon, M. and Ofreneo, R. (1992) *Japanese Industrial Relations Interface in the Philippines*, Quezon City: UP School of Labor and Industrial Relations.

Asper, A. C. (2006) 'Working Paper on Employment, Underemployment, Unemployment and Flexible Work: Realities and Trends: Issues and Responses', Background Paper prepared for the National Convention of the Federation of Free Workers, Manila.

Azucena, C. A. (2006) *Everyone's Labor Code*, Manila: Rex Book Store.

Bacungan, F. and Ofreneo, R. (2002) 'The development of labour law and labour market policy in the Philippines', in S. Cooney *et al.* (eds), *Law and Labour Market in East Asia*, London: Routledge.

Balisacan, A. and Hill, H. (2003) 'An introduction to the key issues', in A. Balisacan and H. Hill (eds), *The Philippine Economy: Development,*

Policies, and Challenges, Quezon City: Ateneo de Manila University Press.

Business World (2005) *Top 1000 Corporations in the Philippines*, Quezon City: Business World Publishing.

Congress of the Philippines (2001) 'Human Capital in the Emerging Economy', Report and Recommendations of the Congressional Commission on Labor.

Constantino, R. (1975) *The Philippines: A Past Revisited*, Quezon City: Tala Publishing.

CRSS-AYC (1997) *Identifying Strategic Industrial Relations/Human Resources Adjustments and Policy Responses to the Challenge of Global Competition*, Pasay City: Philippine Exporters Foundation, Inc.

ECOP (2002) *Cases on Business Initiatives on Work-Life*, Makati City: Ayala Foundation and ECOP.

ECOP (2006) *ECOP Story*, Makati: ECOP.

Fayoshin, T. (2003) *Social Dialogue and Labour Market Performance in the Philippines*, Geneva: ILO.

Imperial, M. L. G., Mangahas, R., Martinez, J. B. and Fombuena, A., Jr. (1997) *Efficacy of Selected Labor Market Reforms in Promoting Globalization with Equity: The Philippine Case*, Manila: Institute for Labor Studies.

Jimenez, R. T. (1993) 'The Philippines', in S. J. Deery and R. J. Mitchell (eds), *Labour Law and Industrial Relations in Asia*, Melbourne: Longman Cheshire.

Kaufman, B. E. (2004) *The Global Evolution of Industrial Relations: Events, Ideas and the IIRA*, Geneva: International Labour Organisation.

Legaspi, N. (2006) 'Paradox: RP among the best but remains a laggard', in *Philippine Graphic*, Makati: Philippine Graphics Publications Inc.

Lim, J. and Montes, M. (1997) *The Structure of Employment and Structural Adjustment in the Philippines*, Employment and Training Papers No. 8, Geneva: ILO.

Lloyd, D. and Salter, W. (1999) *Corporate Social Responsibility and Working Conditions,* Manila: ILO Southeast-Asia and the Pacific Multidisciplinary Team.

Macaranas, F. (2003) *State of Philippine Competitiveness 2003*, Manila: Asian Institute of Management Policy Centre.

Martires, C. (1988) *Human Resources Management: Principles and Practices*, Quezon City: National Book Stores.

National Economic Development Authority (2004) *Medium-Term Philippine Development Plan*, Metro Manila: NEDA.

National Economic Development Authority (2005) 'Second progress report on the MDGs', in *DevPulse*, 30 July, Metro Manila: NEDA.

Nuguid-Anden, C. (2003) 'Enhancing Business-Community Relations: Figaro Coffee Company Case Study', paper submitted to the New Academy of Business, United Kingdom. See www.new-academy.ac.uk.

Ofreneo, R. E. (l993) 'Labor and the Philippine Economy', unpublished thesis, College of Social Sciences and Philosophy, University of the Philippines.

Ofreneo, R. E. (1994) 'Labor control and comparability in Philippine firms', in M. Amante (ed.), *Human Resource Approaches in the Philippines*, Quezon City: UP SOLAIR.

Ofreneo, R. E. (1995) *Philippine Industrialization and Industrial Relations*, Quezon City: UP Centre for Integrative Development Studies.

Ofreneo, R. E. (1996) 'Evolving IR/HR practices in the Philippine commercial banking industry', in J. Lee and A. Verma (eds), *Changing Employment Relations in Asian Pacific Countries*, Taipei: Chung-Hua Institution for Economic Research.

Ofreneo, R. E. (2004) 'Industrial Conflicts in a Globalizing Philippine Economy', paper prepared for the Southeast Asian Conflict Studies Network, De la Salle University.

Ofreneo, R. E. (2005) 'The Philippines under AFTA and WTO: An inquiry into the employment dimensions of regional and global integration', a report to the ILO-ASEAN-UNDP Project on Labour and Employment Implications of AFTA.

Ofreneo, R. E. (2006) 'Philippine Garments: A Year and a Half after MFA', paper presented at the International Workshop on 'Sustaining Development through Garment Exports', Phnom Penh, Cambodia.

Ofreneo, R., Serrano, M. and Marasigan, L. (2001) 'Needs and Demand Assessment of Job Quality in Micro and Small Enterprises (MSEs) in the Philippines', research report submitted to the ILO Small Enterprise Development (SEED) Programme, Geneva.

Ofreneo, R. and Samonte, I. (2002) 'Empowering Filipino Migrant Workers: Policy Issues and Challenges', report submitted to the Department of Foreign Affairs, Manila.

Ofreneo, R. and Samonte, I. (2005) 'Next-Generation Business Leaders in the Philippines', Study of the Economic Elite contributed to the BIR, Washington.

Ramos-Shahani, L. (1993) *Moral Imperatives of National Renewal: Readings on the Moral Recovery Programme*, Manila: Senate of the Philippines.

Selmer, J. and De Leon, C. (2003) 'Culture and management in the Philippines', in M. Warner (ed.), *Culture and Management in Asia*, London: Routledge Curzon.

Sison, P. S. (2003) *Personnel and Human Resources Management*, Mandaluyong City: Personnel Management Association of the Philippines.

Social Watch Philippines (2005) *Race for Survival: Hurdles on the Road to Meeting the MDGs in 2015*, Quezon City: Social Watch Philippines.

Soriano, R. Y. (2005) 'The Employers' Role in Employment Generation', paper prepared for the 'Conference on the Labor Code: 30 Years and Beyond', Manila.

Takahashi, F. (1998) 'Labor-Management Systems in Japanese Companies in the Philippine Setting', unpublished thesis, School of Labor and Industrial Relations, University of the Philippines.

Windell, J. and Standing, G. (1992) *External Labour Flexibility in Filipino Industry*, Geneva: ILO World Employment Research Programme.

WINT-NMYC (1992) 'Survey on the Hiring, Training and Promotion Practices in the Organized Sector', report submitted to the National Manpower and Youth Council, Manila.

Yap, J. (2003) 'A generation of economic orthodoxy: Time to take stock', *Philippine Daily Star*, 21 September.

Ziga, L. (2006) 'Mission-critical skills: professionals in search of a country', unpublished research paper.

Sources of statistical data

Asian Development Bank 2002, *Key Indicators 2002: Population and Human Resource Trends and Challenges*, Mandaluyong City: Asian Development Bank.

Bangko Sentral ng Pilipinas (www.bsp.gov.ph).

Bureau of Labor and Employment Statistics, *Current Labor Statistics*, Manila: BLES DOLE (www.bles.dole.gov.ph).

National Statistics Office, *Philippine Yearbook 2005*, Manila: National Statistics Office (www.census.gov.ph).

National Statistical Coordination Board, *2005 Philippine Statistical Yearbook*, Makati: NSCB (www.nscb.gov.ph).

United Nations Conference on Trade and Development, UNCTAD Database, 2004.

World Bank, World Development Indicators Database, 2004.

5 The changing face of human resource management in Singapore

David Wan and Tak Kee Hui

- Political, economic and social/cultural background and context
- Key labour market features and developments
- Development of PM and HRM and the HR function and profession
- HRM practices
- Case studies of indigenous organisations
- Case studies of individual managers
- Challenges and prospects for HRM
- Conclusion

Introduction

Singapore celebrated its forty-first anniversary of full independence in August 2006. In a relatively short period of time of national development, Singapore has progressed from the Third to the First World. As Professor Jayakumar vividly pointed out, Singapore's success can be summed up in its upholding of certain core principles, namely meritocracy, racial and religious harmony, multi-culturalism, integrity and incorruptibility, as well as the pursuit of excellence (*Straits Times*, 13 February 2006). Indeed, one of the many reasons why the country has achieved its current economic status is the effective investment and utilisation of its human assets and HR (Akdere, 2005). In this respect, the Singapore government has been an indispensable force in spearheading HRM and HRD within a well-established tripartite framework of government, employers and unions (Wan, 1999).

Globalisation generally refers to the worldwide phenomenon of businesses expanding beyond their domestic boundaries. It implies that the world is now a connected economy in which companies do business and compete anywhere and with anyone. However, even in an age of globalisation where competition has taken on a global platform, there would be few countries today in which the government is not involved in one way or another in influencing the country's economic development. Singapore's government has been credited with its ability to quickly adapt policies (even 'unpopular' ones) to meet new challenges and achieve public consensus and support for its economic/social policies (Arun and Lee, 1998; Bae *et al.*, 2003).

In addition to increasing globalisation, technological advances and greater competition from new players like China and India imply that the country must press on with its restructuring efforts. For example, many of the new jobs created after the 1997 Asian Financial Crisis require increased skills and knowledge. Yet, in early 1999 there was still a relatively large proportion of the Singapore workforce (38 per cent) with less than secondary education qualifications (*Straits Times*, 31 August 1999). The mismatch between new job requirements and labour skills requires concerted action by the government, employers and unions (Wan and Ong, 2002).

One consequence of globalisation and heightened competition can clearly be seen in the banking sector. For years, the banking sector in Singapore was dominated by the four big local banks. With the introduction of new technologies (automation) and a global wave of mergers and acquisitions, not only are the local banks pursuing the path of 'right-sizing' by reducing the number of employees, foreign financial institutions in Singapore are also involved in business restructuring. So as to adapt to changes at the workplace, employees need to broaden their skills and pursue cross-training. As for industry, the current focus will be on information ownership, innovation and value creation, mass customisation and effective deployment of social and intellectual capital. These changes will surely have an impact on the deployment and management of HR (Khatri, 2000). Perhaps the biggest challenge for organisations in this new type of employer–employee relationship is how to keep costs down and still retain their treasured staff (Barnard and Rodgers, 2000).

In the next section we discuss forces of political, economic and social changes and the role the government has played in enhancing the country's human assets. This is followed by discussions on the key labour market features and developments. We then focus on the development of HRM in Singapore, by presenting analyses of four key aspects of HR practice, as well as case studies of indigenous companies and individual outstanding managers.

Political, economic and social/ cultural background and context

Political

Mr Lee Kuan Yew was sworn in as the country's first Prime Minister in June 1959. In 1963 the city-state was incorporated into the then newly formed federation of Malaysia. However, on 9 August 1965 Singapore seceded from Malaysia and became a sovereign and independent nation. The immediate implication was that the young country had to be responsible for its own defence and foreign policy. The National Service (Amendment) Bill was passed in March 1967 and compulsory national service was introduced for all male citizens and permanent residents at the age of 18. Singapore also joined Indonesia, Malaysia, the Philippines and Thailand to form ASEAN in August 1967. An intense period of nation building and prosperity engineering followed in the 1970s and 1980s and propelled the country to newer heights of economic development. In the political arena, two opposition Members of Parliament were elected to parliament for the first time in 1984. Since 1990, nominated members of parliament, who can provide a wider representation of independent and non-partisan views, have been appointed to serve for a term of 2 years each.

The political system in Singapore follows the British political framework to some extent. The Cabinet is led by the Prime Minister. On the advice of the Prime Minister, the President appoints other ministers from among the Members of Parliament to form a Cabinet. The Cabinet is responsible collectively to Parliament and Parliament itself has a life span of 5 years from its first sitting. Prime Minister Lee Hsien Loong came into power on 12 August 2004. As the former Deputy Prime Minister and Finance Minister, Lee was seen by many as a capable problem-solver, articulate and intelligent. Under his leadership the country continues to open up and he is able to reach out particularly to younger Singaporeans. A 5-day working week was introduced in the civil service in 2004. Equalisation of medical benefits for married male and female officers in the civil service was also implemented in the same year. Education is given high priority nationwide, with more teachers recruited and the school syllabus shortened; at the same time the government encourages lifelong learning. In short, Singaporeans are encouraged to participate as active citizens (*Singapore Yearbook*, 2005).

Economic

Singapore has been doing well economically due to its continuous effort to restructure and reduce costs. The government has reduced rates of income tax and corporate tax and contribution rates for the Central Provident Fund (CPF). In 2005 growth was at 6.4 per cent (*Business Times*, 16 February 2006). While the Ministry of Trade and Industry estimates that economic growth for the year 2006 is between 4 and 6 per cent, some private sector economists predict a growth rate of 7 per cent. Unemployment rates dropped to 2.5 per cent at the end of 2005 (ibid.). While external demand continues to grow, consumer sentiment and business capital spending are expected to rise. Nonetheless, due to today's competitive business environment and political uncertainties in the region (political succession, terrorism), the future will not always be certain.

China's emergence as an economic power provides both threats and opportunities. While China's economic potential makes it the largest recipient of global foreign direct investments (FDI), thus decreasing the share of FDI for South East Asia, its growing middle class also presents a huge source of demand for goods and services. Equipped with ample knowledge and expertise in hotel management and tourism, logistics, infrastructure, transportation and port management, education and consulting, as well as other niche services, Singaporeans have intensified their presence in the Chinese mainland. At the same time, more and more Chinese firms are utilising Singapore's financial infrastructure and its close networks with the region to establish a foothold in South East Asia. In a similar vein the opening up of markets in India and the Middle East presents Singapore with business and networking opportunities. Meanwhile, competition from Malaysia and Thailand has intensified. Malaysia has expanded its seaport infrastructure in the state of Johor – the southernmost part of mainland Malaysia. With a larger HR pool, lower wages and cheaper land, the Johor seaport is a serious competitor to Singapore. Simultaneously, Bangkok is aiming to be a regional air hub which could seriously rival Singapore's present status.

In addition, globalisation today is more rapid and pervasive than before. Apart from developing its HR capability, Singapore has to step up its effort to attract MNCs that can provide new access to markets, sound management expertise, cutting edge technologies as well as research and development (R&D) and experiences (Hsieh and Tseng, 2002). Promising areas that will broaden Singapore's economic base and add a competitive edge include process engineering, biotechnology, life sciences, product design and development, logistics, e-commerce and management education. Under the country's Science and Technology 2010 Plan the government will spend S$13.55 billion over the next 5 years to enhance Singapore's economic competitiveness. The key strategies include nurturing talent, both local and foreign, and making sure that research is of commercial potential (*Straits Times*, 16 February 2006).

Social/cultural

As of June 2004 the total population of Singapore stood at 4.2 million while the resident population (comprising Singapore citizens and permanent residents) was 3.5 million (Table 5.1). The profile of the resident population comprised 76 per cent Chinese, 13.7 per cent Malays, 8.4 per cent Indians and 1.8 per cent others. Their median age was 35.7 years. Life expectancy in 2004 for males and females

Table 5.1 Population and vital statistics, 2000–2004

	2000	2001	2002	2003	2004
Resident population ('000)[a]	3,263	3,319	3,378	3,437	3,487
Population growth rate (%)	1.3	1.7	1.8	1.7	1.4
Population density (per sq. km)	5,885	6,055	6,086	6,004	6,066

Source: *Singapore Yearbook* (2005: 39).

Note
a   Resident population refers to citizens and permanent residents.

was 77.4 years and 81.3 years respectively. As a multi-racial, multi-cultural society there are four official languages, namely Malay, Mandarin, Tamil and English. While Malay is the national language, English is the language of administration. In 2004 the literacy rate was estimated to be 94.6 per cent (97.3 per cent for males and 92 per cent for females). The Singapore labour force in that year comprised 64.2 per cent of the population aged 15 years and above. In the same year some 84 per cent of the total population lived in public housing (*Singapore Yearbook*, 2005).

Although the majority of the population is Chinese, Singapore is essentially a multi-cultural society and a cosmopolitan city. It is a place where East meets West. There has always been a strong presence of MNCs since the late 1960s and with rapid globalisation the need for foreign talents and skilled labour becomes more evident. Some foreign commentators argue that Singaporeans prefer questions to which there are clear and precise answers, and that managers in Singapore are high in power distance and high on uncertainty avoidance. Things are changing, though, with the continuous modification of the educational system from primary to university levels and the gradual liberalisation of political participation. Creativity, innovation as well as entrepreneurship are considered critical to the future of the country's overall competitiveness. It is still an orderly society that emphasises fairness and impartiality of the law. Multiple viewpoints and democratic participation are encouraged as long as the nation's interests are not compromised. Economic development still dictates that industrial peace with justice must be upheld.

Key labour market features and developments

The economic development of Singapore is heavily shaped by the role of the government. It is indeed an indispensable driving force in the strategic utilisation of HR in the country. For example, a new statutory board under the Ministry of Manpower, the Singapore Workforce Development Agency (WDA), was established in 2003 to assist Singaporeans to cope with economic restructuring through training and skills upgrading. In February 2004 the Ministry of Manpower established a new Quality Workplaces Policy Department to help 'put together a holistic package of policies and schemes to support marriage and parenthood' (*Singapore Yearbook*, 2005: 224).

In 2004 Singapore's labour force totalled 2.2 million people while its labour force participation rate (LFPR) was 64.2 per cent. Total employment growth exceeded job losses and the unemployment rate dropped from 4.7 per cent in 2003 to an average of 4 per cent (*Singapore Yearbook*, 2005). Total employment gains were mainly from the service industries. Table 5.2 provides a breakdown of the employment profile of the Singapore workforce in 2004.

Singapore's workforce is increasingly ageing, a phenomenon that is comparable to trends occurring in many developed countries. By the late 1980s, compared with neighbouring countries, Singapore already had a large proportion of its population aged 65 and above (Wan and Ong, 2002). By 2025 those aged 65 and above are expected to rise to 17 per cent, the highest in ASEAN (ibid.). Increased life expectancy combined with a declining fertility rate (the gross reproduction rate in 2004 was 0.60 per female) prompted the government to increase the minimum retirement age from 55 to 60 in 1993 (ibid.). It was raised to 62 in January 1999 and the long-term target is 67. There is also a possibility that the absolute age limits for jobs be removed altogether (ibid.).

While the government, through discussions with its tripartite partners, namely employers and trade unions, has raised the retirement age progressively over the years, older and less-educated workers continue to form the bulk of those laid off and the jobless rates of this category of workers seem to have worsened even though the economy is improving. Some employers still have an unfavourable view towards older employees and they shed mature workers way before the official retirement age (*Straits Times*, 13 August 2005). The main concerns from the employers' point of view are higher

Table 5.2 Distribution of working persons by industry (%), June 2004

Manufacturing	17.3
Wholesale and retail trade	15.5
Transport, storage and communications	10.3
Business and real estate services	12.2
Community, social and personal services	26.8
Others	17.9

Source: *Singapore Yearbook* (2005: 225).

salaries (because of the seniority pay system) and medical cost risks and trainability. The issue of higher pay for mature workers could be addressed by re-designing new salary packages. Job re-design, re-training and/or re-deployment of older staff should rejuvenate their contributions to organisations.

Another way to utilise HR more effectively can be seen in efforts to increase the employment of women. The number of women working is rising steadily as their educational qualifications continue to improve. In fact, more women aged 55–59 are now joining the workforce (*The Straits Times*, 12 October 2005). In 2001 the LFPR of women was 54.3 per cent (ibid.). The government has been very active in encouraging women to join and remain in the workforce. It has come up with numerous solutions to address problems encountered by the growing number of career women who have families, for instance, tax relief for working mothers, tax rebates for foreign domestic workers, and family-friendly policies (such as the 5-day week). In 2004 maternity leave was extended from 8 to 12 weeks. In 2004 the S$10 million WoW! (Work-life Works!) Fund was launched to provide financial support to companies implementing work–life strategies (ibid.). At the same time a set of guidelines on family-friendly workplaces was issued by the National Tripartite Advisory Panel to promote these practices by employers and employees.

A third response to the generally tight labour market is to develop more flexible work arrangements, such as flexi-hours, job sharing, part-time work and work from home. While part-time work has become more common over the years, increasing from 1.9 per cent of private sector employees in 1998 to 3.4 per cent in 2002, Singapore still lags behind other developed countries (*Manpower News*, March 2003). Some employers in the manufacturing sector have reservations about employing part-time workers on the grounds that they need a longer time to be trained. Employers also perceive that full-timers are more productive and committed to their jobs. In addition, much needs to be done to encourage other forms of flexible work arrangements like flexi-time, telework and conventional home working in the private sector. According to the Ministry of Manpower, in 2002 only 0.22 per cent of private sector employees were on flexi-time; the corresponding percentages for telework and conventional home working were 0.08 and 0.01 (ibid.). Employers still prefer to keep an eye on their employees during regular office hours.

With the swift decline of labour-intensive industries like textiles/ clothing, leather/shoes, steel, metal fabricating, machinery, shipbuilding, traditional business and personal services that once propelled Singapore to an economically developed status, Singaporeans from these sectors are increasingly finding it harder to secure employment in the new high-technology industries. Indeed, many of the newly created jobs are well-paying ones but they are found in higher value-added sectors. Singaporeans need to have the necessary skills and/ or education to take on these better-paying jobs. While it is the lower educated workers in the production or services sector who are most likely to encounter structural unemployment, increasingly, in the new economy, executives, technical staff, managers and professionals alike are confronted with the same challenge of unemployment (*NTUC News*, 13 May 2005). In view of the heightened competition from countries with abundant supplies of labour, old jobs are likely to disappear faster than the growth of skilled jobs and workers have to adapt, be flexible and take re-training and lifelong learning more seriously.

Development of PM and HRM and the HR function and profession

Over the last four decades the HRM function in Singapore has evolved from the type found in traditional family businesses with no proper personnel function to a system that is influenced by the employment policies/strategies of MNCs and the government. The labour movement has also abandoned confrontational bargaining for the establishment of cooperatives and the promotion of workforce flexibility and lifelong learning. Faced with rapid globalisation and intense competition, employers, the government and the National Trades Union Congress are more eager to strengthen their tripartite relationship. As in the past, HRM policies and practices in Singapore will continue to be shaped by the national agenda under the current tripartite arrangement.

HRM at the Singapore workplace continues to focus on the three dimensions of labour market flexibility – in the number of employees (numerical flexibility); in the skills deployed/tasks performed (functional flexibility) and in reward management (financial flexibility).

These dimensions are crucial to organisational survival because of increased business uncertainty, the need to improve productivity, reduction of HR costs and effective utilisation of new technology. In practice, organisations do not restrict themselves to the use of one particular form of flexibility. Among the numerous HR strategies available for companies to achieve numerical flexibility are part-time work, temporary employment, employment of elderly workers, use of foreign workers, sub-contracting work (outsourcing, off-shoring) and encouraging more female participation. Strategies to increase functional flexibility include training and development, elimination of unnecessary job demarcations and negotiating flexibility deals with unions. Flexibility in reward management is achieved via the implementation of flexible wage systems and flexible benefit schemes.

Increasingly companies realise the significance of the HR function and put more emphasis on the role of HR personnel in their firms. If strategically aligned to organisational strategies and goals, HR can help organisations achieve higher performance and attain business excellence (Tiong, 2005). Practitioners in the Singapore HR profession occasionally see the need to uplift its image and reputation. Similar to what accountants, engineers and other professions have done, the Singapore HR Institute initiated a HR accreditation programme in 2006 to enhance the reputation of the HR profession and to provide a clear road map for HR competency and knowledge acquisition. Three accreditation statuses will be accorded: the HR Associate (HRA), the HR Professional (HRP) and the Senior HR Professional (SHRP). The accreditation structure, comprised of the HR accreditation board, a HR accreditation assessment panel as well as a HR accreditation ethics and appeal panel, will ensure the smooth development and running of the accreditation scheme (ibid.).

While the term strategic HRM has been operational in Singapore for nearly a decade, the actual strategic role of HR personnel depends very much on their ability to anticipate new developments, embrace change and provide the needed leadership for organisational success. Several questions need to be answered, for example how do we define and measure HR performance? What strategic role does HR play in an organisation? What is the concrete link between HR interventions and a firm's success? How can we structure HR as a strategic partner in the firm? In what ways do HR professionals drive change and add value to organisational effectiveness? Basically, two sets of questions are being asked: what and how? There is no one path to success and the answers differ from one organisation to another due to, for example, size of firm, ownership type, country of origin, history of the organisation, and competitive environment.

HRM practices

Employee resourcing

The manufacturing sector enjoyed a bumper year for employment in 2005 and 2006. Skills shortages existed in many key industries while job seekers were offered more choice. This positive outlook can be attributed to the government's efforts over the years to turn Singapore into a hub of high value-added activities (such as media/PR/advertising, banking, IT and telecommunications, tourism, logistics and transportation, education, healthcare and life sciences). The talent shortage has also meant that 'poaching' causes employers to raise pay for both existing but deserving employees and new recruits. Positions for experienced sales people, technicians and engineers are among the hardest to fill (*Business Times*, 22 February 2006). Amidst mounting regional and international competition, Singapore International Airlines, for example, finds it difficult to retain their trained pilots. Just relying on competitive remuneration alone may not be sufficient to stop them leaving the company. At the same time some companies are more than willing to discharge their unproductive or troublesome workers rather than spend time and resources in dealing with them.

Recruiting people is not simply about getting the best brains or the most experienced candidates, it is about getting persons with the 'right fit'. That means finding a fit between what the company offers in pay, training and career development, and what the candidate can offer in terms of skills, knowledge and experience, and what they expect of the potential employer and the job. As the economy continues to develop and open up, HR managers will have to recruit and manage global talent. Talent management and the effective management of diversity will become more and more crucial in the HR professional's agenda. As noted by Landau and Chung (2001:210),

Anyone managing in Singapore must be attuned to its cultural complexity. The values, rules and norms may vary considerably, depending not only on the demographic make-up of the labour force, but also the culture of each organisation and the organisation's home country.

The top five challenges facing HR in Singapore in 2006 were, in sequence: recruitment, retention, training and development (tied with compensation and benefits), and talent management (*HRM Magazine*, January 2006). Under the current tight labour market situation, companies will be increasingly forced to refine their recruitment strategies and attract candidates. They will have to consider other options like (a) multi-skilling and cross-training for existing staff; (b) employing part-timers, retirees, housewives and students on flexible work arrangements; (c) sub-contracting non-critical functions to outside suppliers; and (d) overseas recruitment. The Tripartite Committee on Employability of Older Workers has urged HR professionals to re-examine their HR policies on hiring and retention to make them more 'age-friendly' (*The Straits Times*, 22 February 2006). To increase the employability of older workers would require efforts by the government and adjustments to the mindset of both employers and older workers.

As for retention, organisations will have to better understand what motivates their staff. While good pay is certainly high on most employees' lists, personal development, self-esteem and relationships are important considerations too (Fang, 2001; Campbell and Campbell, 2003). A joint study conducted by the *HRM Magazine* of Singapore and JobsDB.com revealed that employees ranked career/learning opportunities as their first priority, followed by recognition, pay, relationships with managers and relationships with colleagues (*HRM Magazine*, Issue No. 5.12, December 2005). On the other hand, employers tend to think that recognition comes first, followed by career/learning opportunities, relationships with managers, pay and the work itself. Interestingly, both groups do not consider job security, work–life balance, non-pay-related benefits and company brand as highly important (*HRM Magazine*, Issue No. 5.12).

Finally, temporary employment in Singapore will become more prevalent since it benefits both employers and job-seekers. Organisations are careful not to increase their permanent staff, and contract/part-time employment provides considerable labour flexibility. As for the individuals, temporary employment offers a viable alternative for desperate job-seekers now that the 'iron rice bowl' (lifetime employment) has become more or less extinct. It provides them with the opportunity to constantly upgrade their skills and experiences by working in different environments. This employment trend is not restricted to secretarial and clerical staff only, but also increasingly embraces people trained in marketing, HR, IT, management, accountancy and engineering (*Business Times*, 19 April 2003).

Employee development

In general, training focuses on improving skills in the current job while development aims to improve the employee's skills and abilities on future jobs. The purposes of training and development are not restricted to removing performance deficiencies or increasing productivity; this HR function also acts as an important tool to attract good recruits and retain staff (Chay and Bruvold, 2003). For expanding enterprises, in addition to recruitment, investment in human capital becomes more crucial for the company's success. However, so as to secure top management's commitment, training and development must be seen as an activity that can help in solving the company's problems and contribute to the bottom line. Some employers choose to focus on the price tag attached to training programmes and ignore the inherent values of training and development. During economic slowdown training and development becomes even more vulnerable.

The Manpower Ministry found that in 2004 some 66.5 per cent of the 2,503 private sector companies surveyed had sent their employees for training (*Straits Times*, 20 September 2005). The construction sector had the largest number of trained workers (76 per cent), followed by the manufacturing sector (65.5 per cent) and the services sector (64.4 per cent) (ibid.). On average companies spent S$511 per employee, or 1.3 per cent of their total payroll, on training (ibid.). As expected, professionals, managers and executives accounted for the bulk of the training expenditure per employee (S$958), followed by clerical sales and service staff (S$364) and production and cleaning workers (S$180) (ibid.). An interesting finding was that, while worker productivity, customer satisfaction, sales and profitability as well as product/ service quality generally improved after employees were sent for training, pay increases and promotion did not follow automatically.

For example, one in two companies reported that there was no wage increase while eight in ten companies increased the incumbents' job responsibilities (ibid.). Perhaps of more significance was that average training expenditure had fallen since 2002. Also, the provision of training was still concentrated among the larger establishments and those with higher skills continued to receive more training.

Employee rewards

In the Singapore context, tripartite effort by the unions, employers and the government together shape the conceptualisation of many labour flexibility schemes. Take the example of wage reform. As part of the total package towards increasing labour flexibility, the government has identified pay flexibility as one of the key cornerstones for continued economic growth. Since 1999 the National Wages Council (NWC) has recommended (in addition to its widely acclaimed 1986 wage reform) the inclusion of the monthly variable component (MVC) as a mechanism for companies to reduce wage costs quickly in a sharp business downturn. Hence, instead of cutting basic salaries or laying off staff, the MVC can be trimmed first. As an example, a more flexible pay system, say, comprising 70 per cent basic wage, 20 per cent annual variable component and 10 per cent MVC, could enhance the link between a company's salary payment and its profitability; motivate employees by rewarding them for their performance (based on individual performance and/or teamwork); and maximise cost-competitiveness.

Wages in Singapore have been moving up and more companies are implementing wage reform. Total wages rose by 3.6 per cent on average in 2004, up from the 1.5 per cent in 2003. The higher pay rises also included a bigger average bonus of 1.87 months, compared with 1.76 months in 2003 (*Straits Times*, 1 July 2005). The 2006 survey conducted by the Ministry of Manpower reveals that, as of June 2005, 90 per cent of workers in large enterprises and 73 per cent in SMEs have some form of flexible wage system (ibid.). The comparative figures for June 2004 were 80 per cent and 42 per cent respectively (ibid.). Meanwhile, the wage ratio (the difference between the maximum and minimum salaries in a given job) has also narrowed, implying that companies now pay more emphasis to performance and less to the seniority of workers. The implication is that employees' basic pay will better reflect the value of their job. Also, with the flexible wage structure in place companies are in a better position to absorb economic shocks and reduce retrenchments, especially of older workers. When economic conditions are good, firms can reward their employees with one-off bonuses rather than built-in wage increases.

Meanwhile, the concept of 'cafeteria benefit' programmes is also spreading. However, compared with the US, its popularity is limited because of high implementation costs and the lack of a local track record. Those companies that offer such flexi-benefit plans tend to be from the hotel, telecommunications and banking sectors. Examples are the Westin Stamford and Westin Plaza Hotels, Raffles International, IBM, Development Bank of Singapore Land and the Singapore armed forces.

Finally, in a tight labour market private sector companies are providing more benefits in an attempt to attract, motivate and retain their employees. For example, many companies, especially in the manufacturing sector, provide attractive family benefits like children's education benefits, compassionate leave to take care of sick children or grandparents, wellness programmes, health screenings, social activities for singles, lunch talks and seminars on parenting and child development, weekend activities for the families, a clubhouse and even child-care centres (Tan, 2004). Provision of work–life balance and family-friendly practices thus help companies to boost their employees' morale and the firm's bottom line.

Employee relations

The role of the Singapore government as a key player in the management of ER is clearly reflected in the administration of employment laws by the Ministry of Manpower. Furthermore, the Ministry assists in the settlement of industrial disputes, and participates in various tripartite organisations. In general, the government's expectations of the Singapore labour movement are diverse: protect the interests of the workers at the workplace; earn the trust and respect of workers and managers; and support the nation's development strategies as well as play an active role in shaping a responsible work ethic. On the other hand, the government expects employers and management to adopt a union acceptance strategy as far as possible, build trust and provide timely information for collective bargaining purposes as well as encourage union roles in activities such as worker training and re-training, employee consultation and employee empowerment.

Tripartism, in terms of an accord between the government, trade unions and employers, is a dominant feature of the ER system in Singapore, the successful practice of which has drawn attention from many countries. Recent examples of employer and union involvement at the national level that have significant impact on the ER scene include the Tripartite Panel on Retrenched Workers (1998); Manpower 21 Report (1999); Tripartite Guidelines on Non-discriminatory Job Advertisements (1999); Code of Responsible Employment Practices (2002); Code on Industrial Relations Practice (2004); National Wages Council Wage Guidelines (yearly); Guidelines on Best Work–Life Practices (2004); Guidelines on Flexible Work Schedule (2004); Guidelines on Family Friendly Workplace Practices (2004); and Tripartite Committee on Employability of Older Workers (2005).

With a well-tested tripartite framework and various institutional structures and procedures in place, for example the NWC, the Ministry of Manpower, the Industrial Arbitration Court, it is up to employer and employee representatives to decide how they should work together. Even though the ER climate in Singapore is generally cordial, some managements frown upon employee representation. Discrimination towards union leaders (in terms of their opportunities for promotion and pay increases) remains, but it is neither open nor widespread. Harmonious ER and greater cooperation depend very much on union/management leadership, their level of trust and the degree of information sharing.

Tan (2004) argued that the presence or absence of a good ER climate in any country depends on: (a) its legal structure (employment laws); (b) the roles played by the government, the labour movement and employer organisations; and (c) national shared values or ideology (such as consensus, harmony). At the workplace level ER depends heavily on management attitude and commitment, objectives of unions, inter-relationships between supervisors and union leaders, and employees' attitudes.

To foster good ER in Singapore, numerous schemes have been tried out and put into practice over the years. These include, for example, labour management committees for joint consultation, quality control circles, grievance handling mechanisms, newsletters, suggestion schemes, safety committees, recreation committees and profit sharing. Whether the presence of these schemes alone is sufficient to counter adverse economic impacts on organisations remains to be seen. Indeed, a relatively long period of industrial peace does not imply that one can take things for granted.

Case studies of indigenous organisations

Having examined the broader aspects of HRM at the national and workplace levels this section will be devoted to two indigenous organisations that have excelled in their HR policies and practices: the National Library Board (NLB) and the NTUC Income Insurance Cooperative Ltd (NTUC Income). Both organisations have won the Singapore HR Awards 2005's Leading Corporate HR Award (local enterprises category) organised by the Singapore HR Institute (SHRI). The Singapore HR Awards provide the platform to honour and recognise individuals and organisations that have made significant contributions in enhancing human capital management and development.

Organisation case study 1: The National Library Board

Established in 1995 to 'expand the learning capacity of the nation so as to enhance national competitiveness and to promote a gracious society', the NLB oversees the management of the National Library, three regional libraries, eighteen community libraries, as well as libraries belonging to government agencies, schools and private institutions (www.nlb.gov.sg). In the age of the knowledge economy the NLB plays a critical role. Libraries in Singapore are not just libraries per se. They provide 'functional space', 'social space' and they are well integrated with the community. Not only do the libraries have to assume new images and attract users young and old, they have to constantly invest in new technologies, innovate and recruit capable persons. In view of its efforts and accomplishments the NLB has won a string of awards, such as the prestigious Singapore Quality Award and the Distinguished Public Service Award.

Without doubt the role of HRM is given the utmost attention at NLB. The Library's CEO, Dr Varaprasad (*Human Capital Magazine*, August/September 2005: 48), comments:

> A world-class library system begins with its people. At NLB, we believe that having motivated and high quality staff is the key to our success and this is what our HR set to achieve. We also have an integrated staff involvement framework that promotes a culture of open communication; working together; a passion of learning; and provides opportunities for innovation.

Examples are numerous and involve the use of cross-functional teams, work improvement teams, business process re-engineering, community of practices, staff suggestion schemes, staff surveys, staff forums and leadership seminars. Indeed, its 'project-centric environment' breaks functional enclosures and provides employees with ample opportunities to be involved in organisation-wide projects, which in turn encourages commitment to teamwork, innovation and achievement of organisational goals and objectives.

Among the various HR initiatives that have contributed to the organisation's success are its innovative practice in enhancing employees' health and wellness. The NLB was the first government organisation to sign the Health-At-Work Charter with the Singapore Ministry of Health in 1997, pledging to invest in the physical health, mental health and social well-being of its employees. This is carried out at three different levels. At the corporate level, employee health and wellness has been singled out as a 'core and effective HR strategy'. At the operational level a Workplace Health Promotion Committee is headed by senior management. There are twenty-nine health facilitators drawn from various divisions and library branches. The objectives of the workplace health programme are to reduce stress and improve the organisational climate, encourage healthy eating habits, increase the level of physical activity and keep employees healthy. At the individual level staff are encouraged to actively participate in the planning of the various health and wellness programmes. An annual sum is provided for every staff member's health-related benefits entitlement. Employees can use the amount to spend on health and fitness classes, health screening, purchase of sports and fitness equipments, spa, massage, foot reflexology, etc.

Source: *Singapore HR Awards 2005.*

Organisation case study 2: NTUC Income

NTUC Income is a cooperative insurance society, formed in 1970 shortly after the 'Modernisation of the Labour Movement' seminar in 1969. It was established in response to a nationwide growing need for affordable insurance. Nowadays, in addition to providing different types of insurance products, NTUC Income also provides special benefits such as competitive loan, repair, domestic cleaning and house moving services, plumbing, renovation, tuition services and health screening. As a good corporate citizen, each year it provides about 1 per cent of its surplus to support the arts, sports, education, healthy lifestyles, charity, trade unions and the environment. It employs 2,500 insurance advisers, 1,400 office staff, and has a network of eleven branches in Singapore.

Over the years of operation it has become a leading insurance firm in Singapore. As the only insurance cooperative in the country it has to compete in a field of more than forty-five local and MNC insurance companies (www.ntuc.org.sg). Since 1999 it has maintained its 'AA' rating by Standard and Poor. This clearly reflects its financial stability and capacity to meet new challenges. Among the numerous awards that the cooperative has received over the years, some noteworthy examples are ISO 9001:2000 Certification (2003), National Work Redesign Model Company (2003), CIO Asia Magazine Award (2003), Family Friendly Firm Award (2000, 2002 and 2004), People Developer Singapore (2001, 2004), Singapore Innovation Class (2004), Sporting Singapore Inspiration Award (2003 and 2004), Singapore Quality Class (1999–2005), Leading Corporate HR Award (2005), Leading CEO Award (2005), Distinguished Patron of the Arts Awards (2000–05). These awards serve to illustrate vividly the cooperative's commitment to innovative HR practices, good corporate citizenship, excellence in leadership, people development, customer service (through innovative solutions) and solid business results.

Its cutting edge in IT development can be seen in the fact that it was the first insurance company in the country to install a mainframe computer system in 1980 and the first to launch an internet website in 1995. The cooperative espouses five core values for its 'internal colleagues': meritocracy, entrepreneurship, respect, integrity and teamwork. This translates into a corporate culture that emphasises promptness, openness and being forward looking. The implication is that recruiting the right people and retaining them will be crucial for the growth of the company. Emphasis will be placed on those who can share the cooperative's values and aspirations.

With an integrated strategy in recruitment, induction, web-based learning, career development, open appraisal system, effective recognition and reward system, workplace wellness programmes, flexible working arrangements and other pro-family practices, NTUC Income has been able to raise its retention rate from 85 per cent in 2001 to 90 per cent in 2004. Its annual turnover rate at 10 per cent was much lower than the turnover rate of 18 per cent in the whole insurance sector. Indeed, employees who contribute to continuous improvements and are actively involved in corporate events are given due recognition. This can be in the form of monetary and non-monetary rewards such as a certificate of appreciation, appreciation lunch with the CEO or priority allocation of concert tickets.

On his leadership style the CEO, Mr Tan Kin Lian (*Human Capital Magazine*, August/September 2005), has this comment: 'I believe in an open and positive style. I like to set the goals and get people to work towards it. I encourage them to be bold, innovative and entrepreneurial. They have to do, learn and adapt.' At the same time, the organisation's human asset has to be properly managed. Hence, 'HR is expensive. HRD is expensive . . . If we can use our HR budget well, we can produce better results. It is a strategic challenge for management.'.

Source: *Singapore HR Awards 2005.*

Case studies of individual managers

This section is devoted to two case studies on individuals who have contributed significantly to the HR profession. During the Singapore HR Awards 2005 competition these two individuals won the Leading CEO Award and the Leading HR Entrepreneur Award respectively.

Manager case study 1: Tan Ser Kiat

Professor Tan Ser Kiat is the Group CEO of the Singapore Health Services, and concurrently the CEO of the Singapore General Hospital. He was appointed as Group CEO of the SingHealth cluster when the government announced the clustering of all public healthcare institutions in 2000. SingHealth comprises three hospitals, five national specialty centres and a network of primary healthcare clinics, and employs over 13,000 employees. A distinguished orthopaedic surgeon by training, Professor Tan received the PPA (Public Administration, Gold) in 1999. He also holds numerous honorary fellowships in the field of medicine. To achieve his vision for SingHealth to become world class and compete side by side with the best hospitals in the world, he knows it is crucial for SingHealth to be an employer of choice and the healthcare cluster must bring out the best in its people and nurture and develop them.

To provide the best care for patients, a well-managed reward system must be in place to recognise various groups of SingHealth employees: medical, nursing, researchers, allied health, ancillary and administration. Professor Tan initiated the GCEO (Group CEO) Employee Excellence Award in 2004. Other recognition programmes include, for example, the SingHealth Investigator Excellence Award for researchers and the House Officer Award for junior doctors. By thoroughly taking care of its staff's welfare and helping them to achieve a healthy and balanced work–life, SingHealth also won the Singapore Family Friendly Employer Award in 2004. A 5-day work week was implemented in 2005.

Underlying the success and growth of the Group are three core values: clinical excellence, commitment and collaboration. Professor Tan strongly believes in his vision of turning SingHealth into a renowned organisation at the leading edge of medicine, and providing quality healthcare to meet the nation's aspirations. As such, harmonious labour relations, employee satisfaction, talent development and a belief in people and talent are championed. The role of the HR function is vividly summarised by Professor Tan (*Human Capital Magazine*, August/September 2005):

> The management at SingHealth sees HR as a strategic partner, not just a department function to meet manpower needs. At SingHealth, HR is involved in the business planning process so they understand the business and share the vision. In this way, our HR department and professionals are better positioned to help grow and motivate our talent towards achieving their goals.

Indeed, business outcomes are measured in KPIs and the balanced scorecard. This is important because of the need to leverage synergies within the cluster, improve employee productivity and contain rising healthcare costs.

On winning the various Singapore HR Awards in 2005, such as the Leading CEO, Leading HR Practices in Learning and Human Capital Development, and Leading HR Practices in Balanced Work–Life, Professor Tan is of the view that through these achievements SingHealth can benchmark itself against industry practices and at the same time use it as a platform to share and learn from the best practices of other organisations.

Source: Singapore HR Awards 2005.

Manager case study 2: Annie Yap

The GMP Group, incorporated in 1991, is the largest HR services provider in Singapore. From its beginning, the company has had a strong vision of its purpose, that is, to 'provide ethical, efficient and effective recruitment through friendly and professional service'. As one of the choice employers in Singapore it is well known as a company with 'warmth, integrity and professionalism'. Today, it has ten offices in Singapore and nine abroad.

The current managing director of the GMP Group, Ms Annie Yap, is the winner of the Leading HR Entrepreneur Award 2005. She is also the President of the

Singapore Staffing Association. She joined GMP in 1991 as a recruitment consult-ant and pioneered the International Recruitment division in 1994. Ms Yap was promoted to senior manager in 1995 and pioneered the Group's Technologies divi-sion a year later. In 1996 she was further promoted to the post of General Manager, Singapore and 2 years later to Managing Director of the GMP Group. Under her leadership, the Group's revenues increased by 150 per cent within a period of 4 years. Moreover, it is the only staffing company to be awarded the Regional HQ status by the Singapore Economic Development Board. Without doubt, as a young and dynamic entrepreneur, Ms Yap has been instrumental in the GMP Group's growth over the past decade. As a regional leader in staffing services she sets her vision to make GMP a global leader.

Under Ms Yap's leadership the GMP Group espouses five core values: PRIDE (professionalism, responsibility, innovation, dedication and expediency). Each of its staff carries a critical role in shaping destinies of the Group's clients. Employees are therefore empowered to make decisions. Having established itself successfully in Singapore, Malaysia and China, the Group is ready to expand further and the future looks bright. In the words of Ms Yap (*Human Capital Magazine*, August/September 2005):

> Today, I have a team of young, dynamic leaders who are as passionate about the company's growth as I am. As you can imagine, my vision and goals alone could not have moved The GMP Group to where it is today. It is my team's effort, creative ideas and dedication that have contributed to The GMP Group's fast growth.

Source: *Singapore HR Awards 2005*.

Challenges and prospects for HRM

The future presents both challenges to and opportunities for effective HRM in Singapore. While the prospect of the long-term job market in Singapore remains optimistic, labour costs are comparatively much higher than its ASEAN neighbours. Globalisation, rapid technologi-cal innovation, company consolidation as well as outsourcing and off-shoring will continue to have significant impacts on employment relations at the workplace. There is, therefore, a constant need for Singapore workers to be highly skilled, innovative and flexible.

The Singapore employment system has already moved into one that can no longer promise lifelong jobs with frequent career advance-ment or predictable pay increases. Examples can be seen not only in private enterprises, but also in the civil service, the statutory boards and other government agencies. For example, since 2003 the government has outsourced S$180 million worth of contracts for non-strategic public services such as car park enforcement, facilities management, IT, audit, customer call centres and libraries to the private sector (*Business Times*, 18 February 2006).

In the face of global competition organisations will continue to restructure so as to compete and survive. In every organisation the top management has to set the right tone for the whole organisation. Managers will have to segregate the revenue earners from the non-performers. They have to work on staff weaknesses and make their jobs more rewarding. Performance-based pay and promotion based on merit have become the norm. The possibility of future retrenchment cannot be ruled out. Individual employees will have to be more proactive in chartering their own futures. They must have pride and motivation in their jobs.

In view of today's competitive business environment, which coincides with an ageing population and a falling birth rate, balancing the interests of employers and their counterparts will require management and workers alike to adopt a fresh look at employee relations and employment practices. A 'win–win' situation will not be easy to achieve given the constant need for companies to address cost-containment and cost-effectiveness. On the other hand, while the economic rationale for downsizing is apparent there is no convincing evidence that employment downsizing will lead to better financial performance.

Compared with earlier generations, individuals are more willing to negotiate their own working patterns and to move from one company or location to another to maximise their career prospects. As highlighted by Cappelli (1999), the biggest challenge for organisations in this new employer–employee relationship will be how to motivate employees and generate commitment when employers are no longer willing to promise long-term security. Bosses that provide frequent feedback on subordinate performances, set clear expectations and care for their workers are more likely to have their staff engaged. Companies that adopt responsible restructuring strategies such as retrenchment only as a last resort, the proper management of the 'survivor' sentiments and maintaining goodwill with those who are asked to leave, will have a better chance to secure the morale and commitment of those who remain (Cascio, 2003).

Conclusion

Even though Singapore features a number of competitive advantages that make it difficult for its close competitors to imitate (access to a talent pool, political stability, proactive government, social harmony, unified labour movement, world class R&D facilities in science and technology, strong enforcement of intellectual property rights), the Singapore government does not believe that the world owes the country a living. To compete with both developing and developed economies the country has to generate investors' confidence and maintain political stability. And to ride successfully on the globalisation process, Singapore has to open up its economy and its labour market to the world. It has to prepare its workforce for the rapidly changing environment through continuous education and training.

Many factors help to account for Singapore's remarkably rapid development. Ghesquiere (2007: 1) attributes the country's success to its 'exceptional cohesion amongst economic outcomes, policies, institutions, values, and leadership over a long period.' While FDI is still crucial, the country has to prioritise and at the same time identify its domestic sources of growth. Faced with increased competition from China, India and the immediate region, Singapore has to move fast to nurture a knowledge-intensive economy within which R&D will play a much more critical role. Promotion of innovation will help Singapore to compete on proprietary knowledge, improve efficiency and move up the value chain in its products and services. Encouragement of entrepreneurship will help the country to realise its dream of becoming an enterprising Singapore. Ultimately, it is the quality of its HR that propels Singapore to compete globally and move on to the next level of economic and social achievements.

Bibliography

Akdere, M. (2005) 'Social capital theory and implications for HR development', *Singapore Management Review*, 27, 2, 1–24.
Arun, M. and Lee, T. Y. (eds) (1998) *Singapore: Re-Engineering Success*, Oxford: Oxford University Press.

Bae, J., Chen, S. J., Wan, D. and Lawler, J. (2003) 'HR strategy and firm performance in Pacific Rim countries', *International Journal of HR Management,* 14, 8, 1308–32.

Barnard, M. and Rodgers, R. A. (2000) 'How are internally oriented HRM policies related to high-performance work practices? Evidence from Singapore', *International Journal of HR Management,* 11, 6, 1017–46.

Business Times, a Singapore newspaper. Various issues.

Campbell, D. J. and Campbell, K. M. (2003) 'Global versus facet predictors of intention to quit: Differences in a sample of male and female Singaporean managers and non-managers', *International Journal of HR Management,* 14, 7, 1152–77.

Cappelli, P. (1999) *The New Deal at Work,* Boston, MA: Harvard Business School Press.

Cascio, W. F. (2003) *Managing HR: Productivity, Quality of Work Life, Profits,* New York: McGraw-Hill/Irwin.

Chay, H. L. and Bruvold, N. T. (2003) 'Creating value for employees: Investment in employee development', *International Journal of HR Management,* 14, 6, 981–1000.

Fang, Y. Q. (2001) 'Turnover propensity and its causes among Singapore nurses: An empirical study', *International Journal of HR Management,* 12, 5, 859–71.

Ghesquiere, H. (2007) *Singapore's Success: Engineering Economic Growth,* Singapore: Thomson Learning.

Human Capital Magazine, Singapore HR Institute. Various issues.

HRM Magazine, Key Media Pte Ltd: Singapore. Various issues.

Hsieh, Y. L. and Tseng, S. F. (2002) 'The welfare state in the information age: Hollowing out or restructuring in the changing labour market in Singapore?', *International Journal of HR Management,* 13, 3, 501–21.

Khatri, N. (2000) 'Managing HR for competitive advantage: A study of companies in Singapore', *International Journal of HR Management,* 11, 2, 336–66.

Landau, J. and Chung, Y. K. (2001) 'Singapore', in M. Patrickson and P. O'Brien (eds), *Managing Diversity: An Asian and Pacific Focus,* Singapore: John Wiley and Sons.

Ministry of Information and the Arts. *Singapore Yearbook* (various issues). Singapore: Ministry of Information and the Arts.

Ministry of Manpower. *Manpower News.* Various issues.

National Trades Union Congress. *NTUC News.* Various issues.

Singapore HR Awards 2005: A showcase of leading HR ideas and practices, Singapore Human Resources Institute.

Straits Times, a Singapore newspaper. Various issues.

Tan, C. H. (2004) *Employment Relations in Singapore,* Singapore: Prentice Hall.

Tiong, T. N. (2005) 'Maximising HR potential in the midst of organisational change', *Singapore Management Review,* 27, 2, 25–35.

Wan, D. (1999) 'Competitive advantage through people – the Singapore experience', in A. R. Nankervis, R. Compton and T. McCarthy (eds), *Strategic HR Management*, Australia: Nelson ITP.

Wan, D. and Ong, C. H. (2002) 'Case study on HRM in Singapore', in A. R. Nankervis, R. Compton and M. Baird (eds), *Strategic HR Management*, Australia: Nelson Thomson Learning.

6 The changing face of human resource management in Thailand

Sununta Siengthai, Uthai Tanlamai and Chris Rowley

- Political, economic and social/cultural background and context
- Key labour market features and developments
- Development of PM and HRM and the HR function and profession
- HRM practices
- Case studies of indigenous organisations
- Case studies of individual managers
- Challenges and prospects for HRM
- Conclusion

Introduction

Since the 1980s many political, economic and social changes have brought about rapid shifts in management concepts and practices in Thailand, particularly for businesses operating in urban areas like the Bangkok metropolis. Thailand was hit hard by the 1997 Asian Financial Crisis, which was attributed to four main factors: mismanagement and lack of transparency in the financial sector; declines in export growth and hence decreases in foreign reserves; the current account deficit; and the government's adoption of a floating exchange rate. Since then changes in both external and internal environments of the country have led to reforms and restructuring in both public and private sector organisations. Many changes, such as business process re-engineering, are more evident in the private sector and are taking place with the availability of advanced information and communication technologies (ICTs). Organisations experiencing rapid changes are induced to be more customer-oriented in order to survive and grow in this competitive environment. Thus, it becomes necessary for organisations to learn faster and to keep being innovative and productive in order to cope with change and maintain their competitiveness. Part of the changes are in the area of HRM, which has experienced shifts as the country developed and opened up to globalisation, with impacts from MNCs.

In this chapter we first outline the political, economic and socio-cultural background and context for management in Thailand. This is followed by a discussion of key labour market features. The development of personnel management (PM) and HRM are presented in the subsequent section. Our discussion of HRM practices focus on four main functional activities, namely, employee resourcing, employee development, employee rewards and employee relations. In order to illustrate HRM practices in actual settings we provide two case studies of indigenous companies: one in energy-related industry and the other a local medium-sized hospital; as well as two case studies of individual Thai managers. We end the chapter by presenting a discussion on challenges and prospects and some concluding remarks.

Political, economic and social/ cultural background and context

In this section we will describe and discuss the political, economic and social/cultural background that has influenced the management philosophy and practices in the country.

Political

Thailand's geographical area is about 513,115 square kilometres and it has a population of over 60 million people (Table 6.1). The historical emergence of Thailand, formerly known as Siam, can be divided into five periods: Sukhothai; Ayudhya; Thonburi; Ratanakosin (in which the Chakri Dynasty was formed); and Contemporary. The Contemporary period began in 1932, when absolute monarchy was replaced by the constitutional monarchy (Samudavanija, 1987, cited in Roongrerngsuke and Cheosakul, 2001). Before the reign of King Rama III of the Chakri Dynasty, the country had very little contact with, or exposure to, the West. Modern Thailand only began during King Rama IV's reign (Ingram, 1955; Riggs, 1967; Samudavanija, 1987; Siffin, 1966, cited in Roongrerngsuke and Cheosakul, 2001).

Table 6.1 Thailand macro-economic indicators, 2000–2006

	2000	2001	2002	2003	2004	2005	2006
Population (millions)	61.88	62.31	62.80	63.08	61.97	62.42	n/a
GDP (baht, at 1988 price)	3,008.4	3,073.6	3,237.0	3,464.7	3,678.7	3,842.7	n/a
GDP growth rates (%)	4.8	2.2	5.3	7.0	6.2	4.5	n/a
Consumer Price Index (2002 = 100)	97.8	99.4	100.0	101.8	104.6	109.3	113.2
% difference	1.6	1.6	0.7	1.8	2.7	4.5	5.9
Trade balance (US$ billion)	5.5	2.5	2.7	3.8	1.5	−8.6	−1.5
Exports (US$)	67.9	63.1	66.1	78.1	95.0	109.2	48.9
Imports (US$)	62.4	60.6	63.4	74.3	3.5	117.8	50.4

Source: Bank of Thailand, www.bot.or.th/bothomepage/databank/Econcond/genecon/thai_glance. htm

In 2001 Thailand had over forty political parties (Roongrerngsuke and Cheosakul, 2001). However, by 2006 the number of political parties had declined to eleven: (1) Thai Rak Thai Party; (2) Chart-Thai Party; (3) Democrat Party; (4) Liberal Democratic; (5) Mass Party; (6) National Development; (7) New Aspiration; (8) Palang Dharma Party; (9) Social Action; (10) Solidarity; (11) Thai Citizen. This seems to suggest a preference for fewer, but stronger, political parties.

Economic

Thailand has gone through various stages of economic and social development with an important role played by foreign direct investment (FDI), particularly that from Japan, which contributed to rapid economic development and internationalisation of the economy. Manufacturing emerged as a leading sector contributing to the economy, both in terms of value-added and export earnings (Akrasanee et al., 1991; Phongpaichit and Baker, 1996; Siengthai et al., 2005; Pholphirul, 2005). The 1985 appreciation in the value of the Japanese yen forced Japanese firms to relocate production facilities overseas to be closer to markets. Japan has been the largest investor in Thailand, focusing on electronics and automotive industries (Julian, 2001; BOI, 2005). Some so-called 'Japanese management practices' have been transplanted and established to a certain extent after some conflict in the early stage of FDI in the country (Siengthai, 1999).

Thailand has been slowly recovering ever since the 1997 Asian Crisis. Economic growth was negative for the first few years after the crisis and then became positive (Figure 6.1). The economy slowed down in 2001 when the GDP growth rate was 2.2 per cent, but rose to 7 per cent in 2003 (see Table 6.1). In 2004 and 2005 growth rates decreased again, mainly due to external shocks from the rising cost of fuel imports and the upward pressure on interest rates. The escalating oil price forced the government to stop subsidies and allow the floating of oil prices. The economy was aggravated further by natural disasters caused by the tsunami in December 2004, a large flood in the north, a drought in the north-east that reduced agricultural output, the outbreak of bird flu, and the political turmoil and violence in the south. Consequently, the economy experienced higher inflation and interest rates.

In addition to the rapidly changing global and regional environment, the slow economic recovery in Thailand may have been due to the country's political system. The Thai Rak Thai Party-led government appeared to have been more focused on the economic front rather than on social and cultural stability in society. In addition, the political turmoil and violence in the three main southern provinces

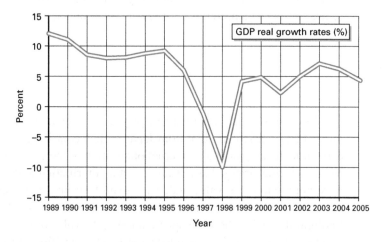

Figure 6.1 GDP real growth rates (%) 1989–2005

deterred investment and contributed to the socio-economic divide, leading to a large gap between 'haves and have-nots' in the country. Also, in urban areas incidences of poverty are clearly observed.

Social/cultural

The population is composed mainly of ethnic Thais and those of Chinese descent through assimilation of Chinese immigrants and ethnic Thais. The intermarriage of ethnic Thais and other ethnic immigrants has become more common but is still not significant. Over 90 per cent of the population practise Buddhism. The census (2000) records that 94 per cent practise Theravada Buddhism. The country has always extended religious freedom to its subjects. Of the remaining 6 per cent of the population, 3.9 per cent are Muslims, 1.7 per cent Confucianists, and 0.6 per cent Christians. Though the King is the designated protector of all religions, the constitution stipulates that he must be a Buddhist. As a result, Buddhism has a significant influence on Thai management philosophy and practices.

In spite of all the changes, the following cultural norms are still recognised. These include *kreng jai* (being considerate of others); *bunk-hun* (reciprocity of goodness; exchange of favour); *jai yen yen* (take it easy); *mai pen rai* (never mind); *sanuk* (fun); and *nam-jai* (being thoughtful, generous and kind). Certainly, these norms are social values emphasising harmonious social relations and consideration for others (Siengthai and Vadhanasindhu, 1991; Kamoche, 2000: 455). They also tend to reinforce hierarchical structures (patron–client systems) in society as well as in the workplace. Therefore, it can be expected that in the family-based small and medium-sized enterprises (SMEs), which are still run by the first or second generation of founders, HRM practices will tend to be reactive rather than proactive, and systematic when compared with the more developed and large-sized family enterprises where professional staff are more prevalent.

Key labour market features and developments

Thailand has a fairly educated workforce. By 2005 the literacy rate among males was about 97 per cent and that among females about

93 per cent (Table 6.2). The level of education of the workforce has increased and is high, particularly at the secondary and tertiary levels (see Table 6.2), suggesting more human capital investment in formal schooling as the government only raised the compulsory level of education to sixth grade in the fifth Five-Year National Economic and Social Development Plan (1977–81) and ninth grade in the tenth plan (2002–06). The fact that there are higher numbers of those at the higher education level after the Asian Crisis suggests more private or individual investment in education and human capital development.

During the economic boom a tight labour market was experienced, particularly in construction and agriculture. Substantial foreign labour was imported into the casual labour market (Siengthai, 1994). The same situation applied to skilled labour. Attracted by job opportunities and wage differentials (higher minimum wage rates), many unskilled and skilled foreign migrants illegally entered the labour market. This suggests the existence of possible less-than-desirable terms and conditions of employment for these immigrants, as there is a possibility of lesser compliance with labour law. At the professional level the shortage of university-trained labour with scientific or technological backgrounds has been met by importing engineers and technicians from more developed or neighbouring countries. In some cases internships and apprenticeships are offered to foreign students who have come to Thailand to attend the various international education programmes which are now available at both undergraduate and graduate levels. Thus, HRM has had to deal with a growing international and diverse workforce.

Table 6.2 Population by educational attainment ('000s)

	1995	2000	2001	2002	2003	2005
No formal education and primary education	31,496	29,692	29,993	30,313	30,696	n/a
Secondary education	7,434	11,159	11,312	11,476	11,666	n/a
Higher education	3,086	4,312	4,421	4,538	4,666	n/a
Literacy rates (%)						
Males	n/a	n/a	n/a	n/a	n/a	97
Females	n/a	n/a	n/a	n/a	n/a	93

Source: Economist Intelligence Unit (2005).

Table 6.3 suggests that, during the period 1988–2005, labour force participation rates in Thailand were the lowest, at 71.2 per cent, in 2004 and highest, at 82.5 per cent, in 1989. Throughout the period participation rates among both males and females were generally high, albeit with slight differences; among males the participation rate was 88.2 per cent in 1989 and 80.2 per cent in 2005, and among females it was 76.8 per cent in 1989 and 62.4 per cent in 2005. The unemployment rates among the male and female labour force have been relatively low, i.e. in the range of 0.8–3.5 per cent, even after the 1997 crisis. This seems to suggest that, while the agricultural sector is still acting as the shock absorber of the economy, some members of the working age population have been discouraged and opted to leave the labour market voluntarily. In addition, it is possible that, even though the manufacturing sector is transforming itself to be more technology-oriented and lean, the service sector is still able to absorb the available workforce. Statistics reveal that urbanisation has been rising in Thailand (Table 6.4). As Thailand is becoming more urbanised, more services are needed and hence more job opportunities are created in the service sector. Wages are also rising, suggesting in part a higher cost of living and higher minimum educational requirements for entry in the labour market, even for the lower level daily-waged jobs (Table 6.5).

The phenomenon of job-hopping is currently less evident, compared with the pre-1997 rapid economic growth period and tight labour market situation. However, staff poaching is still evident. Organisations are carrying out restructuring programmes. Statistics seem to suggest that those in the 50–59 age group are most affected by the organisational restructuring, followed by those in the 40–49 and the 30–39 age groups (Table 6.6). However, as the statistics reveal, the labour force for the 50–59 age group declined dramatically. It seems plausible that large organisations which carried out post-1997 crisis restructuring programmes might have offered early retirement or made lay-offs at different stages.

Development of PM and HRM and the HR function and profession

Until the 1990s, most companies still had so-called traditional PM, which was basically perceived as the payroll function (Siengthai and

Table 6.3 Labour force participation, 1989–2005

	1989	1995	1997	1999	2001	2003	2005
Population aged 15+ (millions)	36,674.8	42,893.9	44,582.8	45,758.1	47,133.6	48,383.8	49,541.0
Male	18,238.6	21,302.0	22,126.3	22,690.1	23,355.0	23,963.0	24,543.7
Female	18,436.2	21,591.9	22,456.5	23,068.0	23,778.6	24,420.8	24,997.3
Labour force (millions)	30,243.3	32,669.9	33,339.2	33,018.7	34,487.7	35,310.5	35,280.2
Male	16,080.9	17,785.5	18,193.7	18,212.6	19,021.6	19,426.6	19,677.1
Female	14,162.4	14,884.4	15,145.5	14,806.1	15,466.1	15,883.9	15,603.1
LFPR (%)[a]	82.5	76.2	74.8	72.2	73.2	73.0	71.2
Male	88.2	83.5	82.2	80.3	81.4	81.1	80.2
Female	76.8	68.9	67.4	64.2	65.0	65.0	62.4
Unemployment (%)	1.4	1.1	0.9	3.0	2.6	1.5	2.5
Male	1.2	0.9	0.8	3.0	2.7	1.6	2.6
Female	1.6	1.3	0.9	2.9	2.5	1.4	2.4

Source: National Statistical Office, Thailand.

Note
a Labour force participation rate.

Table 6.4 Population by urban/rural location (%), 1990–2015

	1990	1995	2000	2005	2010[a]	2015[a]
Urban	18.7	20.0	21.6	23.7	26.2	29.4
Rural	81.3	89.0	78.4	76.3	73.8	70.6

Source: Euromonitor (2005).

Note
a Estimates.

Table 6.5 Minimum wage rates in some selected provinces (baht/day)

	1999	2000	2001	2002	2003	2004	2005	2006
Bangkok, Samutprakarn, Nonthaburi and Pahumthani	162	162	165	165	169	170	175	184
Phuket and Nakorn Pathom	162	162	162	165	168	168	173	181
Chonburi	140	140	143	146	150	153	157	166
Chiangmai, Phang Nga, and Ranong	140	140	143	143	143	145	149	155
Rayong	130	130	130	133	141	143	147	155

Source: Ministry of Labour; Board of Investment, Thailand (as of January 2006).

Table 6.6 Employed persons by age group, Thailand

Age group (years)	2001	2002	2003	2004	2005
15–19	32,104.25	33,060.87	33,841.30	34,728.81	34,050.1
20–24	1,633.74	1,564.36	1,519.87	1,593.79	1,425.4
25–29	4,684.29	4,750.27	4,822.38	4,867.75	4,793.3
30–34	4574.90	4,710.34	4,778.02	4,878.20	4,863.6
35–39	4,286.15	4,409.38	4,506.62	4,596.26	4,520.3
40–49	7,195.89	7,457.46	7,655.96	7,830.11	7,787.2
50–59	4,123.61	4,363.21	4,594.14	4,820.36	4,741.8
60 and over	1,886.39	2,037.21	2,174.63	2,333.93	2,298.9

Source: National Statistical Office, Thailand, several years.

Bechter, 2004; Siengthai *et al.*, 2005). With industrialisation and the inflow of FDI, foreign management concepts were brought into Thailand. The development of PM into HRM is reflected in the different nature and development of firms. The development of HRM has been faster in MNC subsidiaries and joint venture (JV) firms. However, in the early period of economic development, which was based on labour-intensive manufacturing, the concern of HRM was mainly about operational unskilled and skilled workers and a necessity for the promotion and maintenance of an unorganised work force, weak trade unions and dominant employer authority (Siengthai *et al.*, 2005).

The increasingly significant role for HRM in achieving management objectives is reflected in the transformation of the PM function (Silva, 2002). This function was often marginalised in terms of its importance in management activities and hierarchy. PM has evolved from a concentration on employee welfare. The former role had been emphasised in the Buddhist context as it seems to be embedded in family values and some Buddhist values for management, such as compassion, kindness and some others (Siengthai *et al*, 2005). The changing management approach can be through methods that provide employees with both intrinsic and extrinsic rewards. These initiatives are associated with a tendency to shift from a more collective orientation to workforce management towards a more individualistic one. Accordingly, management looks for labour flexibility and seeks to reward differential performance. Communication of managerial objectives and aspirations takes on a new importance.

Indigenous Thai firms fall into different categories with respect to HRM policies. Most private sector firms began as family-owned enterprises closely tied to the Sino-Thai community (Lawler *et al.*, 1997). There are a number of large firms that continue to be managed in that manner and their employment and personnel practices are typically distinct from those with a broad base of investors, especially publicly traded corporations. Another indigenous group consists of SOEs. Most of these firms tend to follow the PM practised in the public sector proper. In fact, many of their personnel managers graduated with a degree in political science and hence the area tended to be influenced by public administration concepts (Siengthai and Bechter, 2004). Other types of firms include JVs and MNCs. These firms practise systematic HRM and prefer to hire foreign-educated graduates.

Large organisations in the service sector, such as banks and particularly some small- and medium-sized banks, have adopted or adapted their HRM practices from the government bureaucratic system, typified by its tall hierarchical organisational structure (Lawler and Siengthai, 1997). However, many large organisations have restructured and implemented business process re-engineering, resulting in flatter organisational structures, thereby introducing the notion of empowerment and to a certain extent the broadbanding concept in employee rewards. Changes in organisational structure have also led to the need to develop multi-skilled employees so as to avoid redundancy. Also, some organisations have altered the name of HR Departments to that of 'Resourcing Departments'. This is in line with a resource-based concept of organisations, which advocates that organisations gain competitive advantage through the development and sustainability of its renewable and inimitable resources, such as HR.

HRM practices

In the following section we describe and discuss HRM practices with respect to four main HRM areas: employee resourcing, development, rewards and relations.

Employee resourcing

Staffing processes in family SMEs are simple and rely on familial relationships. Thus, virtually all higher-level positions are occupied by family members (Lawler *et al.*, 1997), while middle- and even lower-tier positions are typically filled by those who have connections with family members.

Many large organisations manage retrenchment and turnaround strategies by recruiting in only certain necessary positions and the selection process becomes very rigorous (Siengthai and Bechter, 2005). Firms become stricter in the probationary evaluation of new employees. For instance, in the real estate sector most firms recruit employees mainly from the external labour market in order to support company expansion on the basis of specific qualifications, knowledge, competence and experience (Vorapongse, 2001). In most SMEs newspapers advertisements are used (Wailerdsak, 2004). In addition, most large companies use four main channels: campus recruitment, walk-in applications (Wailerdsak, 2004; Kongchan, 2001), informal social networks and, for senior management positions, executive search companies. There is no difference in resourcing between the manufacturing and service sectors (Kongchan, 2001).

Western firms prefer to recruit skills from the external labour market to fill existing openings (Lawler *et al.*, 1997). Recruiting firms are used more often by American and European companies than by Thai companies (Kongchan, 2001). Thai companies prefer personal referrals to other approaches. For operational levels, Thai, Japanese and European companies mostly perform their own recruitment while American companies not only conduct their own recruitment but also use the services of recruiting agencies. For Thai companies, walk-in applications are most popular, followed by internal searches. However, in Japanese firms internal promotion is still a norm. Australian firms pay more attention to cultural aspects of the work environment; thus local culture-fit is taken into account in both internal and external (expatriate) recruitment. However, Clegg and Gray (2002) assert that less attention is given towards team dynamics. MNCs may have paid too much attention to cultural competencies rather than the candidate's ability to develop teams and team dynamics. The adjustment of the expatriate's spouse to the local culture is another factor that has to be considered by JVs and MNCs. This is consistent with the findings of Tung (1982), which suggest that expatriates who are interviewed with their spouses tend to fail less because firms can determine joint suitability for international assignments which enhances their effective adaptation and adjustment to the cross-cultural management context.

Selection processes mostly involved both HR managers and line managers. Interviews were the most frequently used selection device. Companies that are highly visible in the economy do not have difficulty in getting well-educated and well-trained applicants (Lawler and Siengthai, 1997). After the 1997 crisis, the labour market was more of a buyers' market. In addition, with the availability of ICT many firms have started e-recruiting by posting vacancies on websites as well.

Employee development

Orientation is usually provided to new employees (Lawler and Siengthai, 1997). Later on these employees are expected to be acculturated into the company through on-the-job training. Formal training programmes are generally provided at the supervisory level or higher (Siengthai, 1989). From surveys, as well as casual observations, it can be seen that large organisations generally have their own training centres and provide formal training programmes. Executives are usually provided with in-house development programmes as well as short-term training programmes abroad.

Some differences between training and development activities are found between the manufacturing and service sectors. The majority of firms in the manufacturing sector have definite plans for training programmes in both the short and long term, while the majority of firms in the service sector have only short-term training plans. After the 1997 Asian Crisis many companies turned to in-house training and on-the-job training as a result of the recession (Laohathanakul, 1999; Kongsanchai, 2001; Bothidaht, 2001; Chiraratananon *et al.*, 2002). Firms increasingly adopt workforce redeployment and job rotation as a form of on-the-job training. The government currently provides tax deductions for employee training and education expenses as a way of encouraging companies to invest in the intellectual skills development of their employees. Layoffs were used as the last resort in most firms.

In most companies there are no career planning programmes, and if they existed they are not systematic. However, a study on career planning in selected large firms, such as the Petroleum Authority of Thailand, Siam Cement, Advanced Info Service, and Toyota Motor (Thailand), found that there exists an internal labour market at the management level (Wailerdsak, 2004). American companies in Thailand are found to use training and development for long-term planning more than their Thai counterparts. They tend to have clearer career planning programmes more than others. Meanwhile, most Japanese companies do not have career planning programmes. American companies emphasise HRD while European companies focus on IT and communication improvement more than other approaches (Kongchan, 2001).

The majority of both manufacturing and service sectors have annual performance appraisals (PAs) (Kongchan, 2001). Their main objective is administrative, to be used as a basis in rewards, followed by performance improvement. Those responsible for PAs in most companies are immediate supervisors. The PA is formal and uses both qualitative and quantitative criteria. Large organisations, such as banks, generally have very elaborate PA systems, such as self-evaluation versus supervisor evaluation (Lawler and Siengthai, 1997).

With respect to PA, there is no difference between Thai firms and MNCs. Most companies give performance objectives and criteria to their employees. In addition they also have training for appraisers (Kongchan, 2001). American companies provide for the involvement of employees in the PA process more often. However, in American firms there is a tendency to have evaluation of short-term results of performance, while in Japanese-based firms evaluation is more of long-term outcomes (Kongchan, 2001). So, even though there is periodic evaluation in Japanese firms, it is meant to be a feedback mechanism for individuals to improve their performance rather than to be used as a determinant for continuation of employment. For some MNCs, such as those from Australia, technical skills and maturity of Australian expatriates to cope with foreign postings were key factors in gaining their job position (Clegg and Gray, 2002).

Employee rewards

Most organisations provide welfare and benefits, some of which are required by law. Performance reward is based on company profits and employee performance. For example, in the real estate sector most companies set compensation levels according to the standard of living (Vorapongse, 2001). Bonuses are paid depending on profits made by the firms. After the 1997 crisis most companies suspended or reduced monthly payments, bonuses, annual salary increases, overtime, and welfare. Kongchan (2001) found that most companies in both manufacturing and service sectors offered incentives on an individual basis. The criterion used for evaluation is productivity. For American or Western firms, wages or compensation are usually higher than market wage rates. No difference in terms of the compensation system was found between Thai firms and MNCs (ibid.).

Employee relations

ER has been dominated by the government, supposedly the 'umpire' in the system. Since the Public Enterprise Labour Relations Act was abolished in 1990 all public enterprise unions are regulated by the general Labour Relations Act, 1975. This Act guarantees freedom of association and collective bargaining, lays down procedures for settlement of labour disputes and prohibits unfair labour practices. In the private sector, unions are usually organised at the operational level of workers. Employees at the supervisory level cannot become union members.

The influence of the government in ER has been significant. The labour movement was very strong in the public sector before the 1997 crisis. After the crisis many public enterprises came under the privatisation scheme, which required organisational restructuring and consequently weakened the union's role. Furthermore, with the government's policy to deregulate and privatise part of the government sector by 2006, unions have become more low profile and inactive.

With the changes in management concepts, organisational restructuring and empowerment, a more participative management style is needed. Thus, the trend is towards a greater individualisation of ER (Silva, 2002). This implies less emphasis on collective, and more emphasis on individual, relations. It is reflected, for instance, in monetary and non-monetary reward systems.

Case studies of indigenous organisations

We illustrate our analysis by providing case studies of two indigenous companies.

Organisation case study 1: Banpu Public Limited Company

Established in 1983, Banpu Public Limited Company is a pioneer Thai private power plant. It operates in two major businesses: coal mining and power generating. It is one of the foremost energy companies in Thailand and is rapidly becoming a leading regional coal mining company. It has three mines in Thailand, five in Indonesia and one in Shanxi, China. In 2005 it produced around 17 million tonnes of coal, while a target of 21 million tonnes was planned for 2006. The company has grown from 3,000 employees in 2003 to 5,000 in 2006. These include about 2,000 who are unskilled daily workers who earn the minimum wage. The majority of workers are skilled and professionals.

Customers include firms producing animal foods, pulp and paper and cement. Its fast growth in recent years was due to its merger and acquisition strategies. It is a semi-monopoly company in Thailand since there is no significant competitor. Usually, it takes about 3–4 years' lead time for exploration before mining can commence. Thus, the company always performs its strategic planning every 5 years, with annual review based on the company vision that was formulated in 2000. The organisational structure has been flattened as a result of decentralisation that was implemented recently. About 200 employees are at the HQ in Bangkok, Thailand. In Indonesia there are about 100 Thai employees. Currently the company also employs third-country nationals, such as British, Australians and Filipinos. In carrying its corporate transition plan from a local to a global company, the company has developed its code of 'shared values'. Termed the 'Banpu Spirit', the values include innovation, integrity, synergy and care. The company's most distinctive characteristic is its leadership style. All leaders are decisive. The CEO, Mr Chanin Vongkusolkij, is from the company's founding family. He has a very strong interest in HRD activities. He always jointly solves problems with his staff. The company encourages employees to voice their opinions, thus to an extent practising a participative management style. Most of the company's policy implementation is undertaken through employee involvement and with teams (working groups for each project). The HR function is under the Corporate Services Division, which also includes Legal, General Affairs and Quality, Safety and Environment, IT and Corporate System. In the HR unit there are only three employees. In order to standardise HR policies and approaches at the HQ and the foreign subsidiaries, this Corporate Services Division was set up with the aim, among others, of establishing 'best HR practices' in the whole company.

Employee resourcing

The channels used for employee resourcing are mainly newspapers and e-recruitment. Higher-level employees are recruited through recruitment agencies or 'headhunters'. In each job position there are specific competency requirements. Written tests, including a language test, are conducted in the screening process, so as to ascertain an applicant's competency level. The company provides orientation to its employees. Usually an employee is put on probation for a period of 4 months. The company practises promotion from within, at the same time offering a career path for its employees. Thus, it has developed its own internal labour market. However, in the last 5–6 years the company has begun to recruit externally, due to the rapid changes in its business strategies and environment.

Employee development

Employee development programmes are capital intensive and continuous. The company views employee development both as a commitment and a corporate social responsibility to develop HR for the nation. About 3–5 per cent of total annual earnings are spent on two types of training programmes. First, the company offers technical skills training in the areas of mining, IT, quality service enhancement, and total productive maintenance. Second, the company emphasises management training for managers, which is based on its corporate strategic plan especially and the growth of its overseas subsidiaries.

All employees who have been confirmed after the 4-month probationary period undergo training at different stages. New employees on a monthly salary basis are expected to go through twelve basic training programmes within their first year of employment. In addition, there is the Executive Leadership Programme. There is a 'road map' for corporate training strategy implementation for a period of 3–5 years. Additionally, there are programmes that offer international exposure, cultivate work values and develop IT-related skills.

Performance reviews are used as a basis for organisational performance improvement. Performance reviews are undertaken twice a year at mid-year and end of year. Key performance indicators (KPIs) are used for the reviews. Some 60 per cent of the evaluation is based on actual work outcomes and 40 per cent on work behaviour-related evaluation. The supervisor and subordinate identify areas for development to achieve good performance results.

Employee rewards

Reward management and recognition is done through pay for performance (bonus) for line managers and those above them. Compensation for middle-level managers and above depends on market competition but it is at least 75 per cent of the minimum market pay rates. The company has a policy that its salary scale will match the median level of salary in the market even for those below the line management level. The Hays system is used for performance evaluation and compensation management. For lower-level employees the pay scale is of market average. There is a discretion bonus, which is up to the CEO, but with the endorsement of the company's board. In recent years there has been an increase in salaries and the restructuring of salary structure.

Employee relations

The company argues that there is no gap between management and employees. There is a welfare benefits package. In the Indonesian subsidiary there is a union which has a strong link with the national union. So far, the company has been able to develop a harmonious relationship with the union. Currently, difficulties faced by the company include the transformation from a local to a global company, a concept that is not clear to all employees.

Source: interviews with Mr Chaiyaporn Nakasatis, Senior Vice President, Human Resources; Mr Ritthivong Petpragob, Manager, Human Resources; and Mr Veroj Limjaroon, Vice President, Corporate System; conducted in May 2006.

Organisation case study 2:
Nonthavej Hospital Public Limited Company (NTV)

Founded in 1981 and located in Nonthaburi Province, NTV operates as a 280-bed private, general community hospital providing medical care services to both in patients and out patients by specialists in all fields. Its registered capital is 160 million baht (about US$239 million). The hospital places emphasis on the continuing quality improvement of its services. In 2002 the hospital received two recognitions, certification of ISO 9001:2000 by the BM Trada Institute in the UK and recognition by the Department of Medical Science under the Ministry of Health of Thailand for the competency of its medical check-up laboratory for workers aiming to work abroad. The number of personnel has increased steadily, from 1,300 in 2003 to 1,611 in 2006. The management team has a clear workforce ratio policy for full-time and associate appointments (part-time professionals) of 70:30. Among the full-time staff about one-third are medical doctors. Parallel to the organisational corporate brand-building project, NTV emphasises the recruiting and maintaining of medical professionals who have outstanding reputations individually. There is some outsourcing of non-core activities such as security and cleaning services to achieve a more flexible workforce.

The hospital changed its status from 'Limited Company' to 'Public Limited Company' in 1993. Competition in the healthcare market has become more aggressive. The NTV management team, therefore, revised its vision, core values, strategies and work processes in 2006. Thus, the new vision is: 'The best place to get care, the best place to give care.' Its new core values are: (1) customer focus; (2) performance excellence; (3) innovation and learning; (4) system thinking; (5) integrity; (6) management by facts. Additionally, the hospital strives to promote its image as a core value-driven organisation that promises the happiness of the workforce. Organisational restructuring was carried out to improve its service quality and operational efficiency. The HR initiatives were one of the first improvements to be implemented for the new strategic development and implementation.

As NVT is in the service sector, customer satisfaction is paramount. Clear and effective HRM policies are needed for NTV's growth and expansion of services. In 2006 the new hospital director brought about a major change to the existing work culture. His commitment to improve the quality of working life in the organisation has led him to instil a new hospital core value that in turn affects the existing performance measurement systems. What used to be a mere quality- and productivity-driven measurement of organisational outputs has gradually changed to accommodate a more harmonious and content workforce outcome indicator as well. Some innovative measures were recently introduced, such as comprehensive job descriptions, the workforce gold card and HRD according to the quality assurance of the Hospital Accreditation programme. It has yet to be seen how HRM practices at NVT will evolve with the new core values.

Employee resourcing

The number of patients has been increasing, thus expanding the hospital's size. According to one of the hospital's executives, NTV's strengths are its ability to provide good healthcare and the ability to attract good doctors. In the early years of its establishment the hospital concentrated on paediatric care. Thus, there was a large recruitment of medical personnel such as nurses and doctors in this field. Over time the hospital has expanded its service specialties to different fields.

NVT has put much effort in recruiting people who have the potential to grow with the organisation as well as having the mentality for knowledge-sharing. To target qualified candidates the management team defines the NTV internal brand promises (warm, responsive and professional) and brand positioning and communicates them to employees at all levels. They are regarded as standard criteria for recruitment. The hospital gives preferences to the internal labour market in filling vacancies. Government agencies, universities, recruitment organisations and media channels are mainly used for the external recruitment process. Managers are responsible for conducting interviews and attitude tests with candidates. For executive levels, referrals are used as the recruitment strategy.

Employee development

Training programmes are held throughout the year so as to enhance and update the knowledge base of the hospital staff at all levels. The management team recognises the need to build a 'learning organisation' and leadership at the managerial level, as they are accountable for the mindset and attitude, performance and capabilities of their staff. They coax the 'can-do attitude' of management at all levels. Bi-monthly orientation sessions are offered to employees as a means of gradually redirecting their attitudes. Besides implementing an attitudinal change process and general skills and knowledge development programmes on a company-wide basis, specific training needs towards the hospital's strategic directions are identified to suit each level of employee. These strategic oriented programmes are designed together with the respective measurements of success or KPIs. The HRD programmes and internal control/risk management areas were rated highly by NTV's Audit Committee.

Employee rewards

Rewards in terms of salaries and benefits are comparable to other hospitals. However, NTV has yet to establish a formal compensation policy. In 2003 it began compiling job analyses so as to have the description and specification of every job, thus indicating an important step in assessing their HR competencies.

Employee relations

From general observations during interview sessions it appears that there is little gap between administrators and staff members. A participative style of management is practised by the hospital. The hospital frequently utilises cross-functional (cross-departmental) teams to solve problems or generate new business and provide numerous opportunities for employees to exchange and generate new ideas.

Sources: adapted from Siengthai *et al.* (2004); interviews with Ms Pathama Prommas (Member of the Board of Directors), Dr Kamales Santivejkul (Chairman of the Audit Committee), and Ms Prapichaya Prommas (Assistant Hospital Director), May 2006.

Case studies of individual managers

The following section focuses on two Thai managers, Banyong Pongpanich and Somrit Srithongdee. These two case studies are examples of the Thai management style.

Manager case study 1: Banyong Pongpanich

As Chairman of the Phatra Securities Public Ltd Co. (Phatra), Banyong Pongpanich is well known in Thailand's financial market. Banyong, known as Pee Tao to Phatra employees, has a simple vision for Phatra – ensuring the sustainable growth and profitable operations and maintaining the firm's position in the Thai capital market. In 2005 Phatra was listed on the Stock Exchange of Thailand and ever since its stock price has been on average traded at four times its original listing price.

His leadership style can be attributed to one major factor, which is his firm belief in teamwork and merit pay for high performers. Banyong believes that 'the most important asset of the company is people'. Under Banyong's leadership Phatra's reward structure has been carefully crafted in order to ensure that over 200 skilled employees continue to contribute to the company, and rewarding the best employees for their commitment to their jobs. In a good-performing year high-performing employees receive an annual bonus equivalent to 25–30 months of their basic pay. Furthermore, under Banyong's leadership Phatra has won numerous awards from the investment and business community. For example, Asia Money awarded the company the title of the best research broker, and Euro Money and Finance Asia awarded the company the title of the excellent and best equity house in Thailand.

Perhaps the most evident work culture that Banyong has instilled at Phatra is the committee system. Although he values highly the competency of individuals, he is also a true believer of knowledge management. He reckons that tacit knowledge held by individuals at all levels of operations would be disseminated more widely in a committee system. Banyong stresses that:

> We want to make sure that if one person leaves or is not available due to whatever reason, there will be others who can handle the tasks without interruption. That, however, does not reduce the accountability of a supervisor because if anything goes wrong, he/she will be held fully responsible for it anyway.

This practice also serves as a means of ensuring the management succession plan is integrated with on-the-job training and is imparted within the committees. Banyong himself is on many committees, including Strategic Planning, Investment, Business Development, Compensation, and Recruitment. Furthermore, he serves as an ubiquitous advisor to all committees at Phatra. 'Ask Pee Tao's opinion first' is a common phrase at Phatra.

Since companies dealing in stocks (securities) are operating under a dynamic, stringent and regulated environment, creating a sense of professional belongingness is more critical than providing traditional training programmes. Banyong believes

> Professional development is the responsibility of everyone at Phatra. After all a true professional would know when he/she needs to be trained and developed as well as where to get it.

Banyong's conviction for corporate citizenship is evidenced by the establishment of the Phatra Charity Committee, which was launched to innovate philanthropic projects on an ongoing basis as well as to promote cultural heritage activities for younger generations.

Sources: Phatra Homepage: www.phatrasecurities.com; interviews with Mr Banyong Pongpanich (Chairman of the Board) and Ms Patraporn Milindasuta (Executive Vice President of the Office of General Council and Internal Audit), May 2006.

Manager case study 2: Somrit Srithongdee

Somrit Srithongdee is currently the Vice President, HR, Bank of Ayudhya Public Limited Company (BAY). He started his first job in the public sector at the Department of Labour. In 1979 he was recruited by the Bata Company. In 1986 he was offered the position of HR manager at BAY. In his career he has served as a

176 • Siengthai, Tanlamai and Rowley

judge for the Labour Court, participated in the establishment of labour standards for Thailand as well as giving lectures at universities. Somrit has significant work experience related to HRM and industrial relations in two large enterprises, namely Bata and BAY.

The crucial challenge to his career in HR was during the 1997 Asian Financial Crisis. Led by Somrit, the bank streamlined its operations. He initiated changes to the bank's bureaucratic system. Somrit introduced new management practices such as management by objectives and performance management to enhance the bank's performance. Jobs were merged and organisational restructuring was implemented by the HR department. Employees with over 30 years of service were offered early retirement, while workers such as drivers, security guards and cleaners were outsourced from external agencies. The HR department began to implement a 'non-performer programme', which required all HR staff to be trained and serve as advisors to non-performers.

According to an employee: 'Khun Somrit is a very kind-hearted person. He has a strong belief that people can change for the better. His policy for people management is that every employee will be given a second chance to improve their performance.' This is evidenced by the fact that during the bank's restructuring exercise those who could not be relocated to any department were transferred to the HR department for retraining, and subsequently relocated to a department of their own choice. Consequent to these restructuring programmes and by utilisation of the existing personnel's working capacity to a maximum, by 2004 the bank successfully streamlined its operations; it dismissed 2,000 workers and retained some 7,500 employees.

Under Somrit's leadership the HR department created a standard HR flow, with projections for the career paths of employees in each level. Somrit introduced the Management Development programme for new managers, as well as competency building programmes for all levels of employees. One specific training programme was known as the 'Dummy Branch', in which the bank's trainees were able to experience and comprehend the overall day-to-day banking operations.

Somrit furthered initiated the formation of an Employees' Committee comprising line managers and the HR manager, with the aim of eliminating favouritism and thus enhancing the professionalism of employees. Issues and ideas from the HR department are brought to this committee so that they are dealt with democratically by members of the committee and consequently it develops the participation and commitment of line managers. The work of this committee is reviewed annually.

Although each business unit in the bank has been able to achieve their targets, it is still making a loss. Thus, currently the challenge for Somrit Srithongdee, as the Senior Vice President for HR of the BAY, is to increase the bank's bottomline or profits.

Sources: interviews with Mr Somrit Srithongdee (Executive Vice President and Head of HR), and Mr Suvinai Tosirisuk (Senior Vice President), 2004 and 2007.

Challenges and prospects for HRM

Many challenges to the HR function are brought about by globalisation. At the regional level industrialisation and globalisation has
brought about research interests in the convergence of HRM systems
(Rowley, 1997; McGaughey and De Cieri, 1999; Lee, 2002; Rowley
and Benson, 2002; 2003; Lawler and Atmiyanandana, 2003).
However, a number of comparative studies on the impact of globalisation have cast doubts on convergence theory. For instance, studies
on employee relations in the automobile and banking industries in
Australia and Korea seem to suggest that, although there is a similar
pattern of changes which suggests the impact of globalisation, there
seems to be a divergence of practices due to the different institutions
in the national context (Blanpain *et al.*, 2002).

The HR function must be more proactive and take initiatives in this
new role as a business partner. Among these changes are the deregulation policy or privatisation scheme by the government, the restructuring or downsizing policies of firms, the advantages of the new ICT
and firm policies to exploit it, the shift from low-wage to high-wage
and high-skilled labour, as well as the need for management development to cope with these changes. Then there is workforce diversity
which comes with globalisation and the regionalisation process
allowing free flow of products, capital and labour, and at the micro
level of firm operations the need to link HRM and financial performance, innovation and productivity improvements, empowerment,
project-based contracts, redundancy, and bipartite ER.

As observed in recent years, the impact of the 1997 Asian Financial
Crisis is still prevalent. Government and private sector organisations
are still working on the recovery of the economy. Owing to the
extremely competitive economic environment and increasing oil
prices, businesses will continue with their cost reduction strategies,
including downsizing through labour-saving technology, automation
of services and outsourcing of non-core business functions. Even
though the introduction of technology will create the need for skilled
labour, the number of workers needed is less than in the earlier period
of economic development. Another implication is the increase in
overhead costs as higher and multi-skilled employees will also imply
higher levels of wages and salaries, although enhanced productivity
and value added will defray this of course. The dual economy in

Thailand will become more evident as organisations will be divided 'digitally' between those which use ICT intensively and those which use traditional management approaches and are basically small-scale family business enterprises where there is no formal HRM system. Firms that are moving into high technology, where skills are scarce and therefore more capital intensive in nature, will need to resort to individualised terms and conditions of employment in order to retain higher-skilled employees. Examples of such firms are the SMEs participating in the outsourcing businesses in both domestic and international markets, such as software development.

Conclusion

In sum, key factors which brought about high growth rates in Thailand before the 1997 crisis included growth of the export sector, FDI and tourism, all of which had grown considerably faster than projected rates. Yet, after the crisis and with the social problems and turmoil in the south, rising oil prices and natural disasters, Thailand faces pressure in order to sustain its planned growth rate in the years ahead. It is likely that with the government's reinforcement of good corporate governance and self-sufficiency economic development policies, the country is likely to be able to achieve a sustainable economic development growth, although at a lower rate in the next decade. All these macro-environmental factors will lead to the emphasis of management so as to increase innovation, economic performance and productivity.

This chapter has outlined contemporary HRM in Thailand. We have discussed changes in the role and the significance of HRM from a payroll function to a strategic business partner in the business operations in the country. The review of relevant studies suggests that currently the role of HRM practices has become more important in contributing to the competitive advantage of firms. Based on data obtained from studies carried out by HRM scholars as well as from the case studies that are presented in this chapter, the authors offer their observations of the challenges faced by HRM.

The findings in this chapter support the notion that HRM practices do contribute to an organisation's development. Companies cited in the case studies, above all, give prime importance to employee development, so as to ensure the organisation's survival and growth. This study further finds that more organisations, both private and public, use ICT, particularly 'electronic HRM' or 'e-HR' to enhance the efficiency and effectiveness of their HRM practices.

As energy prices and inflation rates increase it is necessary that firms continue with their programmes for productivity improvement, cost reduction strategies and innovation enhancement. Firms will maintain the core workforce and outsource some non-core activities. Needless to say, effective HRM is one of the critical factors that will ensure stability and growth of a company. This is a critical period that demands the competencies and professionalism of the HR managers. Therefore it is necessary that programmes to develop HRM professionals should be expanded so that Thailand can more easily adapt to continuing changes in the economic and business environment.

Bibliography

Akrasanee, N., Dapice, D. and Flatters, F. (1991) *Thailand's Export-Led Growth: Retrospect and Prospects.* Research Report, Thailand Development Research Institute, June.

Aroonrusmeechote, W. (1983) 'A Comparative Study on Management in Textile Industry Between Thai Wholly Owned and Partly Owned Companies', unpublished Master's thesis, Chulalongkorn University.

Bangkok Post (2006) 'Minimum wage rise proposed to reflect costs', 18 June, 3.

Bank of Thailand, GDP of Thailand (% change Q4-05 to Q1-07), available at www.bot.or.th/bothomepage/databank/EconData/Graph/G1e.htm (accessed 5 July 2006).

Bank of Thailand, inflation rates of Thailand, available at www.bot.or.th/bothomepage/databank/EconData/Graph/G2e.htm (accessed 5 July 2006).

Bank of Thailand, Thailand's Macro Economic Indicators, 2002–2007, available at www.bot.or.th/bothomepage/databank/EconData/Thai_Key/Thai_KeyE.asp (accessed 5 July 2006).

Bank of Thailand, Thailand's International Investment Position (IIP), available at www.bot.or.th/bothomepage/databank/EconData/IIP/iip_e.htm (accessed 5 July 2006).

Beer, M. (1997) 'The transformation of the human resource function: Resolving the tension between a traditional administrative and a new strategic role', *Human Resource Management*, 36, 49–56.

Blanpain, R., Lansbury, R. D. and Park, Y. B. (2002) 'The Impact of Globalisation on Employment Relations: A Comparison of the Automobile and Banking Industries in Australia and Korea', *Bulletin of Labour Relations (45)*, The Hague, Netherlands: Kluwer Law International.

Board of Investment (2005) *BOI Investment Review*, September, available at www.kiasia.org/EN/Group_Tier3. asp?GroupTierId=3&SubGroupTier_ID=57&SubTier_ID=139.

Bothidaht, P. (2001) 'Preparing for Organisation Change: A Case Study of TOT', unpublished MBA thesis, School of Management, Asian Institute of Technology, Bangkok, Thailand.

Campbell, D. (2000) 'Recovery from the Crisis: The Prospects for Social Dialogue in East Asia', in *Proceedings of the 12th International Industrial Relations Association (IIRA) World Congress*, Tokyo: Japan Institute of Labour.

Cameron, K. S. (1994) 'Strategies for successful organisational downsizing', *Human Resource Management*, 33, 189–212.

Chaweewattanasakul, N. (1998) 'Human Resource Development in the 21st Century of CP', unpublished Master's thesis, Chulalongkorn University.

Chidchob, O. (1985) 'A Study on Personnel Administration of Toyota Motor Thailand Co. Ltd', unpublished Master's thesis, Chulalongkorn University.

Chiraratananon, S., Ongsakul, W., Singh, S. N., Siengthai, S., Sharma, D., Duval, Y., Lorjirachunkul, V., Rarueysong, C. and Shrestha, R. M. (2002) *Electricity Supply Industry (ESI) Structure and Corporatization: A Case Study of Electricity Generating Authority of Thailand (EGAT)*. A report commissioned by and submitted to EGAT by the Asian Institute of Technology, Bangkok.

Clegg, B. and Gray, S. J. (2002) 'Australian expatriates in Thailand: Some insights for expatriate management policies', *International Journal of Human Resource Management*, 13, 508–623.

Dechawatanapaisal, D. and Siengthai, S. (2006) 'The impact of cognitive dissonance on learning work behavior', *Journal of Workplace Learning*, 18, 42–54.

Devanna, M. A. and Tichy, N. (1990) 'Creating the competitive organisation of the 21st century: The boundaryless corporation', *Human Resource Management*, 29, 455–72.

Directory of Political Parties, available at www.parliament.go.th/files/politi/d02.htm (accessed 5 July 2006).

Duangjai, I. (2000) 'Human Resource Management During the Economic Boom and the Economic Downturn Period: A Case Study of the Viriyah Insurance Co. Ltd.', unpublished Master's thesis, Chulalongkorn University.

Economist Intelligence Unit (2005) *Thailand: Economy: In the doldrums*, September. Available at www.viewswire.com/index. asp?layout=display_print&doc_id=479383633.

Erickson, C. L. and Kuruvilla, S. (2000) 'Industrial relations and the Asian economic crisis: An analysis of the short term impacts and long term implications for industrial relations systems', in the *Proceedings of the 12th International Industrial Relations Association (IIRA) World Congress*, Tokyo: Japan Institute of Labour.

Indhapanya, B. (2001) 'The Roles of Service Marketing and Human Resources Development for the New Market Rules in the Next Decade of The Provincial Electricity Authority', unpublished MBA thesis, School of Management, Asian Institute of Technology.

Ingram, J. C. (1955) *Economic Change in Thailand Since 1850*, Stanford, California: Stanford University Press.

Intho, S. (2003) 'Balanced Scorecard Implementation In Nursing Organisation: A Case Study of a Private Hospital, Bangkok Metropolis', unpublished Master's thesis, Chulalongkorn University.

Jatupornruangrit, S. (2001) 'Human Resources Management by Information Technology System: Case Study of PTT Co. Ltd', unpublished Master's thesis, Chulalongkorn University.

Julian, C. C. (2001) 'Japanese foreign direct investment in Thailand', *Mid-Atlantic Journal of Business,* March.

Kaplan, R. S. and David P. N. (1996) *Translating Strategy into Action: Balanced Scorecard,* Boston, MA: Harvard Business School Press.

Kamoche, K. (2000) 'From boom to bust: The challenges of managing people in Thailand', *International Journal of Human Resource Management,* 11, 452–68.

Kongchan, A. (2001) *Human Resource Management in Thai Firms and Multinational Corporations in Thailand*, research report, Chulalongkorn University.

Kongsanchai, T. (2001) 'Creating Competencies for Strategic TOT Services', unpublished MBA thesis, Asian Institute of Technology.

Laohathanakul, V. (1999) 'Human Resource Management during the Economic Crisis', unpublished Master's thesis, Chulalongkorn University.

Lawler, J. and Siengthai, S. (1997) 'Human resource management strategy in Thailand: A case study of the Banking Industry', *Research and Practice in Human Resource Management,* 5, 73–88.

Lawler, J., Siengthai, S. and Atmiyanandana, V. (1997) 'Human resource management in Thailand: Eroding traditions', in C. Rowley (ed.), *Human Resource Management in The Asia Pacific Region,* London: Frank Cass.

Lawler, J. and Atmiyanandana, V. (2003) 'HRM in Thailand: A post 1997 update', in C. Rowley and J. Benson (eds), *The Management of Human Resources in the Asia Pacific Region: Convergence Reconsidered,* London: Frank Cass.

Lee, J. S. (2002) 'Asia in the 21st century: Challenges and opportunities in work and labour', A Rapporteur's Report (Track 5) in T. Hanami (ed.), *Universal Wisdom Through Globalisation: Selected Papers from 12th IIRA World Congress,* Tokyo: Japan Institute of Labour.

McGaughey, S. L. and De Cieri, H. (1999) 'Reassessment of convergence and divergence dynamics: Implications for international human resource management', *International Journal of Human Resource Management*, 10, 235–50.

Nankervis, A., Chatterjee, S. and Coffey, J. (eds), *Perspectives of Human Resource Management in the Asia Pacific*, Australia: Pearson Education.

National Statistical Office of Thailand, Key Social Indicators of Thailand, available at http://service.nso.go.th/nso/data/data05_3.pdf (accessed 5 July 2006).

National Statistical Office of Thailand, various statistics, available at http://web.nso.go.th/eng/stat/stat.htm (accessed 5 July 2006).

Parapob, J. (2004) 'The Development of 360 Degree Feedback System for Human Resource Management of the Faculty in Rajabhat Universities', unpublished dissertation, Chulalongkorn University.

Park, Y. B. and Siengthai, S. (2000) 'Financial crisis, labour market flexibility and social safety net in Korea and Thailand' in the *Proceedings of the 12th International Industrial Relations Association (IIRA) Congress*, Tokyo: Japan Institute of Labour.

Pholphirul, P. (2005) *Competitiveness, Income Distribution, and Growth in Thailand: What Does the Long-Run Evidence Show?* Thailand Development Research Institute, International Economic Relations Programme, May.

Phongpaichit, P. and Baker, C. (1996) *Thailand's Boom!*, Chiangmai, Thailand: Silkworm Books.

Phongthammarug, K. (2000) 'Impact of Organisational Culture on New Product Development of Food Industries in Thailand', unpublished Master's thesis, Chulalongkorn University.

Pontue, N. (2003) 'Effects of Organisational Culture Factors on the Adoption of Enterprise Resource Planning (ERP) System by Organisations in Thailand', unpublished Master's thesis, Chulalongkorn University.

Riggs, F. W. (1967) *Thailand: The Modernization of a Bureaucratic Polity*, Honolulu: East-West Center Press.

Roongrerngsuke, S. and Cheosakul, A. (2001) 'Overview of HRM in organisations in Thailand', *Sasin Journal of Management*, 7, 1–22.

Rowley, C. (ed.) (1997) *Human Resource Management in the Asia Pacific Region*, London: Frank Cass.

Rowley, C. and Benson, J. (eds) (2000) *Globalisation and Labour in the Asia Pacific Region*, London: Frank Cass.

Rowley, C. and Benson, J. (2002) 'Convergence and divergence in Asian HRM', *California Management Review*, 44, 90–109.

Rowley, C. and Benson, J. (eds) (2003) *The Management of Human Resources in the Asia Pacific Region: Convergence Reconsidered*, London: Frank Cass.

Samudavanija, C. (1987) 'Political history', in S. Xuto (ed.), *Government and Politics of Thailand*, Singapore: Oxford University Press.

Siengthai, S. (1988) *Changes in Wages and Income Level in Thailand in the Last Two Decades*. A report prepared for the National Wages and Incomes

Committee, the National Advisory Council for Manpower Development, June (text in Thai).

Siengthai, S. (1989) *Human Resource Development: A Strategic Factor in the Manufacturing and Services Industries in ASEAN,* Singapore: Institute of Southeast Asian Studies,.

Siengthai, S. (1994) *Tripartism and Industrialization of Thailand,* a research paper prepared for the ILO, December.

Siengthai, S. (1996) *The Impact of Globalisation on HRM Practices: A Case Study of Textile Industry.* A paper prepared for the International Industrial Relations Association 3rd Asian Regional Congress, 30 Sept–4 Oct, Taipei, Taiwan.

Siengthai, S. (1999) *Industrial Relations and Recession in Thailand,* a research paper prepared for the ILO.

Siengthai, S. (2000) *Localization of MNCs Management in Thailand,* published in the Report of the Asian Club Foundation Round Table Discussion, January 27–28, Tokyo, Japan.

Siengthai, S. (2002) 'HRM agenda in Thailand', *The Analyst,* New Delhi, 1, 32–4.

Siengthai, S. and Bechter, C. (2001) 'Strategic human resource management and firm innovation', *Research and Practice in Human Resource Management,* 9, 35–57.

Siengthai, S. and Bechter, C. (2004) 'Human resource management in Thailand', in P. Budhwar (ed.), *HRM in Southeast Asia and the Pacific Rim,* London: Routledge.

Siengthai, S. and Bechter, C. (2005) 'Human resource management in Thailand: A strategic transition for firm competitiveness', *Research and Practice in Human Resource Management Journal,* 13, 18–29.

Siengthai, S. and Leelakulthanit, O. (1993) 'Women in management in Thailand: A participation for national prosperity', *International Studies of Management and Organisation,* 23, 4, 87–102.

Siengthai, S. and Vadhanasindhu, P. (1991) 'Management in the Buddhist society', in J. Putti (ed.), *Management: Asian Context,* Singapore: McGraw-Hill.

Siengthai, S., Tanlamai, U., Bechter, C. and Polprasert, C. (2004) *Strategic Human Resource Management for Firm Innovation and Competitive Advantage,* a research report prepared for Asian Institute of Technology, Bangkok.

Siengthai, S., Bechter, C. and Singleton, H. (2005) 'Human resource management in Thailand', in A. Nankervis, S. Chatterjee, S. and J. Coffey (eds), *Perspectives of Human Resource Management in the Asia Pacific,* Australia: Pearson Education.

Siffin, W. J. (1966) *The Thai Bureaucracy: Institutional Change and Development,* Honolulu: East-West Center Press.

Silva, S. R. (2002) *Human Resource Management, Industrial Relations and Achieving Management Objectives,* paper prepared for East Asia Multidisciplinary Advisory Team, ILO, Bangkok.

Sinthuwong, M, (1999) 'Cultural Training of International Corporations in Thailand', unpublished Master's thesis, Chulalongkorn University.

Smitthikrai, C. (1998) *Recruitment and Human Resource Management of Firms in Thailand: The Comparison Between Organisations with Effective and Non-Effective Performance,* Research Report, Department Psychology, Faculty of Humanities, Chiangmai University.

Srisopachit, P. (1999) 'International Strategy, Human Resource Practices, and Competitive Advantage: A Case Study of the Electronics Industry in Thailand', unpublished PhD dissertation, Chulalongkorn University.

Tung, Rosalie (1982) 'Selection and training procedures of US, European and Japanese multinationals', *California Management Review,* 25, 1: 57–71.

Ulrich, D., Brockbank, W., Yeung, A. K. and Lake, D. G. (1995) 'Human resource competencies: An empirical assessment', *Human Resource Management,* 34, 473–96.

Varanukulrak, S. (2002) 'A System Development of the Learning Center Organisation in the Workplace', unpublished Master's thesis, Chulalongkorn University.

Vattaraphudej, B. (1994) 'A Case Study of Management in Newly Established Small Construction Firms', unpublished Master's thesis, Chulalongkorn University.

Vorapongse, V. (2001) 'Human Resource Management in Economic Recovery: A Case Study of Real Estates Business', unpublished Master's degree thesis, Chulalongkorn University, Bangkok, Thailand.

Wailerdsak, N. (2004) *Managerial Careers in Thailand and Japan,* Chiangmai, Thailand: Silkworm Books.

Wolfe, R. A. (1995) 'Human resource management innovations: Determinants of their adoption and implementation', *Human Resource Management,* 34, 313–28.

Wongsrisakul, D. (1998) 'Ways to Industrial Relations Improvement in Workplace', unpublished Master's thesis (M.Econ.), Chulalongkorn University.

7 The changing face of human resource management in Vietnam

Truong Quang, Le Chien Thang and Chris Rowley

- Political, economic and social/cultural background and context
- Key labour market features and developments
- Development of PM and HRM and the HR function and profession
- HRM practices
- Case studies of indigenous organisations
- Case studies of individual managers
- Challenges and prospects for HRM
- Conclusion

Introduction

With the introduction of the *doi moi* (renovation) policy in 1986 Vietnam enjoyed a rapid and broad-based growth period (*Green Left Weekly*, 2005) which drastically altered the economic landscape of the country with consequent business and management impacts. The country recently decided to embark on a new phase of development placing emphasis on achieving more 'balanced' economic growth while trying to avoid the risk of increasing negative social consequences but ensuring economic sustainability. The new strategic direction, which sets the course for the 2006–10 period and beyond, moves away from the former quantity-oriented obsession (indicated by high annual growth rates) of the last two decades towards a more quality-focused stance (TBKTSG, 2006d). For the first time substantial objectives have been set in qualitative, not quantitative, terms, including quality of life, social development, competitiveness and good governance (Viet, 2006; Doanh, 2006; Ngoc, 2006). This change in development strategy requires management changes in all sectors and organisations, including state-owned, private, JV and fully foreign-owned (Viet, 2006). Under this mounting pressure for internal restructuring, along with world economic integration, improving the country's competitiveness at both macro (country) and micro (enterprise) level by means of HR, HRM and HRD has become more pronounced (Cam Ha, 2006).

Against this background this chapter provides an overview of Vietnam's ongoing development (both internal and international) process and explains the strategic shift towards more 'quality of growth' in which developing and managing HR and assets stand at the centre. The development of PM and HRM is outlined. Key HRM functions are covered and case studies in the Vietnamese context provided. Finally, the challenges and prospects of HRM are discussed and key conclusions drawn at the end.

Political, economic and social/ cultural background and context

The practice of management, and especially HRM, do not operate in a vacuum and are critically influenced by the political, economic and social context and background. Vietnam is a densely populated country of 84.4 million people in South East Asia with a comparatively small size of 329,560 square kilometres and an estimated average birth rate of 1.69 annually in 2005 (Indexmundi, 2006). The country has a heritage of long periods of colonialisation, protracted wars, loss of Soviet-bloc financial assistance, political isolation and economic embargos, a low production base and the rigidities of a centrally planned system.

Political

In 1954 Vietnam was eventually freed from 80 years of French rule. However, as a result of the Geneva Accord the country was de facto divided into a communist north and a pro-Western south. In 1973 a ceasefire agreement was finally reached after 20 years of devastating war, ending US military involvement and economic assistance in the south and paving the way for the country's re-unification under communist rule in 1976.

Following several self-adjustments to cope with changing conditions in the post-war period, Vietnam remains politically a one-party state with the Communist Party of Vietnam (CPV or *Dang Cong san Viet Nam*) at the zenith. Article 4 of the 1976 Constitution firmly reinstates the unchallengeable leading role of the CPV in all aspects of life with the support of the mass organisations, whose staff (cadres or *can bo*) are appointed and treated as government officials. Supreme decision-making rests with the 160-member Party Central Committee, which in turn delegates daily operational tasks to a fourteen-member executive Politburo and its eight-person Secretariat. As a general practice key positions in government and state-controlled organisations are filled by CPV members. Recently the CPV took a drastic departure from its 'revolutionary line' to officially allow its members to 'do business' in newly recognised private enterprises (TBKTSG, 2006d).

Economic

Despite the return of peace, Vietnam experienced only limited economic improvement in the two decades that followed unification. The leading role of the state sector was emphasised and private property was officially denied. To save the country from bankruptcy, the ruling CPV tacitly abandoned Marxist central planning and began introducing some market elements, albeit with socialist characters, as part of a broader economic reform package in 1986. In many respects this was patterned after the Chinese model initiated by Deng Xiaoping some 10 years before and it achieved similar results. As a result of the 'renovation' campaign Vietnam made substantial progress, moving from a low level of development to significantly reduced poverty and enhanced socio-educational conditions. In economic terms, around 8 per cent annual GDP growth was reached in 1990–95, and 7 per cent GDP growth in 1996–2005 (Quang, 2006), even against the background of the 1997 Asian Financial Crisis. Indeed, Vietnam is generally seen as one of the fastest growing emerging economies in the Asia-Pacific region, after only China.

Since 2001 the Vietnamese authorities reinstated their commitment to full-scale economic liberalisation and international economic integration. As preparatory steps to this, several structural reforms aimed at modernising the economy and increasing exports and overall competitiveness were needed. However, the process of 'equitisation' (the Vietnamese version of privatisation) or *co phan hoa* of heavily subsidised loss-making SOEs, and attempts to reduce non-performing loans, have been slow. Despite current efforts to move towards a more market-oriented economy, the government still continues to hold a tight reign over major sectors of the economy, such as the banking system, utilities services, transport and communication, oil exploration, as well as key areas of foreign trade and SOEs.

The quest for competitiveness in the face of increasing free trade agreements has created a sense of urgency for both government and business (public and private sector alike) and has encouraged them to adjust to the new conditions. Significant milestones include membership of the ASEAN Free Trade Area, the conclusion of the US–Vietnam Bilateral Trade Agreement in 2001, and WTO membership in 2006. These have necessitated even more rapid and radical changes in economic and trade structure. Furthermore, access to new and sizeable, yet mature, markets (such as Japan, the US and the EU) and WTO accession will force Vietnam to accelerate its transformation towards a more value-added manufacturing-based and export-oriented economy. To do this Vietnam needs to take measures to promote job creation and to develop a more knowledge-based labour force and enhance HRM.

Social/cultural

One of the important factors influencing management practice is national cultural values. However, Hofstede's (1997) widely cited book on cultural dimensions did not include Vietnam. Research on Vietnamese work cultures following such standard cultural dimensions or others such as those of Trompenaars and Hampden-Turner (1998) is sparse or partial. For instance, one survey on Vietnamese cultural values focused on just collectivism and individualism dimensions (Ralston *et al.*, 1999). It found the transition to a market economy in a Confucian milieu resulted in a gradually merging set of values of individualism and collectivism among Vietnamese managers who over time might embrace more market-friendly values.

Other studies provided qualitative assessments of cultural values. For instance, despite the influence of ostensibly egalitarian socialist ideology employees displayed attitudes towards individualism in that they had no common goals and shared objectives and emphasised individual achievements (Quang, 1997). Likewise, there was an emerging trend of younger generations becoming more individualistic (Nilan, 1999), while the power distance dimension seemed not as high as it appeared at first glance and uncertainty avoidance tended to be reasonably low (Tuan and Napier, 2000), possibly resulting from weak awareness, knowledge or absence of many laws. Others noted a particular set of Vietnamese traits such as proneness to indirect communications, cultural dimensions of 'right relationships', respect and community (Borton, 2000), emphasis on social networks and related reciprocity. Of course, such networks could be beneficial, for example harnessing long-term mutual benefits and cultivating trust and personal relationships (Yeung and Tung, 1996), but in the absence of effective legal systems and social control norms they may also evolve into corruption (resulting from nepotism and cronyism), as recently reported (Vuong Ha, 2005).[1]

As Thang *et al.* (2007) cogently argue, Vietnam has a foundation of ancient literature upon which cultural values are formed, changed, retained and passed across generations. Indeed, in feudal times, which ended less than a century ago, mastery in literature and martial arts were the two key currencies to gain the highest creditability in society. As these authors note, the legacy of such a system is the tendency in daily conversation to use proverbs, sayings and idioms, which are compact, value-carrying and easily memorable messages used as references to guide thoughts, attitudes and behaviours (see also Borton, 2000). Thang *et al.* (2007) conclude that, in the absence of Hofstedian-type measures of cultural values for Vietnam, the rich pool of frequently used proverbs, sayings and idioms can be used complementarily to discern inherent cultural values related to management, for example fear for loss of face, ambiguity and indirectness (Quang, 2006).

Given Vietnam's history and current ideology, in many respects its culture has similarities to China, characterised by relationships, respect for seniority and hierarchy, patronage (mentor/protégé), collective responsibility, promotion from within, etc. Nevertheless, Vietnam enjoys a more pluralistic blend of highly valued 'model' behaviours and practices derived from many sources, for example 'divide and rule', 'law and order', 'individualism', 'elite system', 'gallantry', 'camaraderie' (from France); 'grassroots democracy', 'materialism', 'merit system' (from the US); and 'egalitarianism', 'collective decision and responsibility', 'democratic centralism' (from socialism) (Thang *et al.*, 2007). These can be seen in management, such as in leadership and management styles and practices (see Quang, 2006). In many ways these are different from the 'traditional' culture and practices shaped under the Chinese influence, with some movement towards building a more independent identity for Vietnam (*ban sac dan toc Viet*) (Thang *et al.*, 2007).

Key labour market features and developments

Vietnam enjoys a large and young labour force. The economically active age group (between 15 and 45 years) makes up 78.3 per cent of the working population of 38.6 million; and about half of the total population is under 15 years old (GSO, 2006). Population trends can be seen in Table 7.1. Nevertheless, the country has both qualitative and quantitative problems as untrained workers account for 80 per cent of the labour force and 1.2 million new entrants are entering the market each year (MoLISA, 2006). As a result of expanded international integration, employment in some labour-intensive industries is expected to increase while highly protected industries face challenges.

Until recently Vietnam's economy remained predominantly agri-culture based, with about 80 per cent of the population living in the countryside. Thanks to several land reform measures it is now the second largest net rice exporter in the world. Other main agricultural

Table 7.1 Population over time and by gender and geography ('000s)

Year	Total population	By gender		By geography	
		Male	Female	Urban	Rural
1990	66,016.7	32,202.8	33,813.9	12,880.3	53,136.4
1995	71,995.5	35,237.4	36,758.1	14,938.1	57,057.4
2000	77,635.4	38,166.4	39,469.0	18,771.9	58,863.5
2004	82,032.3	40,317.9	41,714.4	21,591.2	60,441.1

Source: General Statistics Office of Vietnam, www.gso.gov.vn, 2006.

exports, albeit with low monetary values, are coffee (the world's second largest exporter), pepper (the world's largest exporter), cashew nuts, tea, cacao, rubber and fisheries products. The ongoing structural reform has tried to reduce dependency on agriculture and balance labour distribution in the economy. Tables 7.2 and 7.3 outline aspects of employment and economic structure in terms of GDP and employment provided by different sectors.

To further push the strategic shift towards more value-added manufacturing and service-based sectors, the 2006–10 socio-economic development plan has a target of 7.5–8.0 per cent annual average GDP growth broken down into: 3.0–3.5 per cent in agriculture, forestry and fisheries; 10–15 per cent in industry; 7.2–7.5 per cent in services (ADB, 2006). This is ambitious and the plan also aims to create 8 million additional jobs, revamp the state-owned sector, promote private enterprise and boost FDI (Cao Cuong, 2006). With

Table 7.2 Labour force by ownership of enterprises and economic activity ('000s)

	2000	2001	2002	2003	2004
Total	37,609.6	38,562.7	39,507.7	40,573.8	41,586.3
By ownership					
State	3,501	3,603.6	3,750.5	4,035.4	4,141.7
Non-state	33,881.8	34,597	35,317.6	36,018.5	36,813.7
Foreign investment sector	226.8	362.1	439.6	519.9	630.9
By economic activity					
Agriculture, forestry	23,492.1	23,385.5	23,173.7	23,117.1	23,026.1
Fishing	988.9	1,082.9	1,282.1	1,326.3	1,404.6
Industry	3,889.3	4,260.2	4,558.4	4,982.4	5,293.6
Construction	1,040.4	1,291.7	1,526.3	1,688.1	1,922.9
Trade	3,896.9	4,062.5	4,281.0	4,532.0	4,767.0
Hotels, restaurants	685.4	700.0	715.4	739.8	755.3
Transport, storage and communications	1,174.3	1,179.7	1,183.0	1,194.4	1,202.2
Culture, health, education	1,352.7	1,416.0	1,497.3	1,584.1	1,657.4
Other services	1,089.6	1,184.2	1,290.5	1,409.6	1,557.2

Source: General Statistics Office of Vietnam, www.gso.gov.vn, 2006.

Table 7.3 Economic structure and labour distribution

	2001	2005 (plan)
Share of GDP (%)		
Agriculture	23.3	20.0
Industry	37.8	38–39
Services	39.0	40–41
Labour utilisation (%)		
Agriculture	60.5	57–58
Industry	14.4	20–21
Services	25.1	20–23

Source: Earth Trends (2003), Quang and Thang (2004: 177).

this rate of economic growth it is expected that per capita GDP would reach US$950–1,000, approximately double the 2000 level, by 2010 (ITPC, 2005; Viet, 2006).

However, modernisation and industrialisation have resulted in massive labour migration from the countryside to the urban areas and a serious drain of skilled labour to the foreign-owned sector. This phenomenon has in effect widened income gaps among different labour groups and this is expected to become much more serious with WTO membership (MoLISA, 2006). Statistics show a wide discrepancy of six times on average between the lowest and the higher income earners in rural areas and eight times in urban areas (Vietnam Economy, 2005; TBKTSG, 2006c). In addition, the prominence of export industry based on labour-intensive and low value-added content (outsourcing of production and services) together with a problematic education and training system have caused a severe imbalance between supply (surplus of young and unskilled labour) and demand (shortage of skilled workers). This in turn will impact on the country's attempts to go down the route of upgrading quality and sustainability of development.

Development of PM and HRM and the HR function and profession

The recent development of HRM in Vietnam can be divided into two distinct stages closely associated with the two economic development periods (Thang, 2004).

Traditional personnel administration (1975–90)

With the country's reunification in 1976 the communist government started to spread nationwide the centrally planned economic model that had been established in the north in 1954. Under this strict system managing people was typified as a 'command' system of personnel administration in which labour was assigned to all production units by a centralised state plan. In each enterprise the personnel function was carried out by an Organisation Department (*Phong To chuc*), which concerned itself more with political and social issues rather than functional activities. Its principal tasks were to keep cadre records and deal mainly with promotion, salary and benefits. Commonly the department head was a 'compromised' figure for all the parties involved, including the CPV cell, the enterprise's management board and the peripheral organisations, for example trade unions, Youth and Women Association chapters, etc.

In general there was a homogenous pattern of PM across enterprises. In employee resourcing little attention was paid to external recruitment sources. Word-of-mouth, connections and referrals were the most practised methods. Public media was not an option since advertising was not possible. Selection relied heavily on application forms, which mainly sought thorough information on war and post-war activities of applicants and their relatives (parents, spouse, siblings and grandparents). Only a small part of selection actually touched on qualifications. In contrast, family history profiles and involvement in the revolution were closely scrutinised during the selection process and referred to when making staffing decisions. Generally, key positions were filled by discharged revolutionaries and returning graduates from the Soviet bloc, with appointment criteria focusing more on political merit than on professional qualifications, so-called 'red' (*hong*) versus 'expert' (*chuyen*) factors (Quang and Thang, 2004). In addition, labour mobility was discouraged by complicated administrative procedures and regulations.

In terms of employee development, training only took place in on-the-job forms. Personal development and career planning were neglected with the exception of approved potentially high-ranking cadres. No formal PA was held on a regular basis (Quang and Dung, 1998).

In employee rewards the pay system was centrally fixed and standardised for all levels to ensure egalitarianism. Pay and merit increases were not based on performance but more on seniority and personal judgement. Merit increases were often perceived as a 'power reserved' privilege which was exclusively in the hands of managers and at times given to their subordinates as a gesture of 'distributing favours' (*ban phat an hue*) (Quang, 2006).

In terms of ER enterprise management was officially appointed by the government (Vu, 2006). Welfare was a collective task of the enterprise director and the trade union. Overt industrial conflicts were non-existent.

Thus, to maintain social stability the government implemented a low-wage, full-employment policy with lifetime employment guarantees. This practice provided job security but restricted management flexibility in staffing decisions. One possible effect of this egalitarian approach of managing people was to put a limit on individual creativity, productivity and motivation. In other words it was blamed for continued poor performance and low levels of employee satisfaction in the state-owned sector, with more than half of SOEs being loss makers or only marginally profitable (World Bank *et al.*, 2000; Painter, 2003). The urgency to improve SOEs' performance to support the country's development and modernisation brought about fundamental changes which opened a new stage in HRM's emergence in Vietnam.

Building HRM (post 1990)

The major driver for change in HRM as a result of economic transformation was the government's formal recognition of ownership diversity. This represented a breakthrough since entrepreneurs used to be regarded as 'ruthless exploiters' of workers according to Marxist–Leninist dogma and on which basis CPV's members were hitherto not allowed to be involved in any type of profit-making business (Phuong Quynh, 2006). With this ideological adjustment the country also witnessed a fundamental change in the nature of employee relations in SOEs and in effect replaced lifetime employment with a contract employment system. This reshaped the structure of the labour market, putting pressure on all enterprises to improve PM practices. To begin with, ownership diversity gave rise to different types of enterprises, which resulted in a significant divergence in PM practices.

In 1986 the private sector was for the first time formally allowed to join the so-called multi-sector economy (*kinh te nhieu thanh phan*), allowing more 'family-style' and 'patronage'[2] approaches to management. Additionally, since 1988 the influx of MNCs has brought managerial expertise into the rigidly regulated economy in tandem with Western and Asian HR practices and management philosophies. In 1992 the first wave of restructuring of SOEs, by selling parts of their shares to the public (mostly their own employees and management), produced a new genre of mixed ownership organisations known as 'equitised' companies (EQCs) aiming to improve management (Quang and Thang, 2004).

The emergence of new forms of ownership brought in competition among companies for both market and input factors, including HR, a principle that was alien in the pre-*doi moi* period. Consequently, a new form of labour market emerged and labour mobility became increasingly dynamic. This situation required that more attention be paid by companies to better manage and retain their workforces to prevent a 'brain drain' (*chay mau chat xam*) from SOEs to foreign companies, especially in the IT, marketing and high-level executive areas.

Against this backdrop there has been a gradual transformation from the old 'command' personnel administration in SOEs into a new HRM system which puts higher premiums on developing and managing HRs as strategic assets in the long run. Yet some traditional PM practices remain in the majority of SOEs. Meanwhile, other enterprises have begun to adopt some elements of HRM practices (Zhu, 2002). Some noticeable trends include the move towards more formal proactive recruitment, selection, training, PA and performance-related rewards and growing concerns for employee retention (Quang and Thang, 2004).

Nevertheless, to be fully recognised by the whole organisation for its strategic role the HRM function still has to develop itself into a centre of expertise and authority with competencies to become an effective and active strategic partner, change agent, people champion and functional expert. New competencies (such as knowledge and skills in psychology and sociology not just law and foreign languages) should be added to the required profile to make HRM more promising, especially in critical times such as restructuring and downsizing organisations. The next section provides more insight into HRM practices at the operational level.

HRM practices

Employee resourcing

There is a wide gap between industry sectors and organisations in relation to employee resourcing practices. For instance, a 2005 survey ($n = 169$) found FOCs and EQCs were more active than SOEs in matters relating to staffing activities, especially the use of 'modern' recruiting methods, such as internet advertising or professional search firms (Thang and Quang, 2005). Consequently, such enterprises might be in a better position than SOEs to attract candidates. In private companies (PCs) the above popular recruitment channels were comparatively less utilised than in SOEs. In particular, employee referrals remained the most preferred method, being used in about 80 per cent of companies, while only about 10 per cent had internet advertising, the least used method. On the whole, personal relationships still remain an important staffing source in most companies. People are naturally inclined to recommend only those whom they know well. Nevertheless, hiring people who are bound by such relationships may be prone to such negative tendencies as covering each other's back, bias, 'groupthink', favouritism and agreeableness.

There was only a slight difference in the tendency to use selection methods among types of enterprise, with a deviation by PCs, which often appoint people on the basis of close relationships and trust (friends and family) and concern for costs (Thang and Quang, 2005). The use of different resourcing methods results in an unequal level of effectiveness in the search for the best job-qualifications match and the differing quality of the workforce, as seen in Table 7.4.

More modern methods of recruitment have been utilised in the increasing competition for the best qualified candidates. Local companies (such as FPT and TMA in the software development industry) are following MNCs (like Unilever, Nestle, P&G, Johnson

Table 7.4 Effects of recruitment and selection in different types of enterprises

Organisation type	Recruitment principles	Outcomes
State-owned enterprises	May not be based on job requirements, but rather on personal relationships and external interventions	Low quality, ineffective and redundant staff
Private companies	Procedure is applied, but not systematically and consistently	Normal- to low-skilled employees, high turnover rate (especially in the marketing and IT areas)
Foreign-owned companies	Always based on job demand	Best candidates from R&D, effective and dynamic workforce

Source: Quang (2006: 244).

& Johnson, British American Tobacco) in trying to lure young and top-class graduates (especially in the marketing and IT fields) at college campuses. This involves using standard tests (including computerised procedures and simulations), interviews to screen applicants and assessment centres (for a systematic check on leadership and problem-solving ability) to select potential managers and team leaders. Some local enterprises have even begun to make use of selective outsourcing services to help them enhance the cost-effectiveness of their employee resourcing processes.

In addition, the quest for survival has urged local companies to experiment with innovative measures in acquiring high-quality management expertise. Some domestic companies have tried to hire foreigners, even as CEOs, currently in high demand. In this 'war for talent', PCs are ahead of SOEs thanks to their advantages of being more flexible and independent. Many SOEs have asked the government to allow them to hire externally but so far only one (Vinashin, a shipping corporation) has been allowed as a pilot case. As detailed exact procedures have not yet been provided by the authorities there are no cases of hiring external CEOs finalised (Yen, 2005; Dau Tu, 2006). Other practices by local companies to acquire key HRs are presented in the later case study section.

Employee development

Changes in the Vietnamese economic structure require a critical mass of skilled employees and competent business managers. Unfortunately, a majority of the currently available HR managers (especially in SOEs and PCs) not only lack basic knowledge of a market economy but also the managerial skills to lead enterprises to make profits and grow (Quang and Dung, 1998). It is suggested a comprehensive HRD strategy concentrating on enhancing competencies for three key groups in particular (public servants and policy makers, entrepreneurs and workers) is required (MoLISA, 2006).

At the micro level employee development is considered a necessary and useful tool ensuring survival and success of enterprises (Dinh, 1997; Thang and Quang, 2005; Ho, 1999). For instance, in a survey of 679 owners of SMEs most expressed a high need for management and technical training. On a comparative basis management training was given more consideration than technical training. Accordingly, the percentages of companies that reported the need for management training and technical training were 84.4 and 78.8 per cent respectively. However, only about half of companies had sent staff off-site for courses. Several reasons explain why these needs did not fully turn into action. For practical reasons firms expect to be advised on identifying training needs and developing training plans but not many training providers possess this capability (Hieu, 2006). Furthermore, the dearth of competent workers is particularly critical at the high end of the labour market, which, even with the combined efforts of executive search agencies, can only fill 30–40 per cent of demand (Thanh, 2005; Cong and Ly, 2005).

In spite of this common concern the business community has divergent views and practices about the effectiveness of employee development. For example, FOCs see employee development as a motivational tool to make employees capable of meeting performance standards (Schultz et al., 2000) and as an investment that has a high chance of being paid off quickly (*Saigon Times*, 2002). Conversely, most SOEs and PCs still consider employee development as an expense and hence tend to keep allocated budgets for this activity as small as possible. With the exception of some leading SOEs, such as Vietnam Airlines, PetroVietnam, Vietnam Post and Telecommunications and Electricity of Vietnam, which actually have plans and reserved annual budgets for employee development, many SOEs remain reluctant to invest substantially for fear that well-trained employees will leave for better pay and prospects in FOCs (Quang and Dung, 1998) and a threat of 'poaching' of HR too.

There are also divergent approaches with regards to employee development delivery. A survey of enterprises across industries ($n = 166$) found that on-site methods of training were adopted equally by different types of enterprises while off-site training was less preferred by FOCs than by SOEs (Thang and Quang, 2005). In particular, most SMEs relied only on informal training due to budget constraints (Tran and Le, 1999), whilst SOEs and PCs rarely sent people abroad, financed self-study plans or rotated jobs as compared with FOCs (Quang and Thang, 2004).

However, enterprises are focusing on improving competitiveness through investing more in employee development. This new trend is even more visible in EQCs, as shown by a survey ($n = 30$) (*Vietnam Economic News*, 1999). At the same time, to help bridge the competence gap with 'modern' management, HRM as a subject has been introduced into the curriculum of many business administration programmes and training programmes for executive positions (see programme advertisements, for example in TBKTSG, 2005a; 2005b; 2005d). Women entrepreneurs have also been assisted by many types of training courses to enhance their capacity in management, with a special focus on SMEs (Phu Nu Viet Nam, 2005; Phu Nu, 2005; TBKTSG, 2005c). In the same fashion a special certificate short course for HR managers is offered for potential and existing practitioners (TBKTSG, 2005e).

Employee rewards

Despite some changes in the order of preference (i.e. a challenging rather than a stable job), especially at the entry level of the labour market, salary is still regarded as one of the most basic factors job-seekers seriously take into account (Linh, 2005). Indeed, with a gross national income per capita of US$480 (Economist.com, 2005) and a GNP (in purchase parity power) per head of US$2,490 in 2003 (World Bank Group, 2005), most Vietnamese are still concerned with meeting their basic needs. Hence, remuneration can be seen as an effective tool to motivate performance and ensure loyalty. Thus, many non-state local companies established rewards structures with different pay scales and steps to maintain internal pay equity (*Nguoi Lao Dong*, 2006). To build an equitable rewards system both local and foreign companies rely on external salary survey information. For this purpose many domestic companies participate in salary surveys or purchase reports from organisations such as Navigos Group and local branches of Mercer and Watson Wyatt. Contrary to this many other companies, especially SOEs, lag behind the trend in rewards practices.

During the 1990s *doi moi* gradually allowed SOEs more flexibility in determining pay levels according to their ability to pay (Zhu and Fahey, 1999). As a result employees received pay packages that included a basic wage constituting a small element with larger parts coming from benefits and incentives. In effect these changes widened pay differentials between the lowest and the highest earners in SOEs, expanding from 3.5 times in the early 1980s to 13 times in the late 1990s (Quang and Thang, 2004). Despite these adjustments SOEs have failed to catch up with non-state enterprises in competing to obtain and retain the best employees due to rigidity in their rewards mechanisms (*co che*). According to one SOE director he could not implement a pay scale differential of more than five times in order to prevent jealousy among personnel and intervention from the enterprise's mass organisations (Linh, 2005). In principle the trade union could intervene in salary levels or increases but often favoured seniority instead of other criteria/factors. Hence the average salary of the lowest employee was VND1 million while the pay for a director was VND5 million. In contrast, a survey undertaken by Navigos Group in 2005 of 208 local and foreign enterprises showed the difference between SOEs and FOCs was about 35 per cent on average for executive positions, even up to 200 per cent or, in some cases, 500 per cent (Linh, 2005).

Another issue is the official minimum wage (*luong toi thieu*), fixed at US$35 for unskilled workers in 1995. While this was intended to serve as a reference for companies and unions to negotiate further, most labour-intensive companies (especially in the footwear and garment industries) use it as the maximum. Also, the level has not been adjusted, despite the 10 per cent currency devaluation since 1999 (Ngoc, 2005) and the 42 per cent food price increase up to 2006

(TBKTSG, 2006b). However, many SOEs paid substantially higher than the minimum (Kamoche, 2001). After a series of strikes the rate was increased in foreign-invested companies to US$55, US$50 or US$44 per month, depending on geography, in 2006.

Failure to cope with employee expectations will result in bad performance, low morale and satisfaction and high employee turnover, which is especially critical for key staff and which would seriously impact on the core competence of the enterprise. In this respect a recent survey ($n = 81$) revealed that the retention rate has reached 18.3 per cent across the board, with 18.2 per cent for the management group, 14.8 per cent for the expert category and 23 per cent for general employees and workers (Linh, 2005).

State and non-state enterprises alike are trying to include other benefits in their rewards package to retain staff. In addition, several local enterprises have started to link rewards to performance and even the company's strategic focus. For example, since 1992 the Southern Steel Company began to experiment with a pay mechanism which was more in proportion with the quality and material waste rates of workers. V-PACK (a packaging company) defined thirty criteria to reward employee performance, putting more focus on such non-material factors as understanding competitors, willingness to learn, loyalty to the company, wide relationship networks, etc. Consequently, the company's sales grew by 35 per cent per year. Similarly, another company reserved 0.5 per cent of its revenue and 5 per cent of its profit every year to reward the efforts of the production and marketing functions, with the company achieving a higher performance than in the previous year (Duc Hoang, 2005). Another interesting instance can be found in the later case study where the pay-for-performance rewards scheme for a sales director could double their pay compared with that of the CEOs. In addition, stock options are being introduced with an aim to develop a sense of ownership and commitment among employees, especially in law firms, IT development centres and consultancy groups (Quang and Thang, 2004). However, companies still differ remarkably in the stage of adoption and the scope of eligibility for employees to participate in stock option programmes.

In general, benefits packages are more comprehensive for employees in FOCs than in SOEs. Together, benefits and social insurance-related items can amount to as much as 20–35 per cent of salary.[3]

Benefits such as transportation or transport allowances, 24-hour accident insurance, voluntary education funds, health check-ups, overseas study tours, etc. are used more extensively in FOCs (Thang and Quang, 2005). However, all types of enterprises commonly offer a *Tet* (Vietnamese New Year) bonus, usually equivalent to at least 1 month's salary for all employees (*thang muoi ba,* 'the 13th month'). The amount of individual *Tet* bonuses varies substantially across companies depending on the individual and enterprise level of performance in the year. For instance, the distributed bonus for each individual in the lunar new year in January 2005 was VND80,000–121,000,000 (Thuy, 2005). Another development with regard to job security and quality of working life (QWL) is the shift from the subsidised welfare system to a social security system for all workers. Post-1995 all firms were obliged to contribute to its employees' social security, comprising 23 per cent of total gross wages (17 per cent from firms and 6 per cent from individuals).

Performance management is becoming more generally recognised by enterprises in Vietnam as a critical and useful managerial and motivational tool to achieve better productivity and quality levels. However, different PA systems are used in local and foreign enterprises in terms of method, process and frequency. Research ($n = 168$) found that management by objectives (MBO), with its pioneering introduction in FOCs and JVs, was equally practised across companies regardless of ownership form (Thang and Quang, 2005). The two companies used in the later case study section have also been adopting this practice. Peer or 360-degree evaluation methods have been applied in several enterprises, albeit for different purposes. Overall, the effectiveness of the PMS depends a great deal on how well the enterprise manages the process in order to ensure the objectivity, reliability and equity of the process.

In this respect a survey of SOEs ($n = 47$) found that 94 per cent claimed to have applied PA in the form of a dialogue between employees and superiors in combination with self-evaluation (Quang and Dung, 1998). Importantly, following the socialist principle of egalitarianism, PA is often used as a management device in SOEs to maintain harmony in the organisation rather than to stimulate internal competition (Kamoche, 2001). For example, a newly equitised insurance company still applied a form of peer or 360-degree evaluation under the centralised guidelines of the so-called 'annual emulation'[4] campaign (*phong trao thi dua*) despite the very low acceptability (25 per cent) and satisfaction (35 per cent) of employees, as revealed in one survey (*n* =109) (Minh, 2005). The failure of this method in most local enterprises can be traced back to the cultural background of the Vietnamese (see earlier section), which values face-saving, thus making people reluctant to rate others unfavourably in public. To guarantee a higher level of objectivity for the system, FOCs and JVs are more dependent on the ranking of employees, whereas PCs have a lower preference for written self-evaluation and peer evaluation, as in the case of SOEs and joint-stock companies with the government holding the largest share (Thang and Quang, 2005). In this respect FOCs conduct more objective performance evaluations than SOEs (Kamoche, 2001) as they adopt standardised processes from parent companies (Pham, 2001). In contrast PCs pursue much simpler procedures in PA, which tend to be more informal to save time and effort, for convenience and because of a lack of expertise (Vo and Dinh, 1997).

Since transparency and frequency of the PA system are not systematically and formally reflected in their implementation process it is understandable that systems are the target of frequent complaints in many enterprises. The most frequently quoted problems include prejudice, favouritism, insufficient knowledge of performance, ignorance of outcomes, time consumption and deteriorating relationships among workers (Quang and Dung, 1998). One survey (Minh, 2005: 45) found high levels of concern, with 73 per cent arguing PA should be subject to change and adjustment and 24 per cent favouring at least partial change. The outcomes of the PA evaluation are, therefore, not seriously considered in local enterprises as a basis for merit increases, promotions, training opportunities and career development, as is often prescribed.

Employee relations

The Vietnam General Confederation of Labour (VGCL, *Tong Lien doan Lao dong Vietnam*) is the sole national trade union that is officially entrusted with the task of protecting the interest of the workers. The VGCL was founded in 1929 as the Red Workers' General Union (*Cong hoi do*) in the North and was extended to the entire country after re-unification in 1976. Its Chair is often a member of the CPV's Central Committee. In principle the trade union chapter plays a crucial role in the operation of any organisation and enterprise together with the CPV's cell and representatives of other organisations, such as the Youth and Women's Unions.

The development and adjustment of the labour regulatory framework started as far back as the early 1990s. The 1995 Labour Code and the 2002 (revised) Labour Law were developed with the technical contributions from ILO experts (MoLISA, 2006). Nevertheless, despite its 'closed shop' character the representative role of the VGCL has declined over the years (Table 7.5) due to its failure to deliver, especially in the non-state sector, as described below. While the number of members has increased, density has fallen from nearly 86 per cent in 2000 to 67 per cent in 2005.

ER in Vietnam is typified by the traditional patronage or mentor system with the ubiquitous presence of a built-in trade union branch in each organisation (Kamoche, 2001). The impacts of these two aspects are essentially decided by how well they are institutionalised into daily HRM practices. In many ways the patronage or mentor system largely downplays or nullifies the strategic role and professional impact of the HRM function, especially in decisions regarding recruitment and promotion. At the same time it is believed that given the priority of attracting FDI even for unions, they often fail to fulfil

Table 7.5 Trade union membership, 1998–2005 ('000s)

Year	Total number of employees in unionised organisations	Number of union members	%
1998	n/a	3,672	n/a
2000	4,536	3,897	85.9
2001	4,740	4,093	86.4
2002	5,079	4,345	85.5
2003	5,554	4,658	83.9
2004	6,168	5,087	82.5
2005	7,828	5,246	67.0

Source: Vietnam General Confederation of Labor (2006).

their role as workers' champions. Trade unions are also blamed for passive roles in protecting worker interests. Thus, even when present unions often take the employer's side in a common effort to attract FDI at the expense of their own members (Le Do, 2006; Nghia Nhan, 2006). In fact unions have representation in only 20 per cent of enterprises.

The Ministry of Labour and Social Affairs (MoLISA) recently reported an average of 98 strikes a year since the introduction of the (revised) Labour Law in 2002 (Nghia Nhan, 2006). The strained ER actually reached a peak when the consumer price index suddenly increased as a result of the oil price hike. There were 256 'unorganised' (or 'wildcat' because they are not allowed if not 'organised' by unions) strikes in the first 5 months of 2006 alone, much higher than the whole of 2004 (2.2 times) and 2005 (1.9 times). Surprisingly, most of the strikes happened in FIEs (214 strikes or 74.8 per cent) and non-state enterprises (sixty-nine strikes, 24.1 per cent), with only a very few in SOEs (three strikes, 1 per cent). The highest concentration of industrial unrest was in Ho Chi Minh City (sixty-five strikes) and the neighbouring 'development triangle' provinces, such as Binh Duong (115 strikes) and Dong Nai (sixty-four strikes).

The underlying reasons leading to these industrial conflicts were inappropriate wages, unpaid bonuses/allowances for special occasions, unfulfilled contributions to social insurance and working conditions. These complaints (Duc, 2006) were mostly made against Asian-owned labour-intensive factories from Taiwan (ninety-one strikes, 42.5 per cent of the total), South Korea (forty-eight strikes, 22.5 per cent) and Hong Kong (eleven strikes, 5.1 per cent). Only 10 per cent of enterprises have developed a systematic salary scale for employees while another 5,000 FOCs and 20,000 PCs have delayed compliance with the law in the absence of concrete implementation guidelines from the functional authorities (Duc, 2006).

QWL practices, generally seen as an effective source of motivation, are still rarely provided by Vietnamese employers. Other organisational supports include work/family balance, flexitime and other innovative services to make working conditions and environments more ergonomic and stimulating for the employees and to retain them.

Case studies of indigenous organisations

We now present case studies of two indigenous companies. These two companies were once market leaders in their sectors: soft drinks and clinical products. Both are under heavy pressure to compete against well-established MNCs.

Organisation case study 1: Softdrink Company

With total assets of nearly US$3 million and around 1,070 employees, Softdrink has six staff working in the HRM department. Its HRM system is based on a good foundation, that is, a systematic library of job descriptions, the product of its ISO initiative.

Employee resourcing

Recruitment takes several forms depending on the level of vacancy to be filled. 'Promotion from within' is a company-wide policy, with internal applicants being given priority. External recruitment is considered only when internal sourcing is exhausted. The search to fill higher level positions is via advertisements in newspapers, while recruitment for executives is made through KPMG and Ernst and Young. The remarkable feature of resourcing strategy is the hiring of several key positions (such as General Director and Planning, Financial and HR managers) from a direct competitor, one of the world's largest beverage producers. This can be seen as a shortcut approach to accessing management expertise to help close the competitiveness gap with well-established competitors. No real pressure exists on recruitment at lower positions (especially in the factories) since there is a large reserve pool of applications. This results from 'walk-ins' and 'write-ins' as the company encourages job-seekers to hand in resumes even when there are no vacancies. This is also intentionally used as a marketing tool to promote its image as an 'organisation of choice' in attracting applicants.

The selection decision takes into account the company's ability to accommodate a person's needs for job stability and growth after hiring. For this reason there are cases where over-qualified candidates are excluded. Rejecting them is justified by the belief that they would eventually leave since they may have expectations about rewards or advancement opportunities that only other companies could match. Consequently, the company opts to select out qualified people rather than facing disruptions caused by turnover later.

Employee development

A balanced 'make or buy' training policy is used to prepare people for current and future job requirements. Training is implemented in various ways depending on the sophistication level of the production line. On-the-job training for people who work on the semi-autonomous production lines is first provided by the (turn-key) supplier then transferred and managed by experienced groups of supervisors. Training in soft skills (interview, management and supervision skills) is given due attention and conducted by the HR department for potential managers and group leaders. Health and safety training is conducted in-house, while industry-specific training (such as food sanitation) is outsourced to the city's Sanitation Centre. PA is conducted periodically every quarter. The employee's average yearly score is used as the basis for bonus distribution. MBO is applied to set performance objectives with company goals cascaded down into units and then individual objectives. In a structured meeting, immediate supervisors and employees discuss and agree on objectives. Five main criteria are used to evaluate the quality of performance, including the extent of achieving objectives, accuracy of work, obedience to requests, teamwork and attendance. The outcome of the PA is primarily used for administrative purposes, such as bonus distribution, promotion consideration and training opportunities.

Employee rewards

Performance metrics are developed and revised carefully as they are used to link pay to performance. For this purpose a pay structure of twelve grades was developed to maintain equity internally and which is supposed to be industry competitive. Overall, the compensation scale is low as compared with that of top FOCs, but is ranked among the highest for local companies.

Pay for performance is applied at different levels of the hierarchy and linked to both individual and company performance wherever applicable. Thus, drivers who deliver cases of bottles of beverages to distributors are paid contingent on the distance of transportation and the weight of the load. The sales staff receive a base salary and variable incentives depending on sales volumes. At manager level or higher a stock option plan is used. In addition, a profit-sharing scheme is applied based on company-realised profit growth. At the year end, when profit growth exceeds certain set targets, a percentage of that excess amount is set aside to be distributed across work groups. The amount of bonus that each individual employee receives varies in accordance with PA results during the year.

On the whole, the benefits package is undoubtedly limited and less innovative compared with the Fortune 500 'Best Companies To Work For' list offer. However, the company believes that it has been providing good benefits on an industry-comparable basis. One of the company's firm arguments is that its rewards go beyond what is required by law (for example, the company's share in purchasing social insurance and health insurance for employees) to cover more aspects of employee welfare. For instance, while the 'law compliance' portion of benefits applies to every employee without discrimination, the company's extra portion is 'personalised' according to the employee's situation. This includes giving gifts on birthdays, funerals, weddings, etc. and bonuses on National Women's Day (for female workers only) and People's Army Anniversary Day (for war veterans). In addition, 15 days off per year, group vacations, outdoor team-building activities, 13th month bonus, allowances for children with outstanding academic performance at school, company's yearly party events, etc. are also included in the benefits package.

Employee relations

The opinions of the trade union representatives have been often sought to balance the benefits of the workers (welfare) and the company (long-term strategy). This cooperative management approach has helped the company maintain good employee–employer relations, through which the company's competitiveness has been greatly enhanced, even in the face of fierce competition.

Sources: interviews with company HR manager, production director and logistics director.

Organisation case study 2: Healthcare Company

This company was equitised in 1997 and specialises in making medical cotton and sanitary napkins with a total workforce of 315. Despite its relatively small size, personnel matters are entrusted to a fully fledged HRM department (one manager and one professional assistant) recently spun-off from the personnel and administrative department. What is special is that the HR manager enjoys a more strategic standing than his counterpart in Softdrink. The HR manager is an assistant to the Board of Directors whose input is critically sought and valued in the strategic planning process of the company. To some extent the HR manager's credibility and position can be explained by the close personal ties to the company's general director (GD). Confronted by mounting HR problems the company's GD was prompted to attend a seminar on HRM where he and the current HR manager, who at that time was working as an HRM specialist at another local company, first met. They kept in touch for knowledge and experience exchange on HRM matters. Gradually, the GD was impressed with the expertise of this HRM specialist and asked him to provide consultation on HR issues on a part-time basis. After about 18 months the GD made the critical decision to 'acquire' this specialist to come to work full-time for the company. The offer allowed the manager to set up an independent and fully empowered HRM department where he was installed as the functional head. The evolving relationship between them has given the HR manager enough exposure and interaction with the whole company's management and put him on equal standing to other executives on the Board in his attempt to optimise the HR department's contribution to the company's bottom line.

Employee resourcing

Analogous to Softdrink, the annual HR plan is derived from the company business plan, which is also based on the pool of job descriptions as a result of an earlier ISO 9000 initiative. Recruitment activities are active for low- to high-level positions since the company does not enjoy the image of a desired workplace in the labour market. Recruitment sources vary depending on the type and level of vacancies. For example, recruitment for manual labour targets various employment agencies in the city as the main resourcing venue while searching for higher level employees or managerial functions relies on advertisements in newspapers and personal networks. Some recruitment channels seem particularly effective in attracting candidates. For example, a 2005 newspaper advertisement for 40 sales people yielded about 300 applicants. Typically, selection is hinged primarily on the interview, which often focuses on assessing qualifications outlined in job descriptions. In only some positions are selection decisions supported with written job knowledge tests. The criteria for these include both personal qualifications (competences and experience) and judgement on the candidate traits of integrity and perseverance.

Employee development

All newly hired employees are put through an orientation training session led by their direct manager in coordination with the HRM department. This is followed by a report at the end of the probationary period to make sure recruits were actually good choices. At present the severe shortage of people with critical skills forces the company to focus its resourcing strategy more on acquiring than on developing HR. As a consequence, training activities are mainly organised around on-the-job forms. However, a longer-term training initiative is under way to make the company more proactive to changing business conditions. To this effect a training plan has been developed to identify current training needs and the most effective delivery methods. Training topics to be offered include both soft and management skills for development purposes. For example, for the sales force selling and interpersonal skills are the core of the training menu while for line supervisors three key areas of training are organising group work, motivating employees, and monitoring and controlling group performance.

Employee rewards

Salary level is closely monitored in accordance with market rates based on information brought in by employees headhunted from competitors or friends. The reason for not using salary surveys is merely budget constraint not because of mistrust of information reliability, as with Softdrink. On the one hand the company applies a wide range of pay schemes for different types of employees, most of them based on performance. For instance, in the production department, packaging employees manually put pieces of clinical cotton and sanitary napkins into plastic packages and are paid depending on their work volumes. In contrast, sales staff pay is half fixed and half depending on sales volumes. On the other hand the company recognises the important principle of compensation equity that pay should reflect the contribution of the individual to the company. Accordingly, the rewards policy even allows exceptional cases, such as where pay for a sales manager can be double that of the GD. Moreover, an employee stock ownership plan was developed to create a sense of commitment to the company when it was equitised. However, the plan failed to get employee support even though they were allowed to purchase up to 70 per cent of the company's available stock. In the absence of communication and a well-founded development business strategy, most of the new stockholders sold shares for quick cash returns. Nine years after equitisation employees in effect only own less than 10 per cent of the company's total stock value.

Employee relations

To encourage employees to come up with innovative and creative ideas the company introduced the incentive programme 'Bonus For Ideas With Impact'. Under this scheme, individuals or work groups with ideas that could help improve any aspect of work could register them with the company. Feasible ideas are implemented and their impact evaluated in monetary terms and idea initiators are rewarded. This also helps commitment and participation in the long-term business development of the company. A union presence was established in the company, but it has not gained much voice. The president of the union chapter has played only a weak role in fostering the relationship between the employees and senior management according to the HR manager.

Source: interview with company HR manager.

Case studies of individual managers

In the next section, we provide case studies of two local managers. These two managers illustrate the strength of local managers in developing and expanding their business enterprises.

Manager case study 1: Huynh Thi Tue

At the age of 36 Mrs Huynh started up a private enterprise, which officially became Kim Hang Steel Company in 1994. From a small base it expanded to cover twelve production factories over an area of twelve hectares and managed five outlets in Ha Noi, Da Nang, Nha Trang, Can Tho and the eastern part of the south. In total, the company employs 1,000 people. In 1994 the company began to export products to more than sixteen countries in Europe and North America. In 2004 total revenue was VND189.75 billion (US$12.24 million), of which US$3.3 million was exports. In the first 6 months of 2005 the company's revenue reached VND102.65 billion (US$6.62 million), with US$1.78 million from exports.

Huynh admitted to having encountered many difficulties during the process of transforming the company from a small to a larger scale, especially with regard to effective business management. To cope with the new requirements she insisted the company's executives continuously enhanced their management capabilities. Huynh personally explained that the formula for success 'lies with the people'. The foundation of her method of managing people's capacity effectively is to put full confidence in young workers as she claimed they were more creative in dealing with job demands, more sensitive to changing working and business environment, and capable of better handling situations than older generations. At the same time company success can be attributed to having developed a firm relationship of trust with customers (external) and employees of all kinds (internal). On the one hand the company aims to gain customer trust by absolutely delivering the product with the quality as promised. In the case of defects a company technician will be sent on-site to fix the problem within 24 hours of receiving a call from unsatisfied customers. To reinforce this principle of 'quality of service delivery', production workers are paid on defect/scrap rates, and sales representatives and dispatched technicians rewarded in large part according to the customer satisfaction/complaint index. Furthermore, she tries to treat all workers and staff even-handedly. This policy of equity helps unleash people's sense of self-management, self-discipline and commitment, which makes management's control tasks less necessary and more effective. In Huynh's view not a single entrepreneur achieves success without difficulties, especially in this time of fierce competition. It is even more difficult for a female entrepreneur in a still male-dominated business environment. However, she has managed to lead her growing business to its present success by giving attention to the company's human assets, an area she believes women are often good at, thereby being able to retain a remarkable level of productivity and motivation.

Sources: TBKTSG (2005g); round-the-table interview with business school students, Ho Chi Minh City, 22 December 2005.

Manager case study 2: Vo Anh Tai

As the Director of SaigonTourist Travel Services Company, Vo Anh Tai practises this policy:

> The door of my office is never closed so that everybody in the company can come anytime to directly discuss his/her problem with me when proper. Similarly, I always keep my mobile phone open to make myself accessible at all times. I also keep checking my e-mail box on a regular basis to receive feedback from all employees. If wanted, any employee in the company can send an e-mail to his immediate manager, with a copy to me. This is the best way that helps me keep close contact with my workforce.

His 'strategy of quality growth' aims at satisfying four stakeholders: business, customers, employees and community. In fact this people-based management approach had promoted him to the position of Permanent Deputy Director at the age of 36 (in 2003) from the Sales Manager of a hotel belonging to the SaigonTourist Group. As he recalled, by that time the Group had just received a severe blow from the SARS epidemic, impacting on visitors to Ho Chi Minh City. Consequently:

> the company's revenue dropped like a falling rock, people's morale was down to an alarming level, future business plan became hopeless. All we could do immediately to rescue the situation was to stabilise the company's business and the people's mind.

Under these circumstances he decided nothing would be more effective in solving the crisis than to start with employee involvement in the campaign to rescue the company. Instead of developing a strategy and implementation plan of his own he invited 'core' personnel to participate in the process because he reasoned: 'it is they who will be directly executing the strategy, thus it is most logical and effective to discuss and agree on the future course of action with them first'. By doing so, SaigonTourist Travel Services was able to create a consensus for the entire company, *a sine qua non* condition to overcome the crisis. Also, thanks to this people-centred approach the company succeeded in retaining its 'core' human assets and the majority of its workforce throughout the crisis since: 'if people are equally important as material assets in the hotel industry, they mean everything in travel business'. Working on boosting people's morale (through involvement and participation) Vo believed that he had prepared the necessary conditions for growth after the crisis by bringing back stability to both its business (by diversification of its services package) and its workforce.

Vo's participative and communicative approach has proven to be effective in less than 1 year of experimentation, which earned him a full directorship of the company in 2004. In 2005 some 50,000 overseas tourists visited Vietnam in tours offered by SaigonTourist Travel Services. During the same period 90,000 domestic tourists joined the company in eighty travel programmes. Vo now projects a post-SARS business boom which might help his company to score an even higher revenue increase than the 20 per cent or VND411 billion in 2006, an increase of VND68 billion compared with 2004.

Source: TBKTSG (2006a), 5 January.

Challenges and prospects for HRM

Recent research on management practices in Vietnam (Zhu and Fahey, 1999; Zhu, 2002; 2005; Kamoche, 2001; Thang and Quang, 2005; Thang *et al.*, 2007) provides some evidence to support the view that the higher value a company puts on HR, the more extensive is the practice of HRM in those companies. In this context it is observed that the level of HRM practice is generally low in the public sector, relatively higher in the private sector and highest in FIEs in three key aspects: awareness, the recognition of the strategic role of HRM practice; the presence of a HRM function and standardised procedures; effectiveness, in terms of HRM value addition to the final outcomes of the company (Quang, 2006).

A 2006 survey ($n = 41$) of a group of (international) executive MBA students in Hanoi undertaken by the authors on the awareness of HRM's strategic role sheds more light on the growing concerns of managers regarding the issue of building competitiveness through people. Yet it also shows a discrepancy in perceptions in terms of the order of importance with their Asian counterparts in the region. Typically, while sharing the same concerns about critical HRM issues, such as employee resourcing and development, Vietnamese managers seem to worry more about development (Table 7.6), especially for new recruits, than their Singaporean counterparts.

In the case of Singapore the focus is usually put more on acquiring the best-qualified people and retaining them given the highly competitive, yet constrained, labour market in that country. In contrast, Vietnam has an abundant pool of young and dynamic graduates (such as in IT and economics), but due to a severe mismatch between supply and demand in the skilled labour market most companies have to retrain their newly recruited employees to fit the requirements of the job (Huynh Hoa, 2005). Hence, the level of challenges and prospects concerning HRM may differ in terms of urgency, scope and impact from one type of enterprise to another. In short, the prospects for HRM in Vietnam for the coming period are summarised in Table 7.7.

Table 7.6 HRM concerns in Singapore and Vietnam (in order of importance)

Ranking	Singapore[a]	Vietnam[b]
1	Recruitment	Recruitment
2	Retention	Training and development
3	Training	Motivation
4	Compensation and rewards	Retention

Sources

a   Thuc Doan (2006).
b   Survey by the authors ($n = 41$).

Table 7.7 HRM perspectives in Vietnam

HRM areas	Areas for improvement	Solutions
Acquiring	Not regulated and standardised External sources not fully exploited	HR planning and HR information system Job analysis and descriptions, based on job requirements and qualifications Standardisation of processes Focus on skilled labour and high-level executives
Utilising	No orientation Placement and appointment based on relationships rather than merit	Socialisation programmes (corporate culture) Best job qualification match Define core staff Use outsourcing alternatives
Developing	None or improper programmes No career planning Promotion based on seniority	Reserve budget for employee development Career plan for each employee Succession/replacement plan Job rotation Development plan for executives and managers
Retaining	Pay under industry standards Competent and willing performers not recognised and rewarded No link between pay performance Insufficient support from management Working environment not appropriate	Industry remuneration review Pay for performance Link incentives to key business indicators Link goal-setting and performance achievement Performance management system Better employee relations Regular employee satisfaction survey Control turnover by QWL and additional services

Source: adapted from Quang (2006).

With a people-centred HR strategy and/or policy the organisation can ultimately maintain optimal employee relations, high levels of motivation and minimum rates of employee turnover. In the final analysis qualified and motivated people are the key driving force which helps the company to survive and develop further in the new conditions, but this cannot be realised without proper and sufficient support from the organisation (in terms of empowerment, QWL and work–family balance). In other words, an effective HRM formula in Vietnam could be found in a combination of the perceived strategic role of HRM, a well-integrated HR strategy, and a professional HRM function and companies should focus attention on aspects such as recognising the strategic role of HRM and undertaking proper job analysis, as a basis for a more effective HR planning and execution.

Conclusion

This chapter provided an overview of a developing country which has achieved significant progress in many respects in quantitative terms yet has failed to ensure long-term sustainability of its economy. Under the current development conditions of integration and competition worldwide it is realised that in order to be more sustainable a country should put due strategic focus on developing and managing HR – the most critical and valuable assets of all – for short- and long-term growth at all levels of the economy. In this respect Vietnam is no exception given its current development status and its desire to develop further.

However, any attempt to impose imported ethnocentric HRM practices would lead to failure; a warning for those prospective companies interested in entering Vietnam, 'one of the world's last emerging markets' (Von Glinow and Clarke, 1995). Rather, optimal benefits could be more likely by developing full 'polycontextuality' among business partners and different cultures (Von Glinow, 2004; Thang et al., 2007).

However, there is still a long way to go for some firms (i.e. SOEs and PCs) to position themselves in the competitive business environment, due to a lack of awareness and resources as well as the rigidity of systems and lack of motivation to change. More often than not Vietnamese enterprises seem to be more concerned with finding a 'one-fits-all' solution for their growing management problems without first building a solid foundation for an effective HRM system. Companies should focus attention on aspects such as recognising the strategic role of HRM and undertaking proper job analysis as a basis for a HR planning process. In any case, although there is no such common pattern or formula which would guarantee a given enterprise success in importing 'best practices' for its company-specific conditions, HRM policy (in the case of proper adaptation and implementation) is an effective way for an enterprise to become more competitive (Quang, 2006).

It remains to be seen whether Vietnam, while having been successful in providing a quantitative growth pattern in many aspects in the last decade, will also be able to move to a quality development route, which puts a premium on capitalising its own HRs. Without this the future objective to become an industrialised country by 2020 will remain merely rhetoric (Hoang, 2006). All in all, the changing face of HRM in Vietnam has further to go.

Notes

1   In 2005 Vietnam was ranked 107 (together with Belarus, Honduras, Kazakhstan, Nicaragua, Palestine, Ukraine and Zambia) out of 159 countries (scoring 2.6) in terms of corruption (Transparency National Corruption Perception Index, ICP) by the Berlin-based organisation Transparency International, see www.transparency.org.
2   Here a close relationship is built and developed among the patron/mentor and his/her protégé on the basis of camaraderie, cronyism or nepotism, and the latter enjoys protection, support and privileges from the former.
3   Though compulsory it is reported that only 12 per cent of the labour force is covered by a social insurance scheme, leaving in effect a large percentage of informal and agricultural workers 'unprotected' (MoLISA, 2006).
4   'Emulation' (*thi dua*) here means competition, an official word in 'communist' language used to describe the campaign put in place to motivate workers and units to work harder.

Bibliography

ADB (Asian Development Bank) (2006) *Asian Development Outlook 2005: Vietnam*, www.adb.org, accessed 23 February 2006.

Borton, L. (2000) 'Working in a Vietnamese voice', *Academy of Management Executive*, 14, 4, 20–9.

Cam Ha (2006) '197 nam VN moi duoi kip Singapore (Vietnam needs 197 years to catch up Singapore)', *Tuoi Tre Online*, 27 March.

Cao Cuong (2006) 'Nhin thang su that, tiep tuc doi manh doi moi (Facing the reality head-on, continuing to push renovation forward)', *Thoi bao Kinh te Sai Gon*, 20 April, 12–3.

Cong, T. and Ly, A. (2005) 'Tam chan nho, nhieu nguoi keo (Many people sharing a small blanket)', *Thoi bao Kinh te Sai Gon*, 11 August.

Dau Tu (2006) 'San giam doc nuoc ngoai (Hunting for foreign CEOs)', 15 February.

Dinh, H. (1997) *Human Resource Management*, 3rd edn, Hanoi: Education Publishing Company.

Doanh, L. D. (2006) 'Cai cach huong toi mot Viet Nam tu do va tri tue (Reforms leading to a free and knowledge-based Vietnam)', *Thoi bao Kinh te Sai Gon*, 26 January and 2 February, 5–6.

Duc, N. V. (2006) '5 thang, ca nuoc co 287 cuoc dinh cong (5 months, 287 strikes all over the country)', *Lao Dong On-line*, 6 June.

Duc Hoang (2005) 'Luong khong chi la luong (Not only salary)', *Thoi Bao Kinh Te Sai Gon (Saigon Economic Times)*, 14 April.

Earth Trends (2003) *Economic Indicators: Vietnam*. Available at http://earth-trends.wri.org.

Economist.com (2005) *Country Briefings: Vietnam*, www.economist.com/countries/Vietnam/PrinterFriendly.cfm?Story_ID=2681340; accessed 17 September 2005.

Green Left Weekly (2005) 'Vietnam: UN report says Vietnam's social progress "exceptional"', 16 November, www.greenleft.org.au/back/2005/649/649p20.htm, accessed 23 February 2006.

GSO, General Statistics Office (2006) *Population and Employment*, www.gso.gov.vn, accessed 10 October 2006.

Hieu, D. (2006) 'Dao tao cho doanh nghiep: phai coi do la dau tu chu khong phai chi phi (Employee training should be considered as investment, not expenditure)', *VnEconomy*, 1 March.

Ho, V. V. (1999) Experience of SME Development in Asian Countries. *Working Paper presented at Workshop of SME Support Policies in Industrialization and Modernization Process*. Hanoi: Ministry of Planning.

Hoang, D. D. (2006) '"Cung, mem" hay gi khac? ("Hard, soft" or something else?)', *Thoi bao Kinh te Sai Gon*, 30 March, 4.

Hofstede, G. (1997) *Cultures and Organizations: Software of the Mind*, New York: McGraw-Hill.

Huynh Hoa (2005) 'Cung, cau chua gap nhau (Supply and demand do not meet together yet)', *Thoi bao Kinh te Sai Gon*, 22 September, 44.

ITPC (Investment and Trade Promotion Centre) (2005) 'Vietnam targets 7.5%–8% annual GDP growth for 2005 to 2010', http://itpc.hochiminhcity.gov.vn, accessed 23 February 2006.

Indexmundi (2006) *Vietnam Birth Rate*, www.indexmundi.com/vietnam/birth_rate.html, accessed 10 October 2006.

Kamoche, K. (2001) 'Human resource in Vietnam: The global challenge', *Thunderbird International Business Review*, 43, 5, 625–50.

Le Do (2006) 'Chinh sach luong lac hau, dinh cong la tat yeu (Backward wage policy, strikes are inevitable)', *Laodong Newspaper Online*, 11 March.

Linh, L. U. (2005) 'Thu hut nguoi bang luong (Attracting people by salary)', *Thoi bao Kinh te Sai Gon (Saigon Economic Times)*, 11 August.

Minh, N. V. (2005) 'Developing an Effective Performance Management System at Bao Minh Insurance Corporation, Vietnam', *MBA Research Report*, Maastricht School of Management.

MoLISA, Ministry of Labor, Invalids and Social Affairs (2006) *Labour and Social Issues Emerging from Vietnam's Accession to the WTO*, www.worldbank.org/INTRANETTRADE/Resources/WBI-Training/Viet-labor_trao.pdf; accessed 10 October 2006.

Ngan, H. (2006) 'Vi sao cac cuoc dinh cong deu trai luat? (Why all strikes are illegal)', *Vietnam Economy*, 3 February.

Nghia N. (2006) 'Suc nong dinh cong tran vao quoc hoi (The heat of strikes invades the National Assembly)', *Phap luat* (Law), 5 May, 3.

Ngoc, H. (2005) 'Vi sao luong cong nhan qua bot beo? (Why the worker's wage is still so humble?)', *Phu nu (Women),* 16 September.

Ngoc, N. (2006) 'Song trong the gioi hom nay (Living in the contemporary world)', *Thoi bao Kinh te Sai Gon,* 26 January and 2 February, 7–10.

Nguoi Lao Dong (The Labourer) (2006) 'Nhieu doanh nghiep ngoai quoc doanh xay dung thang, bang luong (Many non-state enterprises develop salary scales)', 19 January.

Nilan, P. (1999) 'Young people and globalizing trends in Vietnam', *Journal of Youth Studies*, 2, 3, 353–70.

Painter, M. (2003) 'The politics of economic restructuring in Vietnam: The case of state-owned enterprise "reform"', *Contemporary Southeast Asia,* 25, 1, 20–44.

Pham, N. T. (2001) 'Human Resource Management Practice and SME Performance', unpublished DBA research report, Southern Cross University.

Phu Nu (Women) (2005) Advertising section, 28 August.

Phu Nu Viet Nam (Vietnamese Women) (2005) Advertising section, 31 August.

Phuong Quynh (2006) 'Nhung diem moi cua Dai hoi Dang lan thu X (The new points of the 10th Party congress)', *Thoi bao Kinh te Sai Gon*, 27 April, 12–13.

Quang, T. (1997) 'Sustainable economic growth and human resource development in Vietnam', *Transitions*, 38, 1&2, 257–80.

Quang, T. (2006) 'Human resource management in Vietnam', in A. Nankervis, S. Chatterjee and F. Coffey (eds), *Perspectives of Human Resource Management in the Asia Pacific*, Sydney: Pearson Education Australia.

Quang, T. and Dung, H. T. K. (1998) 'Human resource development in state-owned enterprises in Vietnam', *Research & Practice in Human Resource Management,* 6, 1, 85–103.

Quang, T. and Thang, L. C. (2004) 'HRM in Vietnam', in P. Budhwar (ed.), *Managing Human Resources in Asia-Pacific*, London: Routledge.

Ralston, D. A., Thang, N. V. and Napier, N. K. (1999) 'A comparative study of the work values of North and South Vietnamese managers', *Journal of International Business Studies*, 30, 4, 655–72.

Rowley, C. and Warner, M. (eds) (2007) *Business and Management in South East Asia: Studies in Diversity and Dynamics*, London: Routledge.

Saigon Times (2002) 'Employers prefer new graduates', 5 January.

Schultz, C. J., Speece, M. V. and Pecotich, A. (2000) 'The evolving investment climate in Vietnam and subsequent challenges to foreign investors', *Thunderbird International Business Review*, 42, 6, 735–53.

Son Tung (2006) 'Tao ra su dong thuan (Building consensus)', *Thoi bao Kinh te Sai Gon*, 5 January.

TBKTSG (Thoi bao Kinh te Sai Gon) (2005a) Advertising section, 23 June.

TBKTSG (Thoi bao Kinh te Sai Gon) (2005b), Advertising section 18 August.

TBKTSG (Thoi bao Kinh te Sai Gon) (2005c), Advertising section 25 August.

TBKTSG (Thoi bao Kinh te Sai Gon) (2005d), Advertising section 15 September.

TBKTSG (Thoi bao Kinh te Sai Gon) (2005e), Advertising section 22 September.

TBKTSG (Thoi bao Kinh te Sai Gon) (2005f) 'Giu ca chu tin voi nhan vien (Build trust even with your employees)', *Toa soan & ban doc*, 22.

TBKTSG (Thoi bao Kinh te Sai Gon) (2005g) Successful Businessman section, 22 December.

TBKTSG (Thoi bao Kinh te Sai Gon) (2006a) Successful Businessman section, 5 January.

TBKTSG (Thoi bao Kinh te Sai Gon) (2006b) 'Dinh cong nhin tu luat cung cau (Strikes seen from the law of supply and demand)', 27 February.

TBKTSG (Thoi bao Kinh te Sai Gon) (2006c) Editorial, 'Mot bai toan kho cua nam 2006 (A difficult question for 2006)', 19 January, 1.

TBKTSG (Thoi bao Kinh te Sai Gon) (2006d) Editorial, 'Da chu trong den chat luong tang truong (More focus on the quality of growth)', 4 May, 1.

Thang, L. C. (2004) Managing Human Resources in Vietnam: An Empirical Study of an Economy in Transition, unpublished PhD. dissertation, Asian Institute of Technology.

Thang, L. C. and Quang, T. (2005). 'Human resource management practices in a transitional economy: A comparative study of enterprise ownership forms in Vietnam', *Asia Pacific Business Review,* 11, 1, 25–47.

Thang, L. C., Rowley, C., Quang, T. and Warner, M. (2007). 'To what extent can management practices be transferred between countries: The case of HRM in Vietnam', *Journal of World Business*, 41.

Thanh, P. (2005) 'Mieng banh con lon (The cake is still big)', *Thoi bao Kinh te Sai Gon (Saigon Economic Times),* 11 August.

Thuc, D. (2006) 'Giu loi, nghe thuat giu nguoi (Keep your promise, the art to retain people)', *Thoi bao Kinh te Sai Gon*, 27 April, 32–4.

Thuy, N. (2005) 'Muc thuong cao nhat la 121 trieu dong (The highest bonus is VND121 million)', *Vnexpress*, 31 December.

Tran, K. H. and Le, V. S. (1999) 'HRM and SME Development in Vietnam', paper presented at HRM Symposium on SMEs, APEC, National Sun Yat-sen University, Taipei, Taiwan.

Trompenaars, F. and Hampden-Turner, C. (1998) *Riding the Waves of Culture*, New York: McGraw Hill.

Tuan, V. V. and Napier, N. K. (2000) 'Paradoxes in Vietnam and America: Lessons learned', *Human Resource Planning*, 23, 1, 7–8; 2, 9–10; 3, 8–10.

Viet, V. Q. (2006) 'Tang truong tot nhung van con yeu kem (Good growth but still weak)', *Thoi bao Kinh te Sai Gon,* 9 February, 44–5.

Vietnam Economic News (1999) 'Will equitisation succeed nation-wide', 26 April.

Vietnam Economy (2005) 'Hard to reach 8% growth rate: CIEM', http://vneconomy.com.vn, accessed 23 February 2006.

Vo, N. T. and Dinh, H. (1997) 'Use of Performance Appraisal in Private Enterprises in Ho Chi Minh City', working paper, Hanoi: National Economics University.

Von Glinow, M. A. (2004) 'Do we speak the same language?', *Insights,* 4, 2, 8–9.

Von Glinow, M. A. and Clarke, L. (1995) 'Vietnam: Tiger or kitten?', *Academy of Management Executive,* 9, 4, 35–47.

Vu, Quang Viet (2006) 'Chuyen bien trong lanh dao va he thong lanh dao va nha nuoc Viet Nam tu sau 1945: Kha nang cai cach the che quyen luc de chong tham nhung (Changes of leadership and the leadership structure and the state of Vietnam after 1945: The possibility of reforming the power mechanism to combat corruption)', *Thoi dai moi (New Era),* 9 November.

Vuong Ha (2005) '10 co quan tham nhung pho bien nhat (10 organizations that are most corrupted)', *Dan Tri On line,* www.dantri.com.vn, 30 November.

World Bank, Asian Development Bank and UNDP (2000) *Vietnam 2010: Entering the 21st Century,* Vol. 1, Report No. 21411, 29 November.

World Bank Group (2005) *Vietnam Data Profile,* www.devdata.worldbank.org/external/CPProfile.asp?CCODE=VNM&PTYPE=CP; accessed 17 September 2005.

Yen, H. (2005) 'Vinashin se co tong giam doc nuoc ngoai (Vinashin will have a foreign CEO)', *VietNamNet,* 9 October.

Yeung, I. and Tung, R. (1996) 'Achieving business success in Confucian societies: The importance of *Guanxi* (Connections)', *Organizational Dynamics,* 25, 2, 54–65.

Zhu, Y. and Fahey, S. (1999) 'The impact of economic reform on industrial labor relations in China and Vietnam', *Post-Communist Economies,* 11, 2, 173–92.

Zhu, Y. (2002) 'Economic reform and human resource management in Vietnam', *Asia Pacific Business Review,* 8, 3, 115–34.

Zhu, Y. (2005) 'The Asian Crisis and the implications for human resource management in Vietnam', *International Journal of Human Resource Management,* 16, 7, 1261–76.

8 Conclusion

Chris Rowley and Saaidah Abdul-Rahman

- Review of HRM practices
- Concluding remarks

This particular book has been concerned with HR and the transformation of PM and HRM practices across a broad range of countries, sectors and organisations in South East Asia. During the bubble economy decade prior to the 1997 Asian Financial Crisis many companies were assured of growth and profits despite lacking a proper HRM system. PM was purely routine and regarded as an administrative function within general affairs administration. However, the crisis brought about a different perspective in terms of organisational stability. Organisations as well as researchers began to examine seriously how constructive HRM can contribute to the sustainability of organisations in cases of economic contingencies. Thus, we have set out the objective of reviewing the emerging management context and development of HRM as both a function and set of key practices. Besides, firms in each country began to reappraise their HR strategy and structure in the light of global intensified interest in China's economic ascendancy, regional market integration under the ASEAN Free Trade Accord (AFTA) and the emergence of corporate governance and transparency in business dealings.

We have brought together several specialists from each of the selected countries who have presented separate discourses on PM and HRM in their respective countries. Throughout the book we have been exposed to the details of HRM in each country. Country authors began their accounts with an overview of the political, economic and social/cultural scenarios, followed by in-depth empirical observations and detailed analyses of the HRM structures of mainstream, mainly indigenous companies. Our contributors were instructed to use real-life case studies and adopt an insider perspective; thus the core of the data presented in each chapter was derived primarily from qualitative interviews with managers and practitioners working in the

HRM area. It is further hoped that in turn such a style and structure could be useful in teaching, not only in international and country-specific areas, but also in comparative fields, as well as being a much needed literature resource on these countries. This chapter is divided into three sections: a summary and analysis of the country chapters, followed by a comparative analysis, and the implications for further economic development.

Review of HRM practices

Indonesia

The 1997 Asian Crisis brought about several major changes to Indonesia, the country most adversely affected by the crisis. Politically the country experienced a transformation from authoritarian rule to democracy and regional autonomy. At the same time within the business scenario, despite cumbersome labour regulations, which were a legacy of former President Soeharto's regime, a number of significant changes transpired, especially in the management of HR. The transition from personnel administration to HRM would be challenging for most firms. However, post-Soeharto restructuring programmes have compelled firms to create a more competent workforce and improve on core competencies. However, education and skills need much improvement. Training tends to be more systematic in MNCs and larger domestic firms, and in these cases the HRM departments conduct post-training evaluation and employees are expected to enhance their performance by implementing the knowledge they have gained during the training process. Within the rewards system, firms need to eliminate internal pay inequities, as well as enforce PA and implement performance-based rewards. Nevertheless, due to the vast regional differences as well as ethnic diversity, it is still too early to evaluate the changes that have occurred in the Indonesian HRM area in these last few years.

Malaysia

The Malaysian workforce is composed of diverse ethnic and cultural groups. One consequence of the influx of FDI since the 1960s is the propagation of more systematic HRM practices by MNCs. For instance, the patterns for recruitment and selection, training, job designs and rewards systems were initiated mainly by MNCs. Furthermore, the 1997 crisis proved to be the catalyst for innovation and reform in the HRM scenario. Firms, including locally incorporated companies, began to recognise the strategic importance of the HRM function, thus strengthening the status of HRM departments. The post-crisis era witnessed innovation and reform in HRM practices and policies. In general there is a shift towards more systematic and well-documented HRM policies, procedures and rules, owing to the eagerness of companies in obtaining ISO certification, which categorically elevates their position in the business environment. Nevertheless, due to global competition companies tend to emphasise workplace innovations that will result in a productive and competitive workforce.

HRM in Malaysia since the last two to three decades is more of a blend of Western concepts of HRM practices and Eastern (mainly Japanese-style management practices) as well as local work practices. The success of selective adaptation of HRM practices from both Western and Eastern values and work systems depends entirely on local managers' abilities to harness and interpret them into a course of action suited to the local workforce as well as local cultural values.

The Philippines

The development of HRM in the Philippines may be understood as a derivative of diverse management cultures. The Filipino work ethic has been shaped by influences from several dimensions, particularly due to its colonisation by Spain and the US. MNCs introduced US- and Western-based HR practices such as job evaluation and HRD, while Japanese and South Korean investors introduced concepts like *kaizen*, total quality management and labour management cooperation. Simultaneously, HRM and work practices are influenced by the local Filipino Chinese practices of trust and loyalty, hard work and thriftiness. These concepts are supplemented further by local practices of personalistic relations, mutual help and informal networks.

From the 1990s the Philippines has experienced uneven economic growth patterns that have resulted in a shrinking formal sector and a growing informal sector. More and more Filipinos are seeking job opportunities abroad, and these overseas Filipino workers contribute substantially to the national income. However, the situation has serious implications for HRD; companies may be reluctant to provide higher level training to employees, given the fact that employees may resign at any time. Again, owing to budget constraints, training and skills development in the corporate sector tend to be focused more on core and professional workers. Semi-skilled, periphery and casual workers are catered for by government-subsidised training programmes. The Filipino workforce is educated, highly literate and English-speaking, and if properly mobilised employers will be ensured of its high productivity capability. Indeed, as Ofreneo pointed out in Chapter 4 of this volume, the Philippines has a growing reputation in the IT sector and has big competitive advantages in the off-shore BPO sector.

Singapore

In comparison to the other countries featured in this book, Singapore is a city-state with a population of some 4.2 million and faces an ageing population and a falling birth rate. Currently there are some 600,000 foreign workers in Singapore, equivalent to 30 per cent of the country's total workforce.[1] Hence effective management of its human assets is vital. In the presence of severe global competition and increased business uncertainty, companies focus on flexibility, in terms of numerical, functional and reward management flexibility. Recruitment is more about the 'right fit' between skills, knowledge and experience of the candidates and reward packages and career development prospects offered by the companies. However, in a generally tight labour market, the retention of highly skilled workers becomes a prime challenge. HR managers are compelled to refine their recruitment strategies, including recruiting globally, in order to attract candidates. The flexible reward system motivates employees by the inclusion of a performance-based monthly pay component. Nevertheless, the employment system in the open economy does not guarantee lifelong employment; neither are employees willing to promise long-term commitment. Companies offer attractive family benefits in order to generate commitment and to retain their skilled and trained workers. However, so as to avoid business downsizing and future retrenchment, individuals have to be more proactive with their skills and knowledge improvement.

Thailand

HRM practices developed as a result of industrialisation and the inflow of FDI. Traditionally PM was seen as performing the payroll function; however, with the emergence of foreign companies, HRM gained recognition as a strategic partner in businesses. Consequent to the 1997 Asian Crisis, several significant changes have transpired in the field of HRM. Firms began to impose rigorous recruitment and selection processes. However, there are differences in HRM practices based on the ownership of the firms. In terms of recruitment, Western-owned firms rely on the external labour market, while Japanese-owned firms more commonly utilise the internal labour market. On the other hand, indigenous private companies prefer personal referrals. Rewards and incentives are based upon the individual employee's productivity and performance, which is measured by the PA system. Short-term training is more common than long-term training except in the manufacturing sector, and due to financial constraints companies tend to exercise more in-house training and on-the-job training. Career planning programmes are almost non-existent, except in some large firms. Government legislation has weakened labour unions, which will have far-reaching implications for collective employee relations.

Vietnam

Vietnam's economic reform, which began in 1986, currently focuses on qualitative growth. The influx of MNCs and to a large extent the consequential introduction of international HRM has had a deep impact on HRM, firstly in Vietnam's SOEs and secondly in private companies. Thus, SOEs have moved considerably towards the adoption of a new HRM system – a shift which recognises HR as a strategic asset. New HRM practices adopted by companies include formal recruitment and selection procedures, training and development, performance-related pay and employee retention policies. In response to increased global and regional competition, particularly in attracting FDI, companies are increasingly adopting Western-style HRM approaches. However, in the private sector personal referral continues to be used in recruitment, although there is a move towards the practice of hiring highly qualified foreigners at the top management level. Unquestionably, there is a much wider scope for the development of HRM in this relatively new emerging market. SOEs need to focus attention on ways of retaining their trained workforce, as more foreign companies locate their subsidiaries in Vietnam.

Concluding remarks

This book has outlined the management context and HRM and how it operates in different countries. Our analysis of HRM processes in our six case study countries shows one common trait – that specifically MNCs and FDI have played a major role in initiating more systematic HRM policies and practices; albeit working within a framework of indigenous legislative systems and societal value-sets. Our analysis further shows that business systems in these countries tend to be quite dynamic and constantly evolving due to their rapid growth and changes in the external environment. For instance, in the last decade or so several factors have brought about a reappraisal of HRM policies and practices. Among these are the 1997 crisis and the ensuing economic slowdown in several Asian countries, regional market integration, growth in corporate governance and business transparency, as well as the rise in levels of education.

While it is true that the countries we feature in this book are experiencing rapid social and economic changes, their economies thrive largely upon export-led and investment-led growth, and to a lesser extent consumption-led growth (see also Rowley and Warner, 2006). For that reason Thailand, Malaysia, the Philippines and Indonesia are referred to as the manufacturing powerhouses of the region (Andrews *et al.*, 2003). The most common issue faced by governments of the six countries we have featured in this book is the improvement of the investment environment in their respective countries in order to attract higher amounts of FDI. Unquestionably the host economy benefits directly from FDI in terms of job creation, capital accumulation, transfer of technology and trade flows, as well as technological externalities such as higher productivity for domestic firms. Ulack and Leinbach (2000) assert that South East Asian countries have vast potential for further development by moving towards higher value-added manufactured exports. South East Asian economies are facing stiff competition not only within the region itself but particularly also from China, the world's fastest growing economy.

Table 8.1 shows inward FDI flows for the period 2002–2005 in our case study countries and, as a comparison, China. Singapore continues to be a leader in terms of attracting FDI in South East Asia, despite its heavy reliance on a foreign workforce. The shares of FDI received by Thailand and Indonesia in 2005 surged by 160 per cent and 177 per cent respectively, a fact that could be attributed to both countries' openness to foreign investors. Thailand has a large domestic market, and is recognised as the region's hub for the assembly and export of automobiles. In the case of Indonesia, Zhan and Ozawa (2000) point out that, despite its precarious political and economic environment, Indonesia is progressing well in industrial development. Despite economic instability, Indonesia made headlines in October 2006 by paying off, 4 years early, its outstanding US$3.7 billion debt to the IMF (Gross and Connor, 2006). This indicates a desire on Indonesia's part to be seen as a competitive and fair player in the future Asian economy. Indonesia is still one of the cheapest labour markets in the region, owing to its large population of more than 200 million, thus it is able to attract labour-intensive operations seeking

Table 8.1 Inward FDI overview, 2002–2005, selected South East Asian countries and China (US$ million)

Country	2002	2003	2004	2005	% of GDP 2004	2005
Singapore	7,338	10,376	14,820	20,083	156.2	158.2
Indonesia	145	–597	1,896	5,260	7.0	7.7
Malaysia	3,203	2,473	4,624	3,967	37.2	36.5
Thailand	147	1,952	1,414	3,687	32.9	33.5
Vietnam	1,200	1,450	1,610	2,020	63.5	61.2
Philippines	1,542	491	688	1,132	14.9	14.4
China	52,743	53,505	60,630	72,406	14.9	14.3

Source: adapted from UNCTAD (2006).

to relocate from other less-competitive countries. Wages in Indonesia continue to be among the cheapest in Asia. In 2006, the minimum wage in Jakarta was 819,100 rupiah (about US$89) per month, and is expected to be within the region of 900,516 rupiah (about US$99) in 2007 (ibid.).

On the other hand, Malaysia is losing its competitiveness, judged by a reduction in FDI inflow in 2005. A case in point is that Malaysia tends to lack investment-friendly tax laws compared with Thailand's Board of Investment, which offers 8-year tax breaks and attractive industrial zones (Andrews *et al.*, 2003). As a transitional country, Vietnam has achieved political stability and economic transformation. With a population of 80 million, the country has a large domestic market base. Furthermore, more than 70 per cent of its population are under 25 years old, thus it is able to offer low labour costs compared with other economies in the region; a fact that has contributed to the country's potential in receiving higher levels of FDI in future (see Tables 8.2 and 8.3).

One important factor taken into consideration by foreign direct investors when choosing locations is the quality of the domestic institutional environment, including good governance and transparency and judicial credibility and effectiveness. The quality of HRs is another key factor that determines inward capital flows. Thus, in the present context we need to look seriously at how effective HRM and HRD can enhance the competitiveness of HRs in order for businesses to compete effectively in the global market, as well as increase inward

Table 8.2 Inward FDI performance index 2003–2005, selected South East Asian countries and China

Rank (total 141 countries)	Country	Score
5	Singapore	8.294
53	Vietnam	2.173
62	Malaysia	1.824
96	Thailand	0.867
112	Indonesia	0.537
115	Philippines	0.510
55	China	2.048

Source: adapted from UNCTAD (2006).

Table 8.3 Matrix of inward FDI performance and potential, selected South East Asian countries and China, 2005

	High FDI performance	Low FDI performance
High FDI potential	Front runner China Malaysia Singapore	Below potential Philippines Thailand
Low FDI potential	Above potential Vietnam	Underperformer Indonesia

Source: adapted from UNCTAD (2006).

FDI. An enhanced HRD strategy, for example, strengthens a country's investment climate by producing a highly skilled workforce. At the same time MNCs, too, will intensify HRD as they are known to be providers of training and technology transfers.

Hitherto our analysis has pointed out the effects of FDI and MNCs on the development of internationally endorsed HRM practices, particularly in indigenous business organisations in South East Asian countries. This is the one common trait that appears in all our case study countries. The very existence of FDI and MNCs in the host countries has strengthened the concept of 'dependency development'. Nevertheless 'dependency' in this instance is accompanied by aggressive state intervention in the form of FDI-friendly legislation. Each country strives hard to attract more FDI annually.

Dependency has been defined as 'an explanation of the economic development of a state in terms of the external influences – political, economic and cultural – on national development policies' (Sunkel, 1969: 23), and more appropriate in the case of our present analysis is the fact that dependency is 'a situation in which the economy of a certain group of countries is conditioned by the development and expansion of another economy, to which their own is subjected' (Dos Santos, 1971: 226). Our analysis further shows a trend that is analogous to Wallerstein's world systems theory (Wallerstein, 1974; 1980; 1989) where there is only one world (as opposed to the First World and the Third World) connected by a complex network of economic exchange relationships within a world economy or a world system.

In this instance several Asian countries have developed economically through the process of import-substitution and export-oriented manufacturing financed by FDI – also referred to as the internationalisation of manufacturing production (Sunkel, 1985). Viewed positively, the internationally integrated production systems benefit, albeit asymmetrically, both host and home countries. Foreign firms bring to the host country a package of assets including capital, technology, R&D, managerial expertise and global marketing networks. Sunkel (1985) for instance argues that MNCs engage in continuous technological innovation in products and processes of production, and these corporations are able to convert different kinds of lasting knowledge into commercially viable processes and products. Meanwhile, host countries are likely to maximise the benefits of FDI while minimising the negative impact.

Based on the rapid social and economic changes that have occurred in all countries featured in this book, we expect HRM processes in South East Asia to continue to evolve within the context of each particular country's politics, economic development strategies and labour market policies and conditions, as well as according to global business trends. The internationalisation of business corporations may result in the revision of HRM practices (Cascio and Serapio, 1991), and indigenous firms are expected to adhere to such changes; albeit within a plethora of organisational forms, factors and political situations found in the region (see Chapter 1). In view of the fact that HRM in South East Asia depends on a range of factors including location and culture, we expect in due course new HRM policies and corporate goals, both universal and contingent in nature, may become apparent in South East Asian indigenous business organisations.

Finally, the role of HRM is not only to ensure organisational competitiveness, but also to balance labour and management priorities. As part of contributing to this perspective, this book has shed light on the development of people management and the changing face of HRM in South East Asia.

Notes

1   Figures quoted by Halimah Yaacob of the Singapore National Trade Union Congress (as reported in the *Straits Times*, 19 December 2006).

Bibliography

Andrews, T. G., Chompusri, N. and Baldwin, B. J. (2003) *The Changing Face of Multinationals in Southeast Asia,* London: Routledge.

Cascio, W. F and Serapio, M. G. (1991) 'Human resources systems in an international alliance: The undoing of a done deal?', *Organizational Dynamics*, Winter, 63–74.

Dos Santos, T. (1971) 'The structure of dependence', in K. T. Fann and Donald C. Hodges (eds), *Readings in US Imperialism,* Boston: Porter Sargent.

Gross, A. and Connor, A. (2006) Indonesia HR Update – 2006, www.pacificbridge.com/publications.asp, accessed 30 November 2006.

Rowley, C. and Warner, M. (2006) 'Management in South East Asia: Studies in diversity and dynamism', *Asia Pacific Business Review*, 12, 4, 389–410.

Sunkel, O. (1969) 'National development policy and external dependence in Latin America', *The Journal of Development Studies,* 6, 1, 23–48.

Sunkel, O. (1985) *The Transnational Corporate System*, Geneva: UN Centre for Transnational Corporations.

United Nations Conference on Trade and Development (UNCTAD) (2006) *World Investment Report 2006*, Geneva: UNCTAD.

Ulack, R. and Leinbach, T. R. (2000) 'An opening view', in T. Leinbach and R. Ulack (eds), *South Asia: Diversity and Development*, Englewood Cliffs, NJ: Prentice-Hall.

Wallerstein, I. M. (1974) *The Modern World-System, vol. I: Capitalist Agriculture and the Origins of the European World-Economy in the Sixteenth Century*, New York/London: Academic Press.

Wallerstein, I. M. (1980) *The Modern World-System, vol. II: Mercantilism and the Consolidation of the European World-Economy, 1600–1750*, New York: Academic Press.

Wallerstein, I. M. (1989) *The Modern World-System, vol. III: The Second Great Expansion of the Capitalist World-Economy, 1730–1840s*, San Diego: Academic Press.

Zhan, J. and Ozawa, T. (2000) *Business Restructuring in Asia: Cross-border M&As in the Crisis Period,* Copenhagen: Copenhagen Business School Press.

Index

For Product Safety Concerns and Information please contact our
EU representative GPSR@taylorandfrancis.com Taylor & Francis
Verlag GmbH, Kaufingerstraße 24, 80331 München, Germany